DATE DUE

8223422	SEP 2 3 1996
2/4/97	
MAY 1 3 1998	
APR 2 5 2005	3664281

GAYLORD   PRINTED IN U.S.A.

Social Movements and Culture

Social Movements, Protest, and Contention

Series Editor: Bert Klandermans, Free University, Amsterdam
Associate Editors: Sidney G. Tarrow, Cornell University
                      Verta A. Taylor, Ohio State University

Social Movements and Culture

Hank Johnston and
Bert Klandermans, editors

Social Movements, Protest, and
Contention
Volume 4

University of Minnesota Press
Minneapolis

Copyright © 1995 by the Regents of the University of Minnesota

All rights reserved. No part of this publication may be reproduced, stored in a
retrieval system, or transmitted, in any form or by any means, electronic,
mechanical, photocopying, recording, or otherwise, without the prior written
permission of the publisher.

Published by the University of Minnesota Press
111 Third Avenue South, Suite 290, Minneapolis, MN 55401-2520
Printed in the United States of America on acid-free paper

Library of Congress Cataloging-in-Publication Data
Social movements and culture / Hank Johnston and Bert Klandermans, editors.
     p.   cm. — (Social movements, protest, and contention ; v. 4)
   Includes bibliographical references (p.   ) and index.
   ISBN 0-8166-2574-3 (hardback)
   ISBN 0-8166-2575-1 (pbk.)
   1. Social movements.   2. Protest movements.   3. Culture—Philosophy.
   4. Culture—Methodology.   I. Johnston, Hank.   II. Klandermans, Bert.
   III. Series.
   HN16.S554   1995
   303.48'4—dc20   94-43723

The University of Minnesota is an
equal-opportunity educator and employer.

Contents

Preface

In recent years, to some degree spurred by the discussion of the "new social movements" and by the general turn toward cultural analysis in the social sciences (see, for example, the special issue of *Contemporary Sociology* 19, no.4 [1990]), students of social movements have felt the limitations of excessively structural and interest-oriented perspectives. There appears to be much merit in utilizing the methods and perspectives of cultural analysis in studying movements, and in the past few years a growing interest in culture can be observed among social movement scholars. Not surprisingly, the first attempts to explore this area brought with them a variety of approaches: divergent elements of culture are being investigated, and culture and social movements are being related to each other in many different ways. A common framework for the integration of cultural variables in the study of social movements is clearly missing.

The time seemed ripe for a discussion among social movement scholars about the focus that such a common framework might take. More specifically, we saw the need for discussion and assessment in three areas: (1) the usefulness of different theoretical perspectives on culture as a factor in the emergence of social movements; (2) movement culture as manifested in phenomena such as collective identity, symbols, public discourse, narratives, and rhetoric; and (3) research methods in this context. With this agenda in mind, a three-day workshop, Social Movements and Culture, was organized in San Diego in June 1992. It was sponsored by the Section on Collective Behavior and Social Movements of the American Sociological Association (ASA) and the Working Group on Collective Behavior and Social Movements of the International Sociological Association. It was supported financially by the ASA and the University of California and hosted by the sociology departments of the University of California at San Diego and San Diego State University.

This volume brings together essays by several keynote speakers, who were asked to address questions assigned to them according to the three central themes. We have arranged this volume accordingly. Part I presents different theoretical perspectives in the study of social movements. In the first chapter the editors present a general overview of the ways that culture may be applicable to the study of social movements. This is followed by contributions from Ann Swidler, Alberto Melucci, and Michael Billig, each of whom approaches cultural analysis from a somewhat different angle. Ann Swidler argues that social movement analysis can gain a great deal from a strong cultural perspective, namely, how existing cultural templates shape, constrain, and, in some situations, are used by movement organizations. Melucci's and Billig's essays diverge from the explanatory task implicit in Swidler's by emphasizing process instead of causal progression. Melucci elaborates a processual approach to his concept of collective identity. Billig's rhetorical analysis explicates at a microscopic level of analysis the conflicts and contradictions inherent in culture.

Part II presents four examples of how different cultural elements influence the course of mobilization. A key distinction is between the way a movement processes the dominant culture and culture as a movement characteristic. Chapters by William Gamson, Jane Jenson, and Rick Fantasia and Eric Hirsch provide examples of the performative quality of movements as they seize upon dominant cultural patterns and turn them to their own advantage. Gamson examines public discourse as influenced by media discourse. Jenson shows how the Aboriginal movement in Canada took advantage of changes in public discourse. Fantasia and Hirsch trace how the Algerian revolutionary movement transformed an attribute of traditional Islamic culture to its strategic advantage. The chapter by Gary Fine also looks at the creation of culture but, following his past work on bounded cultural forms, stays within a social movement group proper and emphasizes culture as a movement characteristic. Fine explicates the different narrative forms typical in the Victims of Child Abuse Laws (VOCAL) movement and demonstrates how ritual performance by members functions to solidify the group.

Each of the three essays in Part III describes how to proceed in the task of cultural analysis. Taken along with the examples of cultural analysis in the previous section, these chapters help identify the benchmarks of how cultural analysis might be done. Without shared standards, cultural analysts speak only among themselves, and whatever potential for theoretical advance may reside in the cultural perspective is lost to other researchers. Verta Taylor and Nancy Whittier help prevent such an impasse by identifying four key themes in cultural analysis and by showing that they can be applied practically to movement analysis with reference to the women's movement. John Lofland presents an elaborate taxonomy of movement culture with the aim of providing measures by which the cultural richness of movements might be assessed and compared. Finally, Hank Johnston presents a practical methodology for analyzing social movement frames with the goal of giving greater empirical grounding to this important cultural concept. Together, these essays provide what we hope is a balanced account of the promises and limitations of cultural analysis of social movements.

Part I

Conceptions of Culture
in Social Movement Analysis

Chapter 1

The Cultural Analysis of Social Movements

Hank Johnston and Bert Klandermans

The pendulum of Kuhn's normal science now seems to swing toward culture, gathering speed in what may well be a paradigmatic shift. Mueller (1992) in her introductory essay to *Frontiers in Social Movement Theory*—in more than one sense the predecessor of this volume—refers to a broader paradigm, more sensitive to cultural factors, that is developing. In the collection she and Morris edited (Morris and Mueller 1992), culture as such is not yet central stage, but by placing culture at the center of our concerns the current volume clearly embraces and labels a theoretical trend that was already emerging some years ago. Indeed, the cultural analysis of social movements starts from the same criticisms of the ruling paradigm in social movement literature Mueller describes in her introduction.

Looking backward, we see familiar terrain: organizations, resources, structural preconditions, networks, and rational choice. The view that lies ahead is less clear. Definitions of culture abound, although it is not difficult to extract common denominators: customs, beliefs, values, artifacts, symbols, and rituals are among the elements of culture mentioned in the literature. This indicates that we are headed toward a "softer" set of factors than those of the past—ones that are at their heart mental and subjective, that are difficult to define operationally. *Culture* is a broad and often imprecise term but, as others have noted, at the same time intuitively apparent. Wuthnow's (1987) definition of culture as the "symbolic expressive aspect of social behavior" can serve as a foundation for our discussion. This collection of essays, the fruit of an international workshop, is dedicated to giving shape and focus to cultural analysis applied to social movements.

The movement toward cultural analysis was first perceptible in the early 1980s, and among the early advocates several are contributors to this volume. Gary Fine (1985) noted that small groups produce a culture of their own that shapes the interaction and course of development. Ann Swidler (1986) later comprehensively examined what could and could not be done with cultural analysis, but without specifically addressing social movements. Lofland (1985) sought to classify types of social movement cultures, and in this volume he moves toward the kinds of measures that permit comparison between movements. At the same time, interest in social constructionist approaches to social movements grew rapidly, as witnessed by anthologies such as those edited by Klandermans and Tarrow (1988) and Morris and Mueller (1992). While they are not "cultural" in their focus, these are benchmark studies that emphasize interactional processes and ideational factors that are closely allied to the ways that cultural influences affect social movements.

At this point in the theoretical exchange, the place of cultural analysis applied to social movements remains to be assessed. What are the different foci of cultural analysis? How does one conduct cultural analysis? Where might we be headed? And, finally, are we headed in the right direction? These are the questions we will try to answer in this introductory chapter.

Foci of Cultural Analysis

Compared to social movements, the dominant culture of a society appears stable. Its codes, frames, institutions, and values have evolved over long periods of time and, for the most part, function as the broadest and most fundamental context for social action. Cultures change but, with the exception of revolutionary upheaval, tend to do so over protracted periods of time. Social movements, on the other hand, are quintessentially changeful, and the metaphor of movement itself reminds us that they are in continuous flux. Recent elaborations in both cultural theory and social movement theory challenge this dichotomy of relative stasis versus change. To speak of a dominant culture fails to recognize that the codes, values, and norms of behavior that from a distance appear to be widely shared are far from consensual and hegemonic when they are viewed closer up. Also, recent thinking about new social movements locates these collectivities precisely at the cracks and fissures of the dominant culture that, from macroscopic perspectives, seem so faint they hardly deserve attention. When established identities and social statuses no longer correspond to possibilities that are opened up by advances in knowledge and technology, there arise new movements that blend and meld the analytical distinctions between culture and movements, perhaps more so today than ever before (Inglehart 1990).

For the purposes of an initial assessment, we will take the problematic of stability and change as the starting point and the axis on which the discussion in this essay will turn. Probably more than any other field of study, social movement research can elaborate the relationship between cultural change and stasis because movements arise out of what is culturally given, but at the same time they are a fundamental source of cultural change. First we discuss different ways that culture can be conceptualized. From a systemic perspective, culture can be seen as a characteristic of a movement's environment that functions to channel or constrain its development and that defines what behaviors are legitimate and acceptable. A different approach focuses on how cultural knowledge is performed, sometimes revealing that the dominant culture is riddled with gaps, inconsistencies, and contradictions. From these issues spring forth alternative symbols, values, languages, and frames that can be the seeds of challenge and mobilization. Michael Billig in chapter 4 shows that these oppositions are so fundamental that they are built into the rhetorical structure of normative political discourse. Jane Jenson (chapter 6) and Ann Swidler (chapter 2) emphasize how times of crisis are often the precipitant by which alternative codes are mobilized in political debate.

Second, we will focus on the dynamic relationship between movements and culture from the movement's perspective. Social movements not only can arise from cracks in culture but also can process culture insofar as they consume what is culturally given and produce transmutations of it. The individuals, groups, and organizations that form a movement process culture by adding, changing, reconstructing, and reformulating. Like other aspects of the society that a movement is embedded in, culture is processed through construction of meaning. Questions about meaning construction relate to the processes by which culture is adapted, framed, and reframed through public discourse, persuasive communication, consciousness raising, political symbols, and icons (Klandermans 1992).

Third, cultural analysis can focus exclusively on culture as a movement characteristic—a product of interaction within a movement. Here, of course, the key questions are how movement culture is formed and how it may facilitate or impede mobilization, recruitment, solidarity, and other key movement functions.

Conceptualizing Culture

Debates about the nature of culture have existed for almost a century in sociology, anthropology, and linguistics. While culture is a concept that is intuitively understood, it is also applied to a wide variety of social phenomena that are sometimes quite distinct. Today, with sectors of other disciplines—political science, social psychology, literature, and history—claiming culture as their terrain as well, there is even greater diversity. Moreover, the model of culture changes according to the research questions being asked, the data being used, the analytical distance from the social actors, and commitment to a particular view of scientific enterprise. While it is certain that we will not be able to resolve these divergent perspectives, what we can do in this introduction is identify two global ways of thinking about culture, both of which are relevant to the analysis of collective action.

There is one body of literature, highly diverse within itself, that takes as its goal the description of relationships within a cultural system. This is a "systemic" view of culture, eloquently described by Clifford Geertz (1973, especially 3-30), that affirms the external reality of related conceptions of the world and of patterns of action. A somewhat different approach emphasizes the cultural stock of knowledge that is required to perform as a member of society. This distinction has its roots in an older debate in anthropology regarding the proper epistemological location of culture. Ward Goodenough (1956, 1964) has argued that all the researcher needs to know about culture, insofar as it affects behavior, is located in the minds of social actors. This is a view of society and culture that is essentially Weberian because it takes the social actor as the unit of analysis. It is what also might be called a performative view of culture in that the goal is to see how cultural templates are used to make sense of situations and as a basis for action.

A systemic view of culture can be applied to the emergence and growth of social movements in several ways. In past years, movements were seen as reactions to destabilized systems (the so-called breakdown theories such as Smelser 1962 and Worsley 1957). Another time-honored approach, more useful and without presumptions of movement pathology, looks at the cultural system as an overarching factor that shapes and constrains the course of mobilization much the way political cultures influence the shape of politics in different countries (Almond and Verba 1964). In this view, although movements are defined by their break with the dominant cultural code, they nevertheless are shaped by their inclusion in and modification of aspects of the dominant culture. Diversity in beliefs, values, and norms within society, and the diversity of meanings between individual social actors, are glossed over in favor of aggregated concepts in order to define and isolate cultural factors that constrain and channel mobilization processes. This perspective suggests a positivist spin on cultural analysis—less evident in the early systemic traditions in anthropology—that derives from the application of culture to the explanation of discrete phenomena such as movements, political behavior, or public opinion.

While this approach offers insights, it fails to recognize that there are numerous fissures and lacunae within the dominant sociocultural system that can be primary sources of movement emergence rather than secondary influences. Aldon Morris's (1986) analysis of the civil rights movement emphasizes the structure of southern black communities and aspects of black culture that developed under conditions of oppression. Hank Johnston's (1991, 1992, 1993) analysis of nationalist mobilizations demonstrates how religious traditions and their relation to nationhood shape the course of mobilization in several minority national regions. Moscovici's (1988, 1993) concept of social representations emphasizes the ideational elements of cultures of dissent. They are orienting principles that "point one's attention" and "predispose to an interpretation" as preconditions to action within a social movement. These are middle-level cultural influences that come out of a challenging culture of opposition. They are more dynamic than dominant cultural templates, but more general and less fluid than collective action frames.

One theme that is developed in several chapters of this volume is that oppositional subcultures within the "global culture" function as wellsprings from which oppositional thought and discourse flow. William Gamson's essay on framing and political discourse shows how existing elements of opposition merge with media frames and issue cultures. Michael Billig shows how, at the interactional level, rhetorical contradictions and oppositions are inherent within the dominant discourse. The link between Billig's perspective and that of others is that as researchers become more sensitive to the inherent complexities and contradictions of culture, they will be able to define more relevant variables and to fine tune explanations of movement emergence and success.

In recent years, there has been a shift in cultural analysis toward the performative tradition. Ann Swidler's (1986) discussion of "culture as a 'tool kit' of rituals, symbols, stories, and world-views" that people use to construct strategies of action was an important elaboration of this perspective. Although these strategies are "larger assemblages" that have a systemic quality, there is a strong performative strand because they are applied to help construct social action. These strategies are composed of diverse bundles of symbols, habits, skills, styles, and known and established linkages between them all, whereby given ends can be achieved in appropriate ways. Regarding social movements, Swidler points out that in unsettled times and periods of crisis, mobilizing collectivities reject old cultural models and articulate new ones. These offer new ways of organizing social life, of learning, of "practicing unfamiliar habits until they become familiar" (1986: 278). This performative—and transformative—approach is evident in Fantasia and Hirsch's essay, which traces the changing usages and definitions of the haik, or Islamic veil, in the Algerian revolution. Ritualistic behaviors and symbols such as the veil acquire significance in periods of crisis because they can be transformed to strategic ends, defining new ways of being.

The framing perspective cuts a middle course between a systemic view of culture and its performative aspects. With its theoretical roots in symbolic interactionism, early elaborations of the framing approach (Snow et al. 1986) preserved the emphasis on social process and emergence that presumed the creative intervention of individuals. In the interactive arena are forged schemes of interpretation whereby presenting situations are collectively made sensible. The interactionist tradition is most clearly apparent when frames are conceptualized as cognitive templates applied in similar situations to answer the questions What's going on here? and What am I to do?

More recent elaborations of the framing perspective, however, deemphasize the original cognitive status of frames and shift their constraining and enabling aspects to the collective arena (Snow and Benford 1992). In this process, a shift in the perspective on culture is also presumed. Whereas individuals perform culture by applying frames to situations they encounter, the processes of frame extension and frame amplification, of drawing upon frame resonance or augmenting frame potency, are for the most part treated as strategic actions of social movement organizations and presume systemic relations of social movement culture with the other aspects of culture.

This kind of frame analysis is performed at the level of organizations and institutions, that is, it studies how frames intersect with key cultural patterns and how they might be strategically used in mobilization. These processes are described through organizational documents, key speeches, public records, and media reports. It is an approach that is particularly relevant in today's movement environment, in which groups and organizations strategically consider the effects of their actions on the media and on the public at large. This self-reflective quality is especially characteristic of some new social movement groups that, more consciously than ever before, take steps to construct their own collective identities. Frame analysis at this level unites the systemic perspective of dominant cultural patterns with a performative analysis at a higher level of analysis: that of groups, organizations, and institutions.

The framing perspective has informed several recent studies that combine both performative and systemic aspects of culture. Gamson's (1992) study of issue cultures and public discourse links broad cultural factors with social psychological processes of meaning construction. McAdam and Rucht's (1993) research on protest repertoires links culture and microstructural relations by tracing the diffusion of collective action frames via social networks. What still remains is to link these broad collective action frames with their cognitive equivalents at the level of participant action. This, after all, is where interpretative frames do their real work. As Johnston observes in chapter 11, frames only count insofar as "they penetrate the black box of mental life" to become predicates of behavior. These elements are located at the intersection of social psychology and cultural analysis, especially regarding how social movement participants process culture in the construction of meaning.

Processing Culture

A performative view of culture stresses that social movements are not just shaped by culture; they also shape and reshape it. Symbols, values, meanings, icons, and beliefs are adapted and molded to suit the movement's aims and frequently are injected into the broader culture via institutionalization and routinization. This was documented by the Russian sociologist Elena Zdravomyslova (1992), who showed that the new political rhetoric in Russia stems from democratic movements in the early days of perestroika that adapted the political rhetoric of Western parliamentary democracies for their own use. Similarly, the civil rights movement, the women's movement, the environmental movement, and many other movements that have populated the political arena in the West left their traces in the cultures of their societies. For instance, Gusfield (1981) has observed that the effects of the 1960s counterculture movement were extremely broad, regarding general cultural tolerance for different lifestyles. Similar but more bounded and less long lasting are "mobilization cultures" (Johnston 1991) that endure for periods after significant structural change and can continue to influence contention despite radically changed political opportunity structures. These cultures typically result from long-term mobilization, such as that of the U. S. civil rights movement and the Solidarity movement in Poland, and create patterns of organization and interaction that exert influence several years after demobilization. Similarly, students of the women's movement in the United States have observed less authoritarian and hierarchical forms of organization within the movement, along with a less confrontational and "zero-sum" approach to negotiation and conflict resolution. The implication is that as women increasingly challenge male dominance in all major societal institutions, these patterns of behavior will affect business as usual. On the other hand, as with all new cultural forces, co-optation by existing cultural templates is a real possibility and opens the empirical question of how the cultural influences of different movements mix with dominant patterns.

A central part of the process of culture consumption and production concerns meaning construction. Klandermans (1992) distinguishes between three different processes of meaning construction in the movement context: public discourse, persuasive communication, and consciousness raising during episodes of collective action. At each level the process of meaning construction has its own dynamics, as we can infer simply from the different sets of individuals involved. Public discourse in principle involves everyone in a society or a particular sector within a society. Persuasive communication affects only those individuals who are targets of persuasion attempts; consciousness raising during episodes of collective action concerns primarily participants in the collective action, although sympathetic spectators can be affected as well. Thus, at each level the processes forming and transforming collective beliefs take place in different ways: at the first level through the diffuse networks of meaning construction, at the second level through deliberate attempts by social actors to persuade, and at the third level through discussions among participants in and spectators of the collective action.

The three levels of meaning construction are interdependent. The social construction of protest can be seen as a value-added process in which each level sets the terms for the next level. At the first, the most encompassing, level, the long-term processes of formation and transformation of collective beliefs take place. At the second level, competing and opposing actors attempt to mobilize consensus by anchoring their definitions of the situation in the collective beliefs of various social groups. The degree of discrepancy between an actor's definition of the situation and a group's collective beliefs (formed in the public discourse) makes it more or less difficult to align these groups. And at the third level, when individuals participate in or observe an episode of collective action, collective beliefs are formed and transformed under the impact of direct confrontations with opponents and competitors. At these three levels—in a complex interplay between mass media and social actors such as movements, countermovements, political parties, and authorities, and in interpersonal interaction in social networks and friendship groups—meaning is constructed and reconstructed.

Several essays in this volume move the discussion on meaning construction beyond theoretical exercises. In his analysis of the role of mass media,

Gamson elaborates on the impact of media discourse on the generation of collective action frames. In "What's in a Name?" Jenson describes how naming the nation became a focal theme in Canadian public discourse as reorganized by the actions of nationalist movements demanding rights and power. Fine discusses the use of narrative strategies in the creation of cultural traditions and solidarity. Each of these essays in its own way testifies to what Billig refers to as the practical dilemma facing the ideologists of social movements, whose ideology criticizes common sense, but who seek to attract widespread ideological support. There are different ways of linking one's message to common sense, and Billig provides several examples, but doing so may formulate new words or phrases, new meanings and symbols that become incorporated into commonsense thinking.

As Klandermans (1988, 1989), Ferree and Miller (1985), and Gamson (1992) have pointed out, there is a great deal to learn about the relation of individual social psychological processes to collective processes. Their arguments have in the past been directed at organizational and structural foci characteristic of resource mobilization perspectives, but to these debates we now add the processes of cultural production and cultural influence in social movements. Calling these processes cultural challenges the typically broad and somewhat static definitions of culture-writ-large by emphasizing the situational and interactional elements by which grand cultural templates get translated into behavior. Furthermore, it is our assertion that as interest in new social movements increases, and in reaction to the materialist focus of resource mobilization analysis, what goes on in small, bounded groups as subsets of social movements will increasingly become the focus of investigation. Already, approaches within the framing perspective have focused on group processes in ways reminiscent of interactionist analysis (Snow and Benford 1988). Taylor and Whittier (chapter 9) and Fine (chapter 7) add an important dimension to the debate: groups as places of cultural enactment, where values take form and emotions are expressed, channeled, and redefined and invested in shared meaning through ritual practices—public narration in Fine's Victims of Child Abuse Laws (VOCAL) groups, and an elaborate set of activities that constitute the alternative institutions and cultural events in Taylor and Whittier's feminist groups.

A traditional focus on the interactional level has been the culture produced during key events such as major demonstrations or by core organizations and organizers. More recently, identity movements such as the gay and lesbian movement present more mundane interactive situations—the everyday life within the movement—as the loci of cultural production. Daily interaction is a substantial part of the raison d'être of these movements. Within the context of these submerged networks (see Melucci 1989), and by relating to the dominant culture in a dilemmatic way, as Billig argues, subcultures are created. The point is that the products of this interaction—in the form of verbal and textual production—constitute an important set of data for investigating a movement's cultural work.

Culture as a Movement Characteristic

We discussed earlier how, like the topography of a continent, the dominant culture has isolated valleys, offshore islands, and seismic fissures below the surface. In addition—and often in contrast—to the culture of the larger society, people in groups and organizations develop their own patterns of values, norms, and everyday behaviors. These group cultures are usually categorized according to their distinctiveness from the dominant culture (as are countercultures, subcultures, and lifestyle groups) and according to the size and cohesiveness of the collectivity on which the cultural patterns are based. As we mentioned earlier, there has been a recent trend to characterize even smaller, less enduring, and less encompassing social relationships as having their own unique cultures. From the well-known and time-honored concepts of subcultures and countercultures to Fine's articulation of ideocultures based on more transitory interactional arenas, these dimensions of cultural analysis can be applied to all kinds of social movement groupings—from radical cells, where subcultural elaboration is likely to be dense, to consensus movements like Greenpeace or Ross Perot's United We Stand and to "checkbook movements" like the Cousteau Society, where cultures seem to be quite sparse, and all movement organizations in between.

There are two general ways of looking at movement cultures that parallel our earlier discussion of systemic and performative perspectives. As Lofland points out in chapter 10, systemic assumptions of anthropological analysis characteristic of Radcliffe-Brown and Kluckhohn can be profitably transferred to more bounded social groupings. The emphasis here is on description in order to trace the role of culture in group integration and longevity or in patterning social relationships. Applied to social movements, this approach requires a snapshot of group culture and its relation to the larger culture. Knowing these relationships is useful in the same way that knowing the broader cultural patterns is useful in societal analysis: they specify the constraints and channels of action that are products of human association. The performative approach, on the other hand, captures processes of movement growth and creativity. By conceptualizing culture as a stock of knowledge that allows a person to perform as a competent member of a society, the performative approach allows for creative and adaptive processes within the movement itself.

Describing Movement Culture

Regarding the mapping of cultures, Lofland sets forth in chapter 10 a typology by which movement cultures can be more systematically analyzed. His listing of six basic areas of cultural production is a first step in describing the richness and density of social movement cultures and how the various elements are related. In an unintended way, however, Lofland's essay can be said to represent a more general confluence of cultural analysis and social movement research. Because of the boundedness of social movements, and because their appearance and growth are phenomena that virtually demand explanation, social movement research tends to recast cultural description in terms of variables. The point is that while description alone may suffice in functional analysis of cultures, it is fundamentally a static approach that does not translate well to collective behavior and social movements. Or, in a semiotic vein, a cockfight may embody key patterns of Balinese culture (Geertz 1973: 412-53), but for Johnston, the analysis of social movement texts (written and/or spoken) yields structures of meaning that are useful insofar as they help explain movement growth, recruitment, or mobilization. In social movements, the fundamental quality is change, which in terms of mobilization creates the dependent variables of movement growth or success. Lofland explicitly argues that his enterprise of systemization is necessary if we are to use culture as a variable in explaining movement growth, potential, and success or failure.

A good example of cultural description waxing explanatory is Hunt's (1984) analysis of the symbolic provinces of French revolutionary discourse. Hunt argues a "strong cultural" position that producing revolutionary talk was just as much part of the revolution as were the barricades, and that fashioning a rhetoric was the heart of the revolutionary struggle. It was with revolutionary rhetoric that the break with the past was accomplished and the seedbed for a new order prepared. Moreover, adding a dynamic dimension to the "cultural snapshot," the symbolic framework of the revolution needed constant clarification and updating: "A concern with words, festivals, seals and symbols was essential . . . to the identity of a new political class" (1984: 215). The key to Hunt's argument is that without new vocabularies, new fields of interpretation, new symbols and signs, the revolutionary interpretations would not have been as easily made nor as completely and fully diffused in French society.

An understudied aspect of cultural description, but one that is often crucial to movement success, is the role of "high culture" in mobilization. We have in mind the plastic arts, music and song, literature, poetry, and theater. W. I. Thompson (1967) has chronicled the place of poetry in creating the "imagination" of the 1916 Easter rebellion in Dublin. The nationalist movements and the Young Europe movements (Young Italy, Young Poland, Young Turkey, etc.) of the past century drew heavily on poetry, literature, and song as expressions of national and generational discontent (Smith 1991). More recently, popular cultural forms have been key cultural resources in contemporary movements. In nationalist movements, songs in the native language are common in mass mobilizations, such as those of Québécois chansonniers Pauline Julien, Felix Leclerc, and Gilles Vigneault. Poetry festivals in the Basque and Catalan languages during Franco's rule in Spain and choral competitions in Estonia provided both new idioms and locales for protest. The May 1968 uprising in Paris was known for its artistic element, and the civil rights movement could claim several key works by Ralph Ellison, Stokeley Carmichael, and Malcolm X, not to mention the poetic rhetoric of Martin Luther King's speeches. These kinds of cultural means and resources can greatly facilitate mobilization, depending on the larger cultural and structural context.

Creating Social Movement Culture

So far we have discussed two aspects of the performative approach to movement culture: how the culture of the larger society is imported, processed, and used within the movement's symbol system; and how movement subcultures in turn produce effects on dominant cultural patterns. A third concentrates on cultural processes located wholly within the boundaries of the movement: namely, how the cultural stock of movement symbols and speech is used to accomplish key processes in mobilization.

This is a focus that for the most part emphasizes the Weberian perspective in which culture is internalized by individual social actors and its effects become visible through their actions, precisely the approach that Swidler cautions against in chapter 2. She argues that social movement analysis might draw upon current trends in cultural analysis (especially those informed by the writings of Bourdieu and Foucault) that opt for a stronger view of culture. While Swidler's observations promise to open new avenues of research, we nevertheless believe that there are a number of reasons why

Weberian-nominalist assumptions will continue to be useful in social movement research. First, key concepts such as incentives, recruitment, and participation are defined in terms of voluntary acts of movement adherents. Second, a large proportion of the cultural agenda to date has been in terms of the framing perspective, which carries an individualistic focus in addition to a "strong" cultural focus. Finally, given the predilection for causal explanation in social movement research, there is a tendency (often implicit) toward positivist logic and rules of evidence and proof that do not lend themselves to systemic or semiotic analyses. These assumptions, however, do not go unchallenged. Alberto Melucci in chapter 3 argues persuasively against the traditional positivist approach to social movements by proposing a movement's "action system" as the proper analytical focus. In particular, he suggests that collective identity is better conceptualized as a process, and he argues against the way scientific logic distorts the dynamic nature of mobilization.

Regarding intramovement culture, both Fine (chapter 7) and Billig (chapter 4) represent the shift to looking at the public performance of narratives. Fine looks at how different kinds of talk in movement groupings test and reaffirm movement boundaries. Billig, by analyzing how people debate issues, explores the structures of rhetoric as part of the culture stock of knowledge. He suggests that discussing a topic also embodies an opposite argument that resides in the narrative repertoire of the interlocutors. Suggestive of Swidler's observation about the cultural power of situations, Billig notes how by changing circumstances, different arguments are invoked. Taylor and Whittier's emphasis on discourse echoes these approaches, but they also identify social movement rituals as important hardware in the cultural toolbox of movements. Rituals, like narratives and speech performances, are group-specific normative forms of behavior that foster solidarity and channel emotions. Myths, too, are tales often told that exalt the group, vilify the enemy, and have strong cohesive functions, as in the creation of mythic pasts by nationalist intelligentsias.

Yet, as with cultural influences on a movement, the cultural system of a movement is not irreconcilable with its cultural performance. Description often includes the knowledge that it takes to perform an appropriate behavior. Studying one often shifts the boundary line so that information is gathered on the other, such as when a prescribed narrative form takes on ritualistic characteristics. There remains, however, a distinction that has echoed several times in our discussion. We have in mind the dichotomy between a nominalist view of culture along Weberian lines and the "stronger" view of culture advocated by Swidler. The two are not so easily blended, and they rest on important epistemological distinctions that have implications for how cultural analysis is done. Whether this is a dichotomy that is more perceived than real is revealed in considering the practical issues of doing cultural analysis.

How to Do Cultural Analysis

Because culture in its broadest sense is the very media of interaction, social analysis cannot help but refer to it in one way or another. For much the same reason, however, studying culture systematically becomes an exceedingly difficult undertaking. We cannot here begin to discuss the techniques of cultural analysis; several of the essays that follow present detailed approaches. Rather, what we can do is to indicate how certain assumptions about what cultural analysis can do lead to particular research foci.

A good place to begin is with the shared values of social scientific inquiry. One item that can be agreed upon readily is the desirability of open discussion and debate about ideas, evidence, and the logic of theory construction. The reasoning behind conceptual development and causal relationships should be accessible to readers, and research methodology should be discussed fully to encourage critical scrutiny. Regarding cultural analysis, because of its relative newness as a subfield in sociology and as a perspective in social movement research, an additional task must be to convince others that it truly deepens our understanding of collective action. In this regard, a key issue is the kind of evidence and proof that can be brought to bear. While there is a great deal of good cultural analysis being done, there is some that speaks only to other culturists and does not argue its case in a language or a logic that is widely shared. This sometimes occurs because—simply stated— the evidence is not as interesting as the larger play of ideas and relationships. Other times, and here we echo C. Wright Mills's criticism of structural functionalism's torturous language, it is easier not to bother with translations of complex and detailed material. If we are to talk to a larger audience, the question of how the case for cultural analysis is presented in language and evidence is crucial.

Concerning language, one issue that social movement research can deal with forthwith is the proliferation of terms. It is understood that from slightly different perspectives, or from differing theoretical venues, things get seen in ways just different enough to occasion new terms. It must be granted that the expanded lexicon is partly a function of the vast repertoire of things cultural, and of their changing shadings and forms as one moves between levels of analysis or to different periods in the mobilization process. Lofland's work on the culture of the social movement organization has to date been the most thorough attempt to systematize thinking on this account, and no further attempt to ply the taxonomist's trade will be attempted here. Still, in this volume alone there are numerous invocations of the cultural lexicon: social representations, rhetoric, microdiscourse, macrodiscourse, cultures of solidarity, consciousness raising, oppositional cultures, cultures of mobilization, cultural codes, ideocultures, narratives, stories, and myths, among others. In many cases a winnowing is possible where overlap occurs.

Because of the scope of culture, a useful strategy is to concentrate on key junctures in movement development, key organizational situations, and points of contact with institutional and structural constraints. Swidler's call to look at the situational and institutional sources of cultural influence echoes this point, and it is nicely demonstrated in Fantasia's (1988) analysis of cultures of solidarity. He discusses the way that working-class subcultures become charged in times of crisis, when the cultural and structural constraints of the larger culture are suspended. These are times when "all hell breaks loose," and an emergent set of relations and corresponding cultural understandings guides and solidifies mobilization.

Analytically, what is interesting about Fantasia's approach is the implication that collective behaviorist concepts are applicable to cultural analysis. Fantasia looks at spontaneous and localized actions and situates them within an analysis of bureaucratized labor relations and shared worker grievances. He points out how existing structures channel protest actions that, paradoxically, break the bounds of the same structures. Similar approaches to movement culture are suggested by Whittier and Taylor in chapter 9. They discuss how rituals and emergent norms are taken as elements whereby additions to the subcultural repertoire are made. Movements use rituals in a functional sense to incite and bond members. Emergent norms become components of movement cultures out of the deadly dance that groups—in various stages of organization—engage in with the enemy.

Ultimately, for cultural analysis to be convincing to others it must take as its primary datum some cultural artifact or set of cultural products, either ideational or material, and relate it to changes in collective action. Typically, the validity of interpretations is not in question as much as is their reliability. Here a crucial question is how the cultural product was chosen and whether it is representative. Especially for the several chapters in this volume that focus on narratives and texts (either spoken or written), the keystone to presenting a convincing case is whether they analyze something more than idiosyncratic phenomena. When the focus is on spoken texts, as it is in Johnston's selection of participation accounts for micro–discourse analysis, and in Fine's choice of stories, addressing concerns about representativeness is a way to allay concerns about selective memory, standardized vocabularies of motive, and the situational influences at the point of data collection. In these cases, the accepted canons of social research are necessary: a large enough sample so that representativeness can be assured, random selection if it is practicable, and, if it is not, specification of sampling procedures so that readers might judge the soundness of conclusions.

In the analysis of spoken texts—such as the chapters by Billig, Fine, and Johnston—the problem of selective memory and interactional biases can be particularly acute given the theoretical weight that one or two texts must bear. Johnston points out that there are common linguistic and prosodic markers that can sensitize the analyst to when standardized or programmatic accounts are being offered, as well as when considerations of self-presentation and definitions of the speech situation influence what gets said. The point is that all spoken accounts to some degree are performed, situationally determined, and subject to the selective processing of interactive cues that impart the pace, direction, and tenor of interaction, but rather than assuming that these influences are negligible or not important, we can use tools based on linguistic theory to separate the interactional chaff from the substantive wheat of cultural analysis. How this can be done is outlined in the final chapter.

This kind of textual and narrative data is often gathered through participant observation in movement groups, and it is typically through immersion in group activities that key narratives and texts can be identified. This was the strategy Fine used in isolating several narratives for closer scrutiny. The myths of the movement, rituals that may be central to movement solidarity, intensive situations of consciousness raising, and emergent norms all seem to lend themselves to qualitative methods such as participant observation, sociological intervention, in-depth interviews, and life-story analysis. This is particularly true in light of recent insights about some new social movements regarding their embeddedness in the everyday lives of the adherents.

For the most part, these qualitative approaches assume that whatever cultural production or processing occurs in movement settings is accomplished by the willful actions of adherents, although perhaps as a secondary effect. A further assumption is that cultural influences achieve their significance insofar as they are used by individual social actors to interpret situations and arrive at courses of action. Immersion in group settings, interviews, and feedback sessions are all conceived to collect the relevant perceptions of these "culture producers and processors" in order to make the actions of the movement and actions of the movement adherents more understandable.

There is a fundamental difference between this kind of research focus and one that looks at larger cultural influences on the movement (or the influences of the movement on the larger culture). The components of the dominant culture are more permanent, more deeply embedded, more difficult to change, and often supported by institutional and structural relations. In contrast, movement subcultures are more bounded; they challenge institutional arrangements and typically have cultural patterns that, although they are far from spontaneous—this has been established by research—have roots that are relatively more limited temporally, spatially, and demographically. Movement subcultures rarely have a primary socialization component whereby new generations are fed on the mother's milk of fundamental assumptions and orientations about the world. On the other hand, broadly shared cultural templates tend to be indelible because they are merged with information about core identity. Ethnic and racial dispositions, religious faith, orientations toward marriage, sex, gender, work and leisure are often incorporated into thinking about who one is in ways that, even for those who seek to break the bonds of tradition, make cultural innovation socially and psychologically difficult. In contrast, social movement groups, even those that can claim deep and elaborate histories, must reintroduce this material to new recruits and new believers and, in doing so, transform it.

If we focus on the dominant and more immutable aspects of the larger culture, then interpretative orientations based on observation and participation seem less important. If one presumes that goal-directed voluntary action is shaped collectively by deep cultural patterns, it is the patterns that become theoretically interesting. To date, some of the most engaging work in cultural analysis has been the description of the deep structures of culture. While some movements are sufficiently cohesive and long-lived to generate their own deep structures, this is an approach that is less compelling because movement cultures do not sit still long enough for a persuasive description to make sense without reference to the people who practice them, apply them, and change them.

In a similar vein, Swidler suggests in chapter 2 that social movement research consider the role of broader cultural influences, but it seems to us that the best way to achieve this is with reference to those social actors who "import" cultural patterns to organizational or group settings. These are regions of movement development where "strong cultural" patterning is confronted by challenges to the existing order—a melding of the permanence of fixed cultural templates and the flux of social movements. Although Swidler's point is that the external and constraining effects of culture can blunt movement radicalism, even the diversion of mobilization processes and the stifling of momentum should be considered change. To make a convincing case for the effects of culture, reference to the source of change, to the creative interpretations and adaptive states of mind of the movement adherents, seems to be necessary. The boundedness of the phenomenon requires it since similar effects under comparable conditions cannot be mustered as evidence.

Finally, it bears mention that even received cultural patterns—writ as large as they are—are also in flux, although in slow motion. As they are collectively passed to new generations and their "social facticity" is imparted through primary socialization, they are applied by new generations who come of age and act in creative ways. Change comes through small innovations, as one applies and adapts what is received to everyday life; or change comes in larger bundles as received pasts are subjected to the harsh light of cultural innovation in collective contexts—in "new" social movements that challenge directly dominant cultural codes or by "old" social movements that challenge the institutional and structural frameworks. Either way, even the deepest cultural patterns are in motion as well, motion given impulse by individual social actors.

Where Are We Headed?

In recent years the analysis of culture has been embraced as the answer to many unresolved questions in social movement literature. The shortcomings of resource mobilization, the salutariness of new social movement literature, and the "identity boom" in social movement literature all have been seized upon as an argument in favor of cultural analysis. Admittedly, culture was a neglected aspect of the study of social movements. This is the more surprising because it is so obvious that social movements are shaped by culture and at the same time themselves form and transform culture. Symbols, rituals, patterns of affective orientation, values, discourse, and language—to mention only a few key elements of culture—have always been part and parcel of social movements.

Does this bent for culture mean that we experience a paradigm shift? To the extent that the rediscovery of culture requires new and more elaborate theorizing and methodological innovation, we may well witness something close to paradigmatic changes.

However, it is unlikely that the sociology of culture is able to incorporate the most enduring findings of the past two decades of social movement research, especially regarding the role of organizational and material resources, of political opportunities and constraints, of state structures, and of what we know about movement participation and adherence. The fundamental question as we see it is what answers cultural variables can provide to the core issues of the field, that is, the rise and decline of social movements and the waxing and waning of movement participation, movement success or failure. It is not enough to simply add culture to our list of independent variables. Unless we are able to construct theories that relate culture's impact to variables that we know already to be of influence—such as resources, organizations, political opportunities, and perceived costs and benefits of participation—we will not get beyond the descriptive study of aspects of movement culture. Descriptive studies may result in fascinating portraits of how narratives, rituals, pamphlets, songs, and posters are created. Descriptions of culture can show how cultural items can be strategically used by movement organizations and leaders to navigate the seas of confrontation and contention—in ways reminiscent of the resource mobilization perspective. Cultural analysis may suggest striking parallels between movement culture and larger cultural patterns. But in explaining the growth and trajectory of movements, and the careers of their participants, a decade of research on organizational strategies, networks, political opportunities, and participation makes it clear that cultural factors are not sufficient in themselves.

Cultural analysis, then, ought to become embedded in and related to existing knowledge. Otherwise we run the risk of once again throwing babies out with the bath water. Especially regarding several current themes in social movement theory—framing, collective identity, cycles of protest—theoretical advance comes from incorporating what we know about the role of organizations, material resources, and social structure with culture. We see this in Gamson's essay on public discourse and organizational strategy (chapter 5) and in Fantasia and Hirsch's interest in the changing significance of cultural symbols in response to changing political opportunities (chapter 8). Other themes from the new social movements perspective might be profitably developed with an eye to structure and organization. For example, what is the relation between social structure and new social movement emphasis on collective identity and transient participation (Johnston, Laraña, and Gusfield 1994; Klandermans 1994)? Does this relation differ for the ecology movement or the animal rights movement in comparison with movements where grievances and identity are structurally embedded, as in the civil rights movement in the United States and the antiapartheid struggle in South Africa? Aldon Morris (1992) has persuasively argued that a key distinction between social movements is that some actively create their collective identities, while for others collective identity is to a large extent imposed by repressive structural conditions.

Another juncture for cultural analysis is where institutional and structural constraints confront the actions of social movement organizations. On the one hand, there are some movements for which cultural factors seem to pall in comparison to state violence or insitutionalized oppression. Yet there is an array of structural factors that are at once less draconian and more mutable to the force of culture, such as changing laws on marriage and divorce, sexual harassment, and individual rights demonstrate. Here movements with cultural agendas confront existing structures, with the dependent variable being the degree of success. Regarding the actions of social movement organizations, how structural impediments are interpreted and used for the ends of mobilization, such as strengthening collective identity or congealing ritual and narrative style, is cultural work. Moreover, in situations of structural constraint where the costs and benefits of action are starkly given, the calculus of rational action confronts the value rationality embedded in cultural factors. It is at the level of movement culture that impossible situations are redefined as occasions for sacrifice.

A key issue regarding the cultural analysis of social movements, then, is the interaction between cultural factors and economic and structural determinants of mobilization. Related to this is the growth of new technologies of mobilization (Oliver and Marwell 1993). How has technical and occupational change in the past twenty-five years affected the professionalized mobilization repertoire and how this channels mobilization and even movement success? While they are "rationalized" in terms of means-ends maximization, the forms of social movement fund raising, canvassing, and marketing are wholly within the cultural context of North American consumer culture.

Without providing an exhaustive list of possible research questions, the distinctions proposed in this introduction may help us to suggest three categories of questions in which cultural variables are related to the core questions of social movement research. First, in terms of culture as an opportunity or constraint, we should try to answer questions about why and how movements are stimulated or frustrated by cultural characteristics of host societies. Also important are questions about why and how individuals abide by rules, codes, and institutions or (what is perhaps even more interesting) why they do not. And, as we discussed earlier, how cultural opportunities and constraints are related to structural opportunities and constraints will prove to be a key locus of future research. Second, as far as the processing of culture is concerned, any research that looks for answers to questions of how framing activities penetrate the black box of mental life to affect behavior, how public discourse generates collective action frames, how socially constructed meaning influences action mobilization is extremely relevant for social movement literature. Gamson (1992) argues that social psychology is especially suited for examining these kinds of processes. Ethnographic research on interaction processes can test the generalizability of these findings with data from natural settings. Third, in terms of culture as a movement characteristic, studies that register how interacting individuals produce movement culture and to what extent movement culture fosters or hinders mobilization—through effects on solidarity and collective identity or through their "resourceful" application—are examples of relevant research questions. Aspects of movement culture such as narratives, symbols, myths, and the like ought to be studied in terms of their mobilizing capacity. Also, some movement adherents may be more culturally creative; some may be more influential. In general, individual efforts to reformulate, neglect, emphasize, or deemphasize aspects of movement culture should be part of our models.

Shifts in research interest gain their power not only from theoretical notions, but also from compelling research questions and research methods to answer those questions. Resource mobilization was a powerful paradigm because it offered, in addition to a theoretical framework, questions and methods that had proved their value in organizational sociology. It is here that we are somewhat concerned. What questions that are pertinent to movement growth and decline, and what methods that can speak to (and convince) a broader audience of sociologists, have a cultural perspective to offer? To the extent that the sociology of culture concentrates on culture as a characteristic of societies or movements, with bounded, semiotic analysis of cultural behavior, codes, and "texts" as its major research method (Swidler in chapter 2), its application to the study of social movements will provide only limited answers to our key questions. By definition, social movements are carried by all kinds of interactions between individuals. To be sure, movement culture is among the outcomes of these interactions and they are shaped by the culture of a movement's host society, but the kinds of cultural analysis that leave the interacting individual out will not help much to answer the fundamental questions of the field. After the last paradigm shift to resource and structural analyses, social movement literature reacted by rehabilitating the social psychological study of movement participation (Mueller 1992). Let us not make the same mistake for the second time and turn our backs on those areas where social psychology, structural analyses, and rational choice might prove to be more powerful in favor of a totalizing theory that—ultimately—never can be.

Chapter 2

Cultural Power and Social Movements

Ann Swidler

Culture has always been important for the kinds of processes students of social movements study. But as culture moves to the forefront of social movement research, it is important to address directly the theories, methods, and assumptions different approaches to the sociology of culture carry with them.

I begin by reviewing the basic theoretical approaches in the sociology of culture and go on to suggest that traditional Weberian approaches, which focus on powerful, internalized beliefs and values held by individual actors (what I call culture from the "inside out") may ultimately provide less explanatory leverage than newer approaches that see culture as operating in the contexts that surround individuals, influencing action from the "outside in."

The sociology of culture contains two basic traditions, one deriving from Max Weber and the other from Emile Durkheim. Weber focused on meaningful action, and for him the fundamental unit of analysis was always the individual actor. Ideas, developed and promoted by self-interested actors (rulers seeking to legitimate their rule, elites attempting to justify their privileges, religious entrepreneurs seeking followers), come to have an independent influence on social action. People find themselves constrained by ideas that describe the world and specify what one can seek from it. Thus culture shapes action by defining what people want and how they imagine they can get it. Cultural analysis focuses on the complex systems of ideas that shape individuals' motives for action. In Weber's famous "switchman" metaphor:

> Not ideas, but material and ideal interests, directly govern men's conduct. Yet very frequently the 'world images' that have been created by 'ideas' have, like switchmen, determined the tracks along which action has been pushed by the dynamic of interest. 'From what' and 'for what' one wished to be redeemed and,

let us not forget, 'could be' redeemed, depended on one's image of the world. (1946a: 280)

Weber (1968, 1958) analyzed culture by trying to understand typical world-views, like the Protestant one, that had shaped the motives of historically important groups. Identifying how a worldview motivates action—how one committed to it would act under its sway—*is* explanation in Weberian terms.

The second crucial strand in the sociology of culture comes from Durkheim. For Durkheim (1933, 1965), culture is constituted by "collective representations." These are not "ideas" in the Weberian sense. Collective representations may range from the vivid totemic symbol to moral beliefs to modern society's commitment to reason and individual autonomy (Durkheim 1973). Collective representations are not ideas developed by individuals or groups pursuing their interests. Rather, they are the vehicles of a fundamental process in which publicly shared symbols constitute social groups while they constrain and give form to individual consciousness (Durkheim 1965; Bellah 1973). Durkheim writes not of "ideas" and "world images" but of representations, rituals, and symbols. Symbols concretize "collective consciousness," making the animating power of group life palpable for its members. Symbols do not reflect group life; they constitute it.[1]

Talcott Parsons (1937) made a heroic attempt to synthesize Weber and Durkheim, taking from Weber the image of action as guided by culturally determined ends and from Durkheim the notion of culture as a shared, collective product. The end result was the Parsonian theory of "values," a term that played no important role for either Weber or Durkheim. For Parsons (1951, 1961), "values" are collectively shared ultimate ends of action. "Norms" are shared cultural rules that define appropriate means to attain valued ends. Parsons sees shared values as defining societies, making them what they are, just as Durkheim saw the totem as constituting the Aboriginal clan, making it a society. At the same time, Parsons sees values as governing action in very much the way Weber saw ideas as switchmen. But unlike Weber's concept of "ideas," Parsonian values are very general, abstract orientations of action, rather than the specific, historically grounded doctrines and worldviews that Weber thought shaped action (see Swidler 1986).

Despite its logical appeal and distinguished theoretical ancestry, the Parsonian theory of values was never very successful as a guide to research.[2] Renewed interest in culture emerged from the Parsonian legacy but moved in a different direction. Clifford Geertz (1973), a student of Parsons, followed Weber in much of his substantive work but broke with the Weberian foundations of Parsons's theory of action.[3] He did so by altering both the question and the methods of cultural studies. Influenced by semiotic approaches to language and symbols, Geertz argued that culture should be studied for its meanings and not for its effects on action. He also shifted methodological focus, arguing that the proper object of cultural study is not meanings in people's heads but publicly available symbols—rituals, aesthetic objects, and other "texts."

Despite Geertz's debt to Weber, the effect of the Geertzian revolution in anthropology, history, and literary studies has been to break with the Weberian problematic. Rather than looking at the ideas that motivate individual actors (or even collections of individual actors), Geertz's followers examine public symbols and ritual experiences (see Keesing 1974). Culture cannot be used to explain individual action or even group differences in behavior. Attention does not focus primarily on ideas, belief systems, or dogmas, but on other properties of culture, especially the mood or tone that a "cultural system" gives to daily life through its symbolic vocabulary and through the ritual experiences it makes available (Geertz 1973, 1976). Culture constitutes "humanness" itself as well as the social world: "Man is an animal suspended in webs of significance he himself has spun" (Geertz 1973: 5). If culture influences action, then, it is not by providing the ends people seek, but by giving them the vocabulary of meanings, the expressive symbols, and the emotional repertoire with which they can seek anything at all.

The Revolution in Cultural Studies

Since the mid-1960s, when Geertz's influence began to be felt (with the original publication of "Religion as a Cultural System" in 1966), three dramatic developments have transformed cultural studies. They can best be summarized as publicness, practices, and power.

Culture as Public Symbols

Geertz's work fundamentally redefined the object of cultural analysis, revitalizing the practice of cultural studies.[4] Geertz shifted attention from a question that cultural analysts could rarely answer satisfactorily—How does a person's culture actually influence his or her actions—to one that was guaranteed to produce satisfying and even dazzling results: What does this cultural text, ritual, or practice mean to the people who use, perform, or live it? From Geertz's (1973) unpacking of the multistranded meanings of a Balinese cockfight to a historian unraveling the meaning of a ritual or folk tale (Davis

1975; Darnton 1984) to a literary critic finding deeper cultural patterns that animated Shakespeare's plays (Greenblatt 1980), the technique is similar. Identify a cultural text and then situate it in the rich web of associated cultural practices, beliefs, social structural realities, folk experiences, and so forth that allow its hearers, practitioners, or devotees to find it meaningful. Meaning itself is defined as context, as the other practices in which a text or ritual is embedded. This redefinition of the object of cultural analysis subtly altered what culture was understood to be. The focus on public vehicles of meaning reduced the need to investigate what any given individual or group actually felt or thought. Indeed, public symbols displayed a system of meanings, what some would call a semiotic code, rather than ideas that were in any person's head. The semiotic code was in some sense external to, or at least independent of, the minds of particular individuals. No longer the study of an ineffable subjectivity, the study of culture could now be grounded in accessible public objects.

The focus on public symbols also avoided the question of whether culture is necessarily shared or consensual. Durkheim and Parsons had been forced by the logic of their arguments to claim that cultural meanings were universally shared. But this claim did not hold up empirically. Public symbols, on the other hand, are clearly shared by the people who use them or form around them, and the question of whether these symbols' wider context of meaning is really shared seems unimportant. The analyst's task is to understand a formerly opaque ritual or practice through its context, and that exercise itself seemingly confirms that the context that has made its meaning comprehensible to the analyst also accounts for the ritual's ability to animate its practitioners or devotees.

Focusing on public ideas or texts also reshapes how one describes culture's influence on history. Rather than looking, as Weber did, for the ideas that motivated particular historical actors, the analyst traces changes in the cultural context within which all actors operated. Weber looked for ideas that directed the operation of "material and ideal interests." Contemporary culture analysts trace shifts in "discourses," the larger contexts of meanings within which any particular ideas or interests can be formulated (see Wuthnow 1987, 1989).

Practices

Cultural analysts have externalized the locus of culture in another way, by moving it from the mind's interior (ideas and mental representations) to social practices. The focus on practice has been widespread, from the attempt to revise the Marxian model of culture as "superstructure" (Williams 1973) to the efforts of Pierre Bourdieu and Michel Foucault to locate culture in embodied and institutionalized practices. Indeed, along with the terms *text* and *discourse,* the concept of "practice" is the hallmark of the new approaches in the sociology of culture.[5]

The concept of practice or practices differs from older conceptions of culture in two important ways. First, in reaction against the Durkheimian tradition, it emphasizes human agency. Pierre Bourdieu's *Outline of a Theory of Practice* (1977) conceives of culture not as a set of rules, but as deeply internalized habits, styles, and skills (the "habitus") that allow human beings to continually produce innovative actions that are nonetheless meaningful to others around them. For Bourdieu, active human beings continually recreate culture. They do not dutifully follow cultural rules, but energetically seek strategic advantage by using culturally encoded skills. Because access to those skills is differentially distributed, people's strategic efforts reproduce the structure of inequality (even if the players of the game are slightly rearranged).

Second, locating culture in social practices ties the study of culture to the analysis of institutions. Here the most important innovator is Michel Foucault. Foucault analyzes how systems of categories and distinctions are enacted and made real in institutional practices. For example, the practices that, after the sixteenth century, came to differentiate the sane from the mad— exclusion and confinement in asylums, or the diagnostic criteria later used by psychologists and others in the human sciences—are sets of cultural rules made real by being used to categorize and control human beings (Foucault 1965, 1978).

Foucault's arguments resemble Durkheim's insistence that rituals demarcate cultural boundaries and make symbolic truths real. But Foucault does not emphasize exotic ritual and symbol, nor the shared mental representations that unify a society's members. Rather, Foucault shifts attention to institutions, which use power to enact rules that construct human beings ("the subject") and the social world (Foucault 1983).

Power

The third important element in rethinking culture is a focus on power and inequality (Lamont and Wuthnow 1990). Max Weber (1968) always noted how the struggle for power shaped ideas, arguing that the interests of powerful groups had lasting influence on the shape of a culture. But he was interested in how ideas originally created to serve the powerful came to have a life of their own, constraining rulers as well as those they ruled, forcing elites to preserve their legitimacy by making good on their status claims and leading religious specialists to become preoccupied with distinctively religious problems.

Contemporary theorists instead see culture as itself a form of power. Foucault (1980), for example, analyzes how new kinds of knowledge and associated practices (such as measuring, categorizing, or describing objects of knowledge) in effect construct new sites where power can be deployed. New disciplines, such as psychoanalysis, construct new loci such as the unconscious, new subjectivities, where power can be exercised (and also where resistance can emerge). Foucault (1977, 1983) eliminates the question of who has power, leaving aside the role of interested agents, to emphasize instead that each cultural formation, each technique of power, has a history of its own, and that different actors adopt these techniques for different purposes. Since cultural practices, categories, and rules are enactments of power, Foucault does not think of culture as being used by the powerful to maintain their power. Rather, he thinks of power itself as practices that deploy knowledge to constitute human beings as the subjects of that knowledge.

Pierre Bourdieu focuses less on power than on inequality. He emphasizes that people differ not only in their cultural resources but also in the skill with which they deploy those resources. Bourdieu's (1984) special contribution is to show how deeply inequalities between the more and less privileged penetrate persons, constituting the fundamental capacities for judgment, aesthetic response, social ease, or political confidence with which they act in the world. Actors use culture in creative ways to forward their own interests in a system of unequal power, but the effect of that struggle is to reproduce the basic structure of the system.

Culture and Social Movements

Both opportunities and difficulties await researchers who look to the sociology of culture for fruitful new approaches to social movement questions. On the one hand, as others have noted (Cohen 1985; Tarrow 1992a), culture has always been central to the kinds of processes social movements researchers study, such as formulating grievances, defining a common identity, or developing solidarity and mobilizing action. Indeed, social movements are the sites where new cultural resources, such as identities and ideologies, are most frequently formulated (Friedman and McAdam 1992). Addressing such processes more directly, as several recent researchers have done (see Klandermans, Kriesi, and Tarrow 1988; Morris and Mueller 1992), can only invigorate the field.

On the other hand, the traditional concern of social movement theory with activists and their motives fits naturally with the Weberian focus on how individuals develop understandings that guide their action. Researchers such as Doug McAdam (1988) who study activists, theorists such as David Snow (Snow et al. 1986; Snow and Benford 1988) who analyze the cultural preconditions for activism, and scholars such as William Gamson (1992) who study how ordinary people talk about politics all focus on individuals and their motives. They try to understand actors' experience and the larger forces that shape their motives, ideas, and identities. While such approaches have already proved fruitful, it is important that social movement researchers not become wedded to an implicitly Weberian image of culture just as cultural theory is moving in the other direction—toward more global, impersonal, institutional, and discursive assertions of cultural power.

Turning Culture Inside Out

There is now an abundance of work—that of Foucault and Bourdieu, but also many others (Wuthnow 1987; Sewell 1985, 1990, 1992)—arguing that culture constitutes social experience and social structure, that culture should be seen as socially organized practices rather than individual ideas or values, that culture can be located in public symbols and rituals rather than in ephemeral subjectivities, and that culture and power are fundamentally linked. Yet these more global approaches to the study of culture can also be difficult to grasp firmly, either theoretically or empirically. It would be ideal to marry Weber's concrete, grounded style of causal argument to Durkheim's understanding of the irreducibly collective, encompassing nature of culture.[6]

One new approach to understanding how culture shapes social movements involves rethinking how culture works. Most culture theory assumes that culture has more powerful effects where it is deeper—deeply internalized in individual psyches, deeply integrated into bodies and habits of action, or deeply embedded in taken-for-granted "mentalities." But at least some of the time, culture may have more powerful effects when it is on the "outside," not deeply internalized or even deeply meaningful. Variations in the ways social contexts bring culture to bear on action may do more to determine culture's power than variations in how deeply culture is held. And study of these social contexts may prove a fruitful direction for integrating culture into social movement research.

For Weber's actor-based sociology of ideas, culture has more influence when it is clearer, more coherent, and more deeply held. Protestantism had more influence on economic action than any other faith because its rationalized doctrine cut off "magical paths" to salvation, because it held that salvation was demonstrated in worldly action, and because it demanded that the intensely believing faithful rigorously regulate every aspect of daily life. Although Durkheim's model of culture was different from Weber's, he also held that culture had its greatest effects when it was most deeply part of the collective consciousness. Only universally shared, actively practiced, vivid symbols could constrain individual passions and impose a social reality on individual consciousness.

To analyze culture's power to affect action, independent of whether it is deeply held (either in the sense of deeply internalized, taken-for-granted practices like the habitus or in the sense of deeply held beliefs like those of Weber's Protestant saints), we may focus on three sources of cultural power: codes, contexts, and institutions. In each case we will see how the culture's effects on action can operate from the outside in, as social processes organize and focus culture's effects on action.

Codes

The notion of culture as a semiotic code has been one of the hallmarks of the new cultural studies. But the notion of semiotic code, by analogy with the deep structures that organize language, usually refers to deeply held, inescapable relationships of meaning that define the possibilities of utterance in a cultural universe. Deep, unspoken, and pervasive equals powerful.

Some codes are not deep, however, and not in the least invisible. A perfect example is provided by Theodore Caplow's (1982, 1984) study of Christmas gift giving in Middletown. In an article with the compelling title "Rule Enforcement without Visible Means," Caplow (1984) makes the point precisely. Caplow finds that middle-class Americans do not "believe in" Christmas gift giving. They criticize the commercialization of Christmas; they consider buying Christmas gifts an unpleasant burden; they think most gifts are a waste of money; they often do not like the gifts they receive; and they are unhappy with much of what they buy for others. Thus, Caplow asks, why do they give Christmas gifts, spending a considerable share of their disposable income, if they do not believe in it? Why does the practice persist without normative support and even in the face of widespread criticism?

Caplow uses data on actual gift giving to argue that Christmas gift giving constitutes a semiotic code (that is, a set of relationally defined meanings) in which the relative value of the gifts a person gives others signals the relative importance with which she or he holds those others. Not to give a gift would, independent of the intentions of the giver, be interpretable as a sign that one did not value the (non)recipient. What governs action in this case, then, is not individuals' internalized beliefs, but their knowledge of what meanings their actions have for others.[7]

Speaking of semiotic codes may seem to take us right back into the thickets of French structuralist theories or into a search for the deep underlying meanings that animate Geertzian "cultural systems." But semiotic codes can be much more discrete, more superficial, and sometimes more contested or political than semioticians usually imply. For example, when florists and confectioners try to increase their business by announcing National Secretaries' Week, few are presumably moved by deep belief in the principles that lie behind the announcement. But if every newspaper in the country is for weeks blanketed with advertisements implying that bosses who appreciate their secretaries will give them flowers and take them out to lunch, both secretaries and their employers may be, at the least, uncomfortable about what signals their actions will send. An employer may well think that for twenty-five dollars it is not worth the risk of hurting the secretary's feelings; and even a secretary who has disdain for the occasion may feel offended, or at least ambivalent, if it is ignored.

Much of our cultural politics is fought out on precisely such terrain. Let us imagine that a national secretaries' union launches a "Bread Not Roses" campaign, so that for employers to offer flowers without a raise is redefined as a sign of contempt. This would be a direct use of culture to influence action, not so much by shaping beliefs as by shaping the external codes through which action is interpreted. These are cultural power struggles, in which publicity can be a potent weapon even if no deeper persuasion occurs.

Even without conscious efforts at publicity, one of the most important effects social movements have is publicly enacting images that confound existing cultural codings. From the punk subculture's deliberate embrace of "ugly" styles (meant to muddle standard status codings [Hebdige 1979]) to the Black Panthers' display of militant, disciplined, armed black revolutionaries to the New Left spectacle of middle-class college students being beaten by police (Gitlin 1980), altering cultural codings is one of the most powerful ways social movements actually bring about change.

Recent American gender politics exhibit similar redefinitions of the cultural codes that signal masculinity and femininity. Increasingly in films (a perfect example is *Working Girl*) toughness and ambition are coded as part of earthy, sexy femininity, while classical feminine weakness, lace, and fluffy pillows are identified with a manipulative, dishonest antifemininity. In the same spirit, the very word *macho* makes the traditional hallmarks of masculinity seem suspect—signs of insecurity or weakness. The recent Disney classic *Beauty and the Beast* offers a wonderfully muscled, powerful, handsome antihero, Gaston, who is made utterly ridiculous as he carefully examines his appearance in every mirror he passes. In contrast, the Beast wins Beauty's love through his gentle awkwardness, his eagerness to please her, his love of books, and his distaste for violence. These cultural reworkings may sometimes change people's values or give them new role models. But more important, such cultural recodings change understandings of how behavior will be interpreted by others. If traditional feminine helplessness starts to look manipulative and controlling, and if masculine dominance starts to look pathetically self-absorbed, then men and women do not have to convert to find themselves meeting a new standard. Men may continue to aspire to masculinity and women to femininity, but the content those ideals encode has changed.

The agendas of many social movements revolve around such cultural recodings. Indeed, since most movements lack political power (this is precisely why they use unconventional political tactics) they can reshape the world more effectively through redefining its terms rather than rearranging its sanctions. And of course opponents employ the giant machinery of publicity that defines antiwar activists as unpatriotic, feminists as man haters, and the wealthy as beleaguered taxpayers to subvert social movements and their goals, precisely by winning the battle for symbolic encoding.

Since many of the enduring accomplishments of social movements are transformations in culture—in the legitimacy of specific demands, but also in the general climate of public discourse (see McAdam 1982)—theoretical ideas that focus on global properties of cultural systems may be more valuable than approaches that focus primarily on specific actors or even specific gains.[8] Such analyses would emphasize the flamboyance or visibility of a movement's tactics rather than either its success in mobilization or its gains in more conventional terms (see J. Gamson 1989). Researchers might then seek to understand why some cultural offensives succeed and others fail.

Contexts

One of the persistent difficulties in the sociology of culture is that culture influences action much more powerfully at some moments than at others. I have argued elsewhere (Swidler 1986), for example, that explicit cultural ideologies emerge during "unsettled" historical periods when such coherent, systematic worldviews can powerfully influence their adherents. But sometimes even fully articulated ideologies do not predict how people will act (as the many examples of co-optation, of movements that sell out their principles, or of leaders who betray revolutions attest). And at other times, even inchoate or contradictory worldviews powerfully affect action. To better understand such variations in culture's influence, we need to think more carefully about the specific contexts in which culture is brought to bear.

The contexts in which ideas operate can give them coherence and cultural power. "Context" in the first instance means the immediate, face-to-face situation—whether actors are meeting in public forums such as mass meetings or legislatures where issues are debated and decided. In such settings, the dynamics of the meeting itself can give ideas a coherent, systematic influence, even when the individual participants are confused and ambivalent. Second, context can mean the more general situation of conflict or accommodation, polarization and alliance formation, crisis or politics as usual.

The effect of context is evident in many ordinary political and work activities. In academia, for example, one may be confused or ambivalent about an issue—how good a job candidate's work is, whether a colleague merits tenure, whether a departmental decision is genuinely feminist. But in a meeting where sides polarize, where one group defines the issue one way and their antagonists define it in another, these ambiguities fall by the wayside. When politics polarize and alliances are at stake, the public culture crystallizes. Ideas that may have had only loose associations become part of a unified position; other ideas, which may originally have been intermingled with the first set, become clearly opposed. To back the side one supports comes to mean holding a particular ideological line, casting one's lot with a given framing of the situation. It is the conflict itself, the need to separate allies from foes and the need to turn general predispositions into specific decisions, that structures ideological debate.

Certain contexts, particularly those that are important in many social movements, give culture a coherent organization and consistent influence that it normally lacks in the minds of most individuals. This accounts for some of the difficulty in trying to pin down just where and why culture makes a difference in social action (see, for an example, the revealing debate between Sewell [1985] and Skocpol [1985] on the role of culture in the French revolution). If we think of culture either in the Weberian sense, as ideas deeply internalized in individual psyches, or in the more recent semiotic sense as broad, encompassing discourses that shape all social discussion in a given historical era, we will miss the more specific ways cultural power varies by context.

Social movements play out in contexts such as revolutionary committees, public meetings, and constituent assemblies, where stakes are high, risks are great, and political alliances are both essential and uncertain. When activists demand ideological purity to undermine their enemies and consolidate their alliances, they make ideas powerful from the outside in. When a political meeting decides that individual leadership violates its principles, or that fetal tissue research threatens the right to life, ideas can acquire a power to affect action that they normally lack. Of course there is a relation between such context-specific amplifications and clarifications of ideological effects and the wider beliefs, commitments, and values that individuals use to think about their lives in ordinary times. But ordinary culture is fluid, multistranded, and often inconsistent. Specific contexts turn inchoate individual beliefs and broad cultural idioms into particular demands for action. To use contemporary jargon, political actors know the "correct line" even if they remain uncertain about their personal beliefs. And specific political contexts lead actors to draw lines of ideological division sharply, to develop the action implications of their ideological stances, and to make adherence to one side or another of a debate an important sign of alliance or opposition. As the song says, "Which side are you on?"

Institutions

To explain how culture can have consistent effects on action even when people's beliefs are inconsistent, ambiguous, or lightly held, I have suggested that semiotic codes and political contexts can make ideas and symbols culturally constraining, irrespective of whether people believe them. Institutions can have similar effects, by another route.

Institutions are well-established, stable sets of purposes and rules backed by sanctions. One example is legally structured marriage. Others, less formal but no less powerful, are the employment relationship and the established norms about buying and selling that define consumer transactions.[9]

Institutions create obdurate structures that are both constraints and opportunities for individuals. For sociologists of culture, what is interesting about institutions is that individuals create culture around their rules. Individuals can then come to act in culturally uniform ways, not because their experiences are shared, but because they must negotiate the same institutional hurdles.[10]

For example, in a college where students must have a major in order to graduate, they need to be able to answer the question, What do you plan to major in? They may also ask themselves and each other, What am I interested in? because the institution contains the presumption that focused interests guide the choice of major. Moreover, students may develop cultural lore about how to select a major, identities based around the choice of major, and categorizations of others ("techies" versus "fuzzies") on the basis of their majors. In a similar way, the American institution of voting presumes that citizens have ideas or opinions about public issues. Those who do not have opinions or ideas may feel that they are missing some crucial ingredient of selfhood. The tasks an institution requires make sense only if people have or can develop corresponding orientations. Widely shared cultural accounts for those orientations ensue, creating collective consistencies and resonances that the actors might not possess otherwise.

Similarly, the cultures of social movements are shaped by the institutions the movements confront. Different regime types and different forms of repression generate different kinds of social movements with differing tactics and internal cultures. Dominant institutions also shape the movements' deeper values. The most obvious case is the institution of suffrage itself. From Chartism to women's suffrage to the civil rights movement, Western democracies have witnessed the drama of people denied suffrage organizing extralegal protest to batter their way into the system, making claims for equal dignity and equal moral personhood. In such systems, to be a legitimate political actor is to be one who can vote.

Social movements develop their cultures to fit extant institutions in other ways as well. Where, for example, the state is responsible for public order, movements can induce state action by threatening the public peace. French workers, for example, protested against employers, not directly, but by barricading streets, marching to the town square, and demanding state involvement (Reddy 1984). In the weaker American state, with powerful market institutions but weak centralized police powers, workers defined their battles as struggles with employers over benefits and wages.

Institutions affect the formulation of social movement identities and objectives in yet more central ways. Where the state enshrines "rights" as the crucial legal claim that trumps all others, both individuals and social movements will conceive of the claims they make as "rights" (Glendon 1991). And where legal claims are tied to group identities, as they long have been for American Indians (Cornell 1988) and increasingly have become for women, the disabled, and members of many ethnic and racial groups, identity becomes a central focus for social movements. When institutions make questions of group identity salient, they generate identity-oriented movements and a quest for identity on the part of individuals.

If institutions shape cultural responses in these ways, then the "frame alignment" of which David Snow and his colleagues (Snow et al. 1986; Snow and Benford 1988) have written is not just a matter of individuals' getting their frames in sync. Rather, individuals develop common scripts in response to the features of the institutions they confront. Commonalities in movement cultures are, at least in part, responses to the institutions the movements are trying to change.

The implication of all this for social movement researchers is in part to change the ordering in their implicit causal models. Gamson's *Talking Politics* (1992), for example, looks carefully at discourse—at what ordinary people say about politics when they are stimulated to think about it in a group situation. Gamson is interested in delineating the elements from which an active, oppositional culture could be built. But on the evidence of the ways people in Gamson's focus groups talk, one might well conclude that social movements in contemporary America are a near impossibility. While respondents demonstrate intelligence and occasional indignation over social wrongs, their information is fragmentary, their conversation meandering, and their worldviews concatenations of numerous overlapping frames, many of which are nearly self-canceling. But perhaps this search for a popular culture that could support activism starts in the wrong place. How people organize the cultural resources at their disposal depends very much on the kinds of institutional challenges they face.

Conclusion

I began this essay by stressing the two great wellsprings from which much of contemporary culture theory derives. In a sense Weber and Durkheim still define the range of alternatives available to sociologists who want to use culture to explain things. I have suggested that while the Weberian image of culture as belief carried by committed individual actors seems easier to work with, recent developments in cultural studies have moved in a more Durkheimian direction, seeing culture as constitutive, inherently collective, imbedded in symbols and practices, and necessarily infused with power (see Alexander 1988). But culture in this sense—public practices infused with power—can also be extremely hard to grasp concretely. Indeed, too-easy embrace of the notion that culture is ubiquitous and constitutive can undermine any explanatory claims for culture. Then emphasis on culture becomes a species of intellectual hand waving, creating a warm and cozy atmosphere, while other factors continue to carry the real explanatory weight.

I have tried to offer four concrete suggestions about how culture might be conceived as a global, collective property without becoming only a diffused mist within which social action occurs. I have argued first that, to think more powerfully about culture, we must entertain the possibility that culture's power is independent of whether or not people believe in it. I have then gone on to suggest that culture can have powerful influence if it shapes not individuals' own beliefs and aspirations, but their knowledge of how others will interpret their actions.

My third suggestion is that students of culture in general, and social movement scholars in particular, need to pay close attention to the public contexts in which cultural understandings are brought to bear. Reminding ourselves of the power that meetings and other group forums have to crystallize ideological splits and recode public speech and action, I suggest that culture can have consistent, coherent effects on action in particular contexts even if individuals and groups are divided and inconsistent in their beliefs.

Finally, I have suggested that institutions structure culture by systematically patterning channels for social action. In a sense this simply reinforces the insights of the "political process" model of social movements, which notes that movements respond to the wider structure of political constraints and opportunities (McAdam 1982). But I have tried to push the cultural dimension of such processes, arguing that even cultural patterns that appear to be independent inventions (or innate needs) of individuals or groups can be produced or reproduced by the challenges with which institutions confront actors. Thus many movements may invent simultaneously what seem to be common cultural frames (like the many rights movements of the 1960s or the identity movements of the 1980s). But these need not be matters either of independent discovery or of cultural contagion. Rather, they may be common responses to the same institutional constraints and opportunities.

Rethinking how culture might work from the outside in is a large task. I do not think the suggestions I have made here about codes, contexts, and institutions are the only ways the issue might be approached. But I am convinced that if interest in culture is restricted to studying the inner meaning systems of deeply committed activists, or if culture is relegated to a vague—if "constitutive"—penumbra, we will sacrifice more incisive ways of thinking about its power.

Notes

I would like to thank Claude Fischer and Kim Voss along with the editors and reviewers of this volume for helpful comments and advice.

1. See the analysis of Durkheim's view of symbols as constitutive in Bellah 1973.

2. The two major lines of empirical work on values are the anthropological, comparing values of different social groups (Kluckhohn and Strodtbeck 1961), and the social-psychological, comparing the values of individuals (Rokeach 1973).

3. Geertz's early classic, *The Religion of Java* (1960), is overtly Weberian in inspiration and execution, tracing the influence of differing religious ethics on economic action. Geertz (1966) also emphasizes the problem of theodicy (explaining suffering and injustice in the world God controls), which was central to Weber's analysis of the dynamics of religious change. And Geertz has returned repeatedly to the problem of rationalization in non-Western religious traditions (1968, 1973).

4. See Keesing 1974 for a detailed treatment of this issue.

5. See Sherry Ortner's (1984) insightful and entertaining analysis of shifts in culture theory, "Theory in Anthropology Since the Sixties."

6. This is the theoretical strategy Randall Collins (1981, 1988) has called "microtranslation." The theorist attempts to provide concrete, individual-level causal imagery even for macro or global causal processes, without making the micro reductionist claim that the underlying causal dynamics operate at the micro level.

7. Careful readers of Weber will note that such an explanation of action is perfectly compatible with his theoretical orientation. "Social action" is, after all, action whose "subjective meaning takes account of the behavior of others and is thereby oriented in its course" (Weber 1968: 4). Weber (1946b) also argued clearly that the Protestant sects continued to influence action long after intense belief had faded because members knew that sect membership gave visible social testimony to their worthiness. Nonetheless, Weber and most of his followers have been preoccupied with the inner workings of the religious psyche rather than with more external forms of cultural power.

8. William Sewell Jr. (1985, 1990) analyzes how dramatic social movements shift an entire pattern of public discourse and thus remake future forms of collective action.

9. See Jepperson 1991 and Scott 1992 for fuller treatments of institutions and problems of institutional analysis.

10. I develop this argument more fully for the case of marriage in *Talk of Love: How Americans Use Their Culture,* forthcoming from University of Chicago Press.

Chapter 3

The Process of Collective Identity

Alberto Melucci

Culture and Collective Action

Interest in cultural analysis has grown in the past two decades together with an extraordinary cultural transformation of planetary society. We are witnessing, with mixed feelings of amazement and fear, the impressive development of communication technologies, the creation of a world media system, the breakdown of historical political cleavages, the impact of cultural differences on national societies and at the world scale. Never before have human cultures been exposed to such a massive reciprocal confrontation, and never has the cultural dimension of human action been directly addressed as the core resource for production and consumption. It is not surprising therefore that social sciences are rediscovering culture, that a new reading of the tradition is taking place through the lens of this key concept, and that a wave of interest in cultural analysis is bringing a new vitality to theoretical debates in sociology.

Social movements, too, seem to shift their focus from class, race, and other more traditional political issues toward the cultural ground. In the past twenty years emerging social conflicts in advanced societies have not expressed themselves through political action, but rather have raised cultural challenges to the dominant language, to the codes that organize information and shape social practices. The crucial dimensions of daily life (time, space, interpersonal relations, individual and group identity) have been involved in these conflicts, and new actors have laid claim to their autonomy in making sense of their lives.

This essay addresses the concept of collective identity that was introduced in my previous contributions to the analysis of contemporary social movements (see especially Melucci 1989), and that has already stimulated a promising discussion (Bartholomew and Mayer 1992; Laraña, Johnston, and Gusfield 1994). Why should the issue of collective identity be a concern and, more specifically, in the context of a book on social movements and culture? From the theoretical point of view, interest in cultural analysis corresponds to a shift (see Swidler, chapter 2 in this book) toward new questions about how people make sense of their world: How do people relate to texts, practices, and artifacts so that these cultural products are meaningful to them? And, ultimately, how do they produce meaning? These new questions raised by the recent reflections on culture are paralleled by the increasing evidence of the weaknesses of traditional sociological theories when they are confronted with contemporary social movements.

The study of social movements has always been divided by the dualistic legacy of structural analysis as a precondition for collective action and the analysis of individual motivations. These parallel, and sometimes intertwined, sets of explanations never fill the gap between behavior and meaning, between "objective" conditions and "subjective" motives and orientations. They never can answer the questions of how social actors come to form a collectivity and recognize themselves as being part of it; how they mantain themselves over time; how acting together makes sense for the participants in a social movement; or how the meaning of collective action derives from structural preconditions or from the sum of the individual motives.

The development of a new interest in culture and the related attention to hermeneutics, to linguistics, and to the many methodological warnings coming from ethnomethodology and cognitive sociology have also made more evident the low level of epistemological awareness and self-reflexivity typically implied in traditional research on collective phenomena. With few exceptions (for a good example see Johnston, chapter 11 in this volume), research on social movements has been led so far by a widespread "realistic" attitude toward the object, as if collective actors existed in themselves, were unified ontological essences that the researcher had to understand by referring them to some underlying structural condition or by sorting the motives behind the behaviors. The position of the observer is of course that of an external eye, as objective as possible, and very little attention is paid to questions such as how the relationship of the researcher to the field contributes to the construction of it. The present book is in itself a significant example of a turning point on these matters and a sign of an increasing epistemological awareness.

A thorough rethinking of the concept of collective identity is necessary to confront the dualism between structure and meaning. The concept, as we will see, cannot be separated from the production of meaning in collective action and from some methodological consequences in considering empirical forms of collective action. This strategic role of the concept in dealing with the questions that are coming to the forefront of contemporary sociological debates probably explains the parallel interest in both cultural analysis and collective identity. By asking the question of how individuals and groups make sense of their actions and how we can understand this process, we are obliged to shift from a monolithic and metaphysical idea of collective actors toward the processes through which a collective becomes a collective. A processual approach to collective identity helps account for such a theoretical and methodological shift. But the concept is often used in social movement studies in a reified fashion, a new passe-partout that simply substitutes the old search for a core "essence" of a movement. This essay stresses three basic points that are fundamental to a processual approach to collective identity: (1) collective identity implies a constructivist view of collective action; (2) it has some epistemological consequences on the way one considers the relation between observer and observed in social research; and (3) it affects the research practices themselves.

Defining Collective Identity

Action and Field

I consider collective action as the result of purposes, resources, and limits, as a purposive orientation constructed by means of social relationships within a system of opportunities and constraints. It therefore cannot be considered either the simple effect of structural preconditions or the expression of values and beliefs. Individuals acting collectively "construct" their action by means of "organized" investments: they define in cognitive terms the field of possibilities and limits they perceive while at the same time activating their relationships so as to give sense to their "being together" and to the goals they pursue.

The empirical unity of a social movement should be considered as a result rather than a starting point, a fact to be explained rather than evidence. The events in which a number of individuals act collectively combine different orientations, involve multiple actors, and implicate a system of opportunities and constraints that shape their relationships. The actors "produce" the collective action because they are able to define themselves and their relationship with the environment. The definition that the actors construct is not linear but produced by interaction, negotiation, and the opposition of different orientations.

Individuals or subgroups contribute to the formation of a "we" (more or less stable and integrated according to the type of action) by rendering common and laboriously adjusting three orders of orientations: those relating to the ends of the actions (the sense the action has for the actor); those relating to the means (the possibilities and the limits of the action); and finally those relating to relationships with the environment (the field in which the action takes place). The action system of a collective actor is thus organized along a number of polarities in a state of mutual tension. The collective actor seeks to give an acceptable and lasting unity to such a system, which is continuously subject to tensions because action has to meet multiple and contrasting requirements in terms of ends, means, and environment. Collective mobilizations can occur and can even continue because the actor has succeeded in realizing, and in the course of the action continues to realize, a certain integration between those contrasting requirements. This "social construction" of the "collective" through negotiation and renegotiation is continually at work when a form of collective action occurs. A failure or a break in this constructive process makes the action impossible.

The question How is a collective actor formed? at this point assumes a decisive theoretical importance: what was formerly considered a datum (the existence of the movement) is precisely what needs to be explained. Analysis must address itself to the plurality of aspects present in the collective action and explain how they are combined and sustained through time. It must tell us, therefore, what type of "construct" we are faced with in the observed action and how the actors themselves are "constructed."

A Definition

I call collective identity this process of "constructing" an action system. Collective identity is an interactive and shared definition produced by several individuals (or groups at a more complex level) and concerned with the orientations of action and the field of opportunities and constraints in which the action takes place. By "interactive and shared" I mean a definition that must be conceived as a process because it is constructed and negotiated through a repeated activation of the relationships that link individuals (or groups).

First, collective identity as a process involves cognitive definitions concerning the ends, means, and field of action. These different elements or axes of collective action are defined within a language that is shared by a portion or the whole of a society or that is specific to the group; they are incorporated in a given set of rituals, practices, cultural artifacts; they are framed in different ways but they always allow some kind of calculation between ends and means, investments and rewards. This cognitive level does not necessarily imply unified and coherent frameworks (as cognitivists tend to think: see Neisser 1976; Abelson 1981; Eiser 1980), but it is constructed through interaction and comprises different and sometimes contradictory definitions (see Billig, chapter 4 in this volume).

Second, collective identity as a process refers thus to a network of active relationships between the actors, who interact, communicate, influence each other, negotiate, and make decisions. Forms of organizations and models of leadership, communicative channels, and technologies of communication are constitutive parts of this network of relationships.

Finally, a certain degree of emotional investment, which enables individuals to feel like part of a common unity, is required in the definition of a collective identity. Collective identity is never entirely negotiable because participation in collective action is endowed with meaning but cannot be reduced to cost-benefit calculation and always mobilizes emotions as well (Moscovici 1981). Passions and feelings, love and hate, faith and fear are all part of a body acting collectively, particularly in areas of social life like social movements that are less institutionalized. To understand this part of collective action as "irrational," as opposed to the "rational" (which in this case means good!) part, is simply a nonsense. There is no cognition without feeling and no meaning without emotion.

Let us try now to understand more closely this interactive and communicative construction, which is both cognitively and emotionally framed through active relationships.

Process and Form

The term identity is most commonly used to refer to the permanence over time of a subject of action unaffected by environmental changes falling below a certain threshold; it implies the notion of unity, which establishes the limits of a subject and distinguishes it from all others; it implies a relation between two actors that allows their (mutual) recognition. The notion of identity always refers to these three features: the continuity of a subject over and beyond variations in time and its adaptations to the environment; the delimitation of this subject with respect to others; the ability to recognize and to be recognized.

The notion of a certain stability and permanence over time seems to contrast with the dynamic idea of a process. There is no doubt that at any given moment social actors try to delimit and stabilize a definition of themselves. So do the observers. But the concept of collective identity as defined here can precisely help to explain that what appears as a given reality, more or less permanent, is always the result, at least to a certain extent, of an active process that is not immediately visible.

Such a process involves continual investments and as it approaches the more institutionalized levels of social action it may increasingly crystallize into organizational forms, systems of rules, and leadership relationships. The tendency and need to stabilize one's identity and to give it a permanent form create a tension between the results of the process, which are crystallized in more or less permanent structures, in more or less stable definitions of identity, and the process itself, which is concealed behind those forms.

The concept of collective identity as defined here can help catch the interactive and sometimes contradictory processes lying behind what appears to be a stable and coherent definition of a given collective actor. I am aware of the fact that I am using the word *identity*, which is semantically inseparable from the idea of permanence and is perhaps, for this very reason, ill-suited to the processual analysis for which I am arguing. Nevertheless, I am still using the word *identity* as a constitutive part of the concept of "collective identity" because so far I have not found a better linguistic solution. Because, as I will argue, this collective identity is as much an analytical tool as a "thing" to be studied, it is by definition a temporary solution to a conceptual problem and can be changed if other concepts prove to be more adequate. In the meantime, I work within the limits of the available language, confident that the shift toward new concepts is a matter not just of different words but of a new paradigm. The way out from the legacy of modernity is a difficult process, and we will realize that our time is over only at the end, when we will find ourselves in a new conceptual universe. Meanwhile, for the sake of communication, we cannot help but use old words to address new problems.

One way to overcome the apparent contradiction between the static and the dynamic dimensions implied by collective identity is to think of it in terms of action. Collective identity enables social actors to act as unified and delimited subjects and to be in control of their own actions, but conversely they can act as collective bodies because they have achieved to some extent the constructive process of collective identity. In terms of the observed action, one may thus speak of collective identity as the ability of a collective actor to recognize the effects of its actions and to attribute these effects to itself. Thus defined, collective identity presupposes, first, a self-reflective ability of social actors. Collective action is not simply a reaction to social and environmental constraints; it produces symbolic orientations and meanings that actors are able to recognize. Second, it entails a notion of causality and belonging; actors are, that is, able to attribute the effects of their actions to themselves. This recognition underpins their ability to appropriate the outcomes of their actions, to exchange them with others, and to decide how they should be allocated. Third, identity entails an ability to perceive duration, an ability that enables actors to establish a relationship between past and future and to tie action to its effects.

The Relational Dimension of Collective Identity

Collective identity therefore defines the capacity for autonomous action, a differentiation of the actor from others while continuing to be itself. However, self-identification must also gain social recognition if it is to provide the basis for identity. The ability of a collective actor to distinguish itself from others must be recognized by these others. Therefore it would be impossible to talk of collective identity without referring to its relational dimension.

Recent advances in the neurosciences and cognitive sciences on what is innate to human behavior and what is acquired (Omstein and Sobel 1987; Gazzaniga 1987) provide a formal model for the present discussion of collective identity. Although some extreme positions have been taken up, contemporary brain research tends toward the intermediate view that the relational and social aspects of human behavior lie within its biological constitution. In the functioning of our brains, heredity lays down a neural program that governs the growth of an individual's nervous system. As far as the constitution of individual identity is concerned, the program creates conditions under which individual differentiation comes about as a result of interaction with the environment. Psychoanalysis, genetic psychology, and symbolic interactionism, investigating the early structuring of individual identity, had already demonstrated the crucial role of primary interactions—recognizing and being recognized—in the most deep-lying experiences of the life of an infant.

In a similar way, therefore, we can say that social movements develop collective identity in a circular relationship with a system of opportunities and constraints. Collective actors are able to identify themselves when they have learned to distinguish between themselves and the environment. Actor and system reciprocally constitute themselves, and a movement only becomes self-aware through a relation with its external environment, which offers to social action a field of opportunities and constraints that are in turn recognized and defined as such by the actor.

Therefore the unity of collective action, which is produced and maintained by self-identification, rests on the ability of a movement to locate itself within a system of relations. A collective actor cannot construct its identity independently of its recognition (which can also mean denial or opposition) by other social and political actors. In order to act, any collective actor makes the basic assumption that its distinction from other actors is constantly acknowledged by them, even in the extreme form of denial. There must be at least a minimal degree of reciprocity in social recognition between the actors (movement, authorities, other movements, third parties) even if it takes the form of a denial, a challenge, or an opposition ("We are for You the You that You are for Us"). When this minimal basis for recognition is lacking there can only be pure repression, an emptiness of meaning nullifying the social field in which collective identity can be produced.

The autonomous ability to produce and to recognize the collective reality as a "we" is a paradoxical situation: in affirming its difference from the rest of the society, a movement also states its belonging to the shared culture of a society and its need to be recognized as a social actor. The paradox of identity is always that difference, to be affirmed and lived as such, presupposes a certain equality and a certain reciprocity.

Identity and Conflict

Collective identity as a process can be analytically divided and seen from internal and external points of view. This separation of two sides is obviously a way of describing what should be seen as a basically unified process. Collective identity contains an unresolved and unresolvable tension between the definition a movement gives of itself and the recognition granted to it by the rest of the society.

Conflict is the extreme example of this discrepancy and of the tension it provokes. In social conflicts reciprocity becomes impossible and competition for scarce resources begins. Both subjects involved deny each others' identities and refuse to grant to their adversary what they demand for themselves. The conflict severs the reciprocity of the interaction; the adversaries clash over something that is common to both of them but that each refuses to grant to the other. Beyond the concrete or symbolic objects at stake in a conflict, what people fight for is always the possibility of recognizing themselves and being recognized as subjects of their action. Social actors enter a conflict to affirm the identity that their opponent has denied them, to reappropriate something that belongs to them because they are able to recognize it as their own.

During a conflict the internal solidarity of the group reinforces identity and guarantees it. People feel a bond with others not because they share the same interests, but because they need this bond in order to make sense of what they are doing (Pizzorno 1978, 1986). The solidarity that ties individuals to others enables them to affirm themselves as subjects of their actions and to withstand the breakdown of social relations induced by conflict. Moreover, they learn how to gather and focus their resources in order to reappropriate what they recognize as theirs. Participation in forms of collective mobilization or in social movements, involvement in forms of cultural innovation, voluntary action inspired by altruism—all these are grounded in this need for identity and help to satisfy it.

Collective Identity over Time

Collective identity is a learning process that leads to the formation and maintenance of a unified empirical actor that we can call a social movement. As it passes through various stages, the collective actor develops a capacity to resolve the problems set by the environment and become increasingly independent and autonomously active in its relationships. The process of collective identity is thus also the ability to produce new definitions by integrating the past and the emerging elements of the present into the unity and continuity of a collective actor.

It is above all situations of crisis or intense conflict that challenge the identity of a movement, when it is subjected to contradictory pressures that set a severe test for the ability of the collective actor to define its unity. It can respond by restructuring its action according to new orientations, or it can compartmentalize its spheres of action so that it can still preserve a certain amount of coherence, at least internally to each of them. The most serious cases provoke a breakdown or fragmentation of the movement or a breach of its confines. This can lead to the incapacity to produce and maintain a definition of the movement that has a certain stability or, vice versa, to the compulsive assumption of a rigid identity from which it is impossible to escape, as in sects or terrorist groups.

Collective identity ensures the continuity and permanence of the movement over time; it establishes the limits of the actor with respect to its social environment. It regulates the membership of individuals, and it defines the requisites for joining the movement and the criteria by which its members recognize themselves and are recognized. The content of this identity and its temporal duration vary according to the type of group.

When we consider organizational structures, leadership patterns, and membership requisites, we deal with levels of collective action that presuppose the notion of collective identity: they incorporate and enact the ways a collective actor defines ends, means, and field of action. One should consider those levels as empirical indicators of a possible collective identity and, conversely, should use this concept as an analytical tool to dismantle the "reified" appearance of those empirical dimensions of a social movement and to attain the constructive process behind them.

Dereification of Collective Identity

In sum, one cannot treat collective identity as a "thing," as the monolithic unity of a subject; one must instead conceive it as a system of relations and representations. Collective identity takes the form of a field containing a system of vectors in tension. These vectors constantly seek to establish an equilibrium between the various axes of collective action and between identification that an actor declares and the identification given by the rest of the society (adversaries, allies, third parties).

Collective identity in its concrete form depends on how this set of relations is held together. This system is never a definitive datum; it is instead a laborious process in which unity and equilibrium are reestablished in reaction to shifts and changes in the elements internal and external to the field. Collective identity therefore patterns itself according to the presence and relative intensity of its dimensions. Some vectors may be weaker or stronger than others, and some may be entirely absent. One may imagine it as a field that expands and contracts and whose borders alter with the varying intensity and direction of the forces that constitute it.

At any given moment both actors and observers can give an account of this field through a unified, delimited, and static definition of the "we." This "reification" tendency is always part of a collective actor's need for continuity and permanence. But today this unsurmountable necessity has to confront important changes in the ways identification takes place.

Identification processes are today gradually transferred from outside society to its interior. From transcendent and metaphysical entities—from metasocial foundations like myths, gods, and ancestors, but also from the more recent avatars of God like History or the Invisible Hand of the market—identification processes shift to associative human action, to culture and communication, to social relations and technological systems. As identity is progressively recognized as socially produced, notions like coherence, boundary maintenance, and recognition only describe it in static terms; but in its dynamic connotation collective identity increasingly becomes a process of construction and autonomization.

For recent social movements, particularly those centered on cultural issues, collective identity is becoming the product of conscious action and the outcome of self-reflection more than a set of given or "structural" characteristics. The collective actor tends to construct its coherence and recognize itself within the limits set by the environment and social relations. Collective identity tends to coincide with conscious processes of "organization" and it is experienced as an action more than as a situation.

To express this increasingly self-reflexive and constructed manner in which contemporary collective actors tend to define themselves, I suggest that we coin a term: *identization*. Within the boundaries of our language, it is a rough and provocative acknowledgment of a qualitative leap in the present forms of collective action and also a call for an equivalent leap in our cognitive tools.

The Lens of Collective Identity: What One Can See Through It

Collective identity is a concept, an analytical tool, not a datum or an essence, not a "thing" with a "real" existence. In dealing with concepts, one should never forget that we are not talking of "reality," but of instruments or lenses through which we read reality. The concept of collective identity can function as a tool only if it helps to analyze phenomena, or dimensions of them, that cannot be explained through other concepts or models and if it contributes to new knowledge and understanding of these phenomena.

As I said in the opening section of this essay, the concept of collective identity was devised in order to overcome the shortcomings of the dualistic legacy still present in the study of collective action and the difficulties of the current approaches in explaining some dimensions of contemporary social movements, particularly the central role of culture and symbolic production in recent forms of action. It also addresses the naive epistemological assumptions implied very often by many contemporary approaches to the study of social movements. It is then a concept that is intended to introduce changes in our conceptualization of social movements, and for this very reason should contribute to a different understanding of the changing significance of social movements in contemporary society.

These two levels, changes in conceptualization and changes in our understanding of the significance of collective phenomena, are connected by a circular relation. The circle is not a vicious one if concepts help us to see more of the phenomena to which they apply, to see them differently. Moreover, if these empirical phenomena are filtered and interpreted through these lenses, they may help us to refine and improve the quality of the lenses themselves.

Let me try to indicate what one can see through the particular lens of collective identity.

First, the notion of collective identity is relevant to sociological literature because it brings a field view of collective action and a dynamic view of its definition. It implies the inclusion of the social field as part of the movement construction and it means that beyond the formal definitions (speech, documents, opinions of participants) there is always an active negotiation, an interactive work among individuals, groups, or parts of the movement. This shifts attention from the top to the bottom of collective action and it does not consider only the most visible forms of action or the leaders' discourse. It looks to the more invisible or hidden forms and tries to listen to the more silent voices.

Processes of mobilization, organizational forms, models of leadership, ideologies and forms of communication: these are all meaningful levels of analysis for the reconstruction from within of the system of action that constitutes a collective actor. But also relationships with the outside—with competitors, allies, adversaries, and especially the reaction of the political system and the apparatus of social control—define a field of opportunities and constraints within which the collective actor takes shape, perpetuates itself, or changes (the importance of this dimension has been stressed by, for example, Gamson, Fireman, and Rytina 1982; Gamson 1990; Tarrow 1989b).

Second, the concept of collective identity can also contribute to a better understanding of the nature and meaning of the emerging forms of collective action in highly differentiated systems. In the past ten years, analysis of social movements and collective action has further developed into an autonomous sector of theory and research in the social sciences, and the quantity and quality of work in the area has increased and improved our understanding of recent phenomena (McCarthy and Zald 1987; Jenkins 1983; Cohen 1985; Turner and Killian 1987; Klandermans, Kriesi, and Tarrow 1988; Snow and Benford 1988; Melucci 1989; Gamson 1990). The autonomy of the conceptual field relating to analysis of social movements has developed, not by chance, in parallel with the increasing autonomy of noninstitutional forms of collective action in complex systems. The social space of movements has become a distinct area of the system and no longer coincides either with the traditional forms of organization of solidarity or with the conventional channels of political representation. The area of movements is now a "sector" or a "subsystem" of the social arena.

Recognizing this autonomy forces us to revise concepts like "state" and "civil society" (Keane 1988), "private" and "public," "expressive" and "instrumental"; distinctions break down and signal a change in our conceptual universe. The notion of "movement" itself, which originally stood for an entity acting against the political and governmental system, is now inadequate to describe the reality of reticular and diffuse collective phenomena. Contemporary "movements" take the form of solidarity networks with potent cultural meanings, and it is precisely these that distinguish them so sharply from political actors and formal organizations.

The concept of collective identity helps to make distinctions that separate this level from others (particularly from political dimensions of collective action). These dimensions do not disappear from the scene, but come to play different roles that can be caught only if one relies on conceptual tools that allow one to recognize the complexity of present collective actors and that do not take for granted "social movement" as a unified and homogeneous reality.

Third, we have passed beyond the global and metaphysical conception of collective actors as historical heroes or villains. By identifying specific levels that enter the construction of collective identity, we can see movements as action systems. They are not entities that move with the unity of goals attributed to them by their ideologues or opponents. They are systems of action, complex networks among the different levels and meanings of social action. This is particularly true of contemporary forms of collective action that are multiple and variable. They lie at several different levels of the social system. The consequence for the analysis of contemporary conflicts is that we must therefore begin by distinguishing between the field of a conflict and the actors that bring such conflict to the fore.

In the past, studying conflicts used to mean analyzing the social condition of a group and using this analysis to deduce the cause of the collective action. Today we must first identify a social field where a conflict emerges and then explain how certain social groups take action within it. Moreover, the actors in a conflict cannot be easily linked to a social condition because they are very often a social composite. Their condition as such does not explain their involvement in a conflict. Since actors are not inherently conflictual, by their social "essence," the nature of action is temporary; it may involve different actors, or it may shift among various areas of the system. This multiplicity and variability of actors make the plurality of the analytical meanings contained within the same collective event or phenomenon even more explicit.

Fourth, the concept of collective identity has important consequences in clearing up some misunderstanding on the so-called new social movements. Paradoxically, the result of the recent debate on "new movements" has been that the image of movements as metaphysical entities has been deeply questioned. Contemporary movements, like all collective phenomena, are not "new" or "old" but bring together forms of action that involve various levels of the social structure. They comprise different orientations that entail a variety of analytical points of view. Their components belong to different historical periods. We must, therefore, seek to understand this multiplicity of synchronic and diachronic elements and explain how they are combined into the concrete unity of a collective actor. The notion of collective identity can help to describe and to explain this connection between the apparent unity, which is always our empirical starting point, and the underlying multiplicity, which can be detected only by an appropriate analytical tool.

Fifth, another important consequence of the concept of collective identity has to do with the theory of domination and conflict. Once one has clarified the epistemological premise concerning the "newness" of contemporary movements, the notion of collective identity can prevent sociological analysis from too quickly getting rid of the theoretical question of whether a new paradigm of collective action is now taking shape. The question occurs not in the empirical sense of taking the observed phenomenon as a whole, but rather analytically, in terms of certain levels or elements of action. We must ask ourselves, therefore, if there are dimensions to the "new" forms of action that we should assign to a systemic context other than that of industrial capitalism, if these dimensions express new systemic conflicts and challenge new forms of social domination, a question that is dismissed by critics of "new movements," who place these phenomena on an exclusively political level.

I have suggested that collective action in many recent social movements, by the very fact that it exists, represents in its form and models of organization a message broadcast to the rest of society concerning new powers and the possibilities of new challenges. Instrumental and political goals are still pursued, but they become precise in their scope and replaceable. Action affects institutions by modernizing their culture and organization as well as by selecting new elites. At the same time, however, it raises issues that are not provided for by instrumental rationality, which requires only the implementation of whatever has been decided by anonymous and impersonal power.

Sixth, this level of analysis cannot explain everything, and the concept of collective identity is a permanent warning about the necessity of recognizing a plurality of levels in collective action. Contemporary movements, in particular, weave together multiple meanings, legacies from the past, the effects of modernization, resistances to change. The complexity, the irreducibility, the intricate semantics of the meanings of social action are perhaps the most fundamental contributions that the concept of collective identity can bring to the field of social movements studies.

Finally, collective identity has some radical methodological implications. Sociological analysis is not free from the risk of reducing collective action to just one of its levels and considering it as a unified empirical object. If sociology still rests on an essentialistic idea of social movements as characters acting on the stage of history, it may thus contribute, even unwillingly, to the practical denial of difference, to a factual and political ignorance of that complex semantics of meanings that contemporary movements carry in themselves. Not taking collective action as a given reality and questioning what is usually taken for granted—namely, the existence of a movement as a homogeneous empirical actor—are what analysis is about. To understand how a social movement succeeds or fails in becoming a collective actor is therefore a fundamental task for sociologists.

Of course actors have to reify their action in the making in order to speak about it. So do the opponents and the observers, including the researcher. "Objectifying" is a basic trait of human cognition and also a cognitive economy used in speaking about the world. But it does not mean that, as researchers, we have to take this reification for granted. The task of analysis is precisely that of deconstructing this apparent reality and letting the plurality of relations and meanings appear.

How are ends and means interpreted by different parts of the movement? How are resources and constraints held together in the movement discourse? What kind of relation with the environment shapes the movement and how do the different parts interpret it? What kind of conflicts, tensions, and negotiations can be observed during the process of construction and maintenance of a movement as a unified empirical actor? These are some of the questions that can be derived from the concept of collective identity and that lead to a different research practice.

How to Study Collective Identity

Research Methods on Social Movements

I would like to discuss here the consequences that posing the question of collective identity has for research practice. In the field of social movements, research has reflected the actor-system dualism inherited from the nineteenth-century legacy. This dualism has been present in three major and recurrent practices. First and most commonly, in the observation of behaviors variously defined as movements, protest, mobilizations, and so on, the researcher seeks to discover a particular social condition. This has meant investigating whether the structural conditions that define the actor, or rather the alleged actor, are capable of explaining the types of behavior observed.

The second area deals with the perceptions, representations, and values of actors. In this case, surveys are conducted, normally about activism, to delve into the motivations of individuals to participate in social movements. A subcategory of this approach is the analysis of documents produced by collective actors, that is, of the ideologies that have been articulated in written form. This entails working on organized (and organizational) representations. In this case, one can take the framing activity of "movement" leaders (those who have the power to speak on behalf of a movement) as a point of reference. Obviously a constant and recurring possibility is that of relating these two levels: certain representations and opinions are correlated with certain structural conditions.

The third type of research practice concerns the quantitative analysis of collective events, a relatively recent approach that Charles Tilly (1978, 1986) has systematically developed with very important results (see also, in the same direction, Tarrow 1989b). Here the empirical units are protest events. Such events, further classified by their specific characteristics (size, type of actors, repertoire of actions used, response on the part of the authorities), are then correlated with structural factors or different states of the political, economic, or other systems.

Each of the foregoing research practices provides useful information and helps clarify some aspect of collective action. Each of them indicates a research path that, explicitly confined to its own epistemological limits, could increase our understanding of collective action. But when an approach becomes the only tool for the interpretation of "a movement as such," then it easily becomes an undue extension and generalization that is also colored by a metaphysics of the actor that tends to consider it an "essential" subject instead of a system of relationships.

In the first case it is assumed that the structural "thickness" of a social condition should explain action, which is not able in itself to carry the "true" meaning of what is observed. One has to refer to a more substantial reality beyond the appearance of the phenomenon. A self-restrained application of this approach could provide useful information on the social profile of participants in social movements and on some societal macroprocesses that affect collective action.

In the second case, when inquiries concern the participants' motivation, the assumption is that by comparing individual opinions and representations and by relating them to some structural variables (e.g., social condition) one can draw a picture of the movement as a collective actor, which is supposed to be the sum or the combination of those individual opinions. When, on the other hand, one refers to documents, the discourse of the leaders and their framing activities are taken, mostly implicitly, as representative of the movement as a whole: the actor is conceived therefore as a unified reality that is interpreted in a transparent way by the leaders and by the organizational discourse. Here too a self-restrained use of these sources and methods could tell us what participants and leaders think.

The third case is concerned with protest events, and it is based on public records. In this case the reification of the collective actor is produced first by the fact that it is reduced to a political actor: given the nature of the data, the only forms of action that can be considered are those that challenge a public authority and are recorded by the police, the press, or other public sources. Second, in the definition of the movement, all the submerged relationships, the everyday activities that are part of a movement culture cannot be taken into account, or can be referred to only indirectly. But, of course, a self-restrained use of this method could give us important answers to the question of how an actor confronts a public authority and how the action is affected by the opponent.

When these approaches are used to provide general interpretations of "a movement as such," what disappears from the scene in all three cases is collective action as a social production, as a purposive, meaningful, and relational orientation, that cannot simply be derived from structural constraints (first case), cannot be reduced to the unity of leaders' discourse or to the sum of militants' opinions (second case), or cannot be reduced to being merely public behavior (third case).

The recent developments of discourse analysis applied to social movements are aware of this complexity and try to creatively approach the multiplicity of levels implied in a collective discourse (Johnston, chapter 11 in this volume). They bring a different point of view that is more concerned with meaning and its construction. Also, the recent wave of interest in biographical methods (see for a synthesis Bertaux 1981; Della Porta 1992) has also brought new attention to the subjective and discursive dimensions of collective action. But here there are also some risks related to a new version of the naive assumption that the meaning of a collective action will be the sum of the representations of individual actors (see Melucci 1992). Moreover, the assumption that a narrative will somehow adequately reveal the meaning of an action—above and beyond the relationship with the researcher in which the narrative is produced and the particular relationship of the narrator with his own memory—can easily end up identifying action with the ideology of the actor (and of the researcher) instead of revealing the nature of action as an interactive construct. If attention is not paid to the conditions of production of a text, to the reception and interpretation of it by the researcher, a new kind of "objectivism" can be the outcome of a very "subjective" source as biographical data.

Action research and research intervention, particularly as developed by Alain Touraine (1978), directly address the question of how action is constructed and attempt to observe action as it takes place, as a process built by actors. But these approaches assume a kind of missionary task on the part of the researcher, who ends up playing the role of deus ex machina, providing the actors with a consciousness that they are apparently not able to produce for themselves (this is particularly true of Touraine 1974, 1984). Second, they ignore the relationship between the observer and the observed, a problem that is crucial for any form of research that entails a direct interaction between researcher and subject. Finally, research-intervention methods underestimate the fact that a researcher intervening in a field of action does not work under "natural" conditions but modifies the field and may even manipulate it, beyond his or her intentions (this point has been particularly developed by the French *analyse institutionnelle;* see Lapassade 1981; Loureau 1977).

Conditions for Studying Collective Identity

If collective action is conceived as a field of meanings and orientations that are constructed through social relationships within resources and limits, further steps must be taken to address empirically the shortcomings of these attempts. Since collective identity is not a "thing" but a process of construction through active relationships, a research practice focusing on process should at least fill three conditions.

First, it should recognize that actors understand the meaning of their actions, independent of the redeeming or manipulative intentions of researchers.

Second, it should recognize that the researcher-actor relationship is itself subject to observation.

Finally, it should recognize that any research practice that requires an intervention in the field of action of a given actor creates an artificial situation that must be explicitly acknowledged. Such a practice therefore requires a high degree of self-reflexivity and a capacity for metacommunication regarding the circular relationship between the observer and the observed.

A research practice capable of responding to these requirements needs to concentrate more on processes and less on contents. It is toward this end that my research experiments in the field of collective action have been directed. This experience has resulted in my conviction that the three directions I have indicated here constitute a proving ground for any method that wishes to escape dualism between structure and intentions, observer and observed. In following these recommendations, research on collective identity casts off the illusion of being a reflection of the "true" reality and moves closer to understanding its very nature: action is a self-reflecting process socially constructed within the limits of a given social and cultural field; research is that particular kind of social action where chances or opportunities for self-reflexivity are higher.

Collective actors are never completely in control of their own actions. They are acted upon and lived by the process of the construction of a "we" even as they act and live that very process. There is an opaque, hidden aspect of collective action that is a result of the impossibility of an actor's simultaneously assuming the position of actor and the point of view of the relationship in which it is involved and to which it contributes. The relational point of view is not inaccessible to a collective actor, but one cannot simultaneously act and be an analyst, as each of us knows from our own personal experience. Analysis requires the distance that permits us to assume the point of view of the relationship itself and to metacommunicate about the limits and the possibilities by which action is delimited.

Only by keeping this distance and at the same time being close to the action can one observe that intense, plural, and sometimes contradictory system of meanings that constitute the collective identity of a social movement. Without access to the invisible network of negotiations and interactions among different parts and levels of an empirical movement, it is difficult not to reduce action to behaviors and opinions. But this access requires some conditions in the relationship between researchers and collective actors.

A Contractual Relationship

Knowledge about collective identity assumes a decisive role in rendering accessible a specific potential for action; it functions as a multiplier of processes for change because it gives the actors responsibility for the choices they make. Action research is sometimes close to this purpose and result, but it is often led by a missionary spirit that too easily transforms the researcher into an activist or a preacher.

Knowledge today becomes a desirable resource for actors, allowing for the recognition of a difference between actors and researchers in terms of skills and interests. The researcher is a particular type of actor who can provide cognitive resources, which help to make the relational point of view more transparent. This helps bring about the possibility of a negotiated relationship between actors who professionally control some cognitive resources and others who need to clarify their capacity for action but in turn control expertise and information relative to the action itself.

The meeting point between these two groups of actors is necessarily contractual. There is nothing missionary about it. Nor does this relation imply expectations about the destiny of the actors for the point of view of researchers. This might be true of some researchers as individuals, as citizens, as political activists, but not as scientists. In their institutionalized role, researchers are called upon to produce knowledge. In this capacity, they have to take ethical and political responsibility for the production and destination of cognitive resources; they do not have the privilege of being able to guide the destiny of a society as advisers of rulers or ideologues of protest.

The meeting ground between actors and researchers, and in this case I am not thinking only about the study of social movements, is the recognition of a demand for cognitive resources. Two distinct interests, that of the researcher who gathers information and that of the actor who improves his or her capacity to act consciously and meaningfully, can temporarily meet and create the possibility of an exchange.

An Example

In my own research practice, which is based on group experiential and videorecorded sessions (Melucci 1984), I have tried to apply these methodological guidelines to different social movement networks. The goal of my methodology is to break the apparent unity of the discourse of movements and to observe the interactive construction of the unity through differences and conflicts. The particular methodology is intended to address not individual opinions, but the system of interactions in its making. It assumes that it does not address only discourses, but discourses constructed through actual interactions involving the internal and external action field: actors are confronted with their internal tensions and with the external relationships with researchers, leaders, other actors, observers, opponents. The procedure is intended to allow the multilevel, multifaceted, often contradictory aspects of identity to emerge. Through a structured and process-oriented intervention it aims at the reconstruction of a field of meanings and relationships that is often dilemmatic (as the rethorical approach in social psychology has also shown; see Billig, chapter 4 in this volume).

Let me take as an example the women's movement of the 1970s. My example is based on the movement in Italy (Melucci 1984, 1989), but many characteristics resulting from this particular research are comparable to similar phenomena in other Western countries. Usually the women's movement has been analyzed either as a political actor or as a feminine culture spread in the life world. Through the reconstruction of the collective identity I was able to detect the action system of this collective actor and the ways the different components of women's action are kept together and translated in visible mobilization.

The women's movement reveals the tensions between consciousness-raising groups centered on the transparency of internal affective needs and the professional groups committed to conquering a public space for the feminine difference; between the groups producing "women's culture" (writing, art) for internal consumption and those engaged in the production of services (lodging, health, welfare); between the groups giving priority to research on the self and individual differences and those that put the accent on "sorority." These are not the only types of groups within the movement, but orientations that are present within a single group or portion of the movement. The integration of these orientations is assured by the high degree of elasticity of a very adaptable organizational form, simultaneously self-reflective and productive (the main production is that of "feminine" cultural codes). Starting from this identity structure, the mobilization of women is thus possible and assumes the characteristic double-level (visibility-latency) form: brief and intense public mobilization campaigns that are fed by the submerged life of the networks and their self-reflective resources.

This example shows how important the notion of collective identity can be in revealing collective action as a system of tensions. Applied to empirical cases, it accounts for different outcomes of the movement, which are related to the different internal field and to different answers from the external environment. Collective action should be thought of as a construct, putting an end to the structure-intentions duality. Action is an interactive, constructive process within a field of possibilities and limits recognized by the actors. The accent on the limits to the process of construction, which always take place within the boundaries of a given field, avoids the risk of a radical constructivism that would be difficult to sustain (Giddens 1984). Nevertheless, without the capability of perceiving and making sense of its boundaries, action would not be possible. In fact, radical constructivism finishes by destroying the relational dimension of social action and presents itself as the ultimate version, perhaps more sophisticated, of a voluntaristic paradigm.

Some Conclusions

At this point I would like to discuss some more general consequences concerning the position of the researcher and the role of scientific knowledge. Today scientific knowledge increasingly enters into the constructive process of collective action as a particular form of social action with a high self-reflective capacity. Knowledge is not a mirror revealing in a linear way the causal chains that govern reality. Instead, it is a circular process of modeling (of its subjects) and self-modeling (of its instruments). It is a process that is anything but "pure," in which the contaminating factors of emotions, subjective evaluations, and the limitations of the observer interact in a decisive manner. But also different fields of knowledge interact to an ever greater degree, continuously calling into question the conventional disciplinary boundaries and their institutional settings. Thus defined, scientific knowledge takes on the aspect of a bricolage, the gathering and combining of cues, whose meanings depend upon variations in point of view, from the particular perspective of the observer (Bateson 1972, 1979; Gilligan 1982).

Studying collective identity means redefining the relationship between the observer and the observed because we are dealing not with a thing, but with a process continuously activated by social actors. Acknowledging both in ourselves as scientists and in the collective actors the limited rationality that characterizes social action, researchers can no longer apply the criteria of truth or morality defined a priori outside of the relationship. Researchers must also participate in the uncertainty, testing the limits of their instruments and of their ethical values. They cannot avoid freezing in a definition "what a social movement is," as very often is the case for actors themselves. But they must be aware that collective identity is just a tool for analysis, not a reality in itself.

Thus the two models that have always characterized the relationship between researcher and actor in social sciences fall to pieces before our very eyes: that of identification and that of distance. "Understanding" or "empathetic" researchers share with ideologues, from whom they nevertheless intend to distance themselves, the illusion of the power to destroy the gap between reflection and action. The myth of transparency or of total communication seems to feed in a recurrent manner the need to transform the scientific work into maieutics or into pedagogy, exposing the "cold" body of science to the fire of action. But the model of distance, of the neutrality of the researcher, high priest of a "truth" and a "reality" that are beyond the comprehension of the actors, also seems to be obsolete. After all, just what is this "reality" of which researchers speak, if not that constructed together in a circular interaction with their "subjects"?

Giving up the role of the demiurge, the great suggestor or the eye of God, researchers can take responsibility for their work of knowledge, and they can offer the actors the possibility to develop their capacity to learn how to learn, to produce their own codes.

The particular form of action that we call research introduces into the field of social relations new cognitive input derived from the action itself and from the observation of its processes and effects. In complex societies, research could be conceived as a process of metacommunication, a second-degree learning process, as the development of the formal abilities that an era of accelerated change such as ours requires of knowledge. Providing an account of the plurality and tensions constituting a collective actor, collective identity, is a cognitive tool for this learning process.

Chapter 4

Rhetorical Psychology, Ideological Thinking, and Imagining Nationhood

Michael Billig

Alberto Melucci, in his book *Nomads of the Present,* pointed to a gap in current ways of studying social movements. According to Melucci, structuralist theories try to explain collective protest by discovering the strains in social systems. In so doing, the structuralist approach fails to describe how social movements are established. On the other hand, resource mobilization theorists devote their attention to examining how collective action is accomplished. In their turn, such theorists overlook the meaning of collective action for the participants. Melucci argues that both approaches ignore how social movements produce new collective identities and cognitive interpretations. He claims that "collective identity is . . . a process in which actors produce the common cognitive frameworks that enable them to assess their environment and to calculate the costs and benefits of their action" (1989: 35).

It would be easy to interpret Melucci in disciplinary terms, as if he were calling for social psychology to be added to the sociological analysis of social movements. The argument might run along the following lines. Sociologists, whether they analyze the social structure of macrosociety or the sociological organization of movements, tend to disregard the identities and cognitive frameworks of actual participants. By contrast, social psychologists, especially cognitive social psychologists, take frameworks of meaning, "identity systems," and attitudinal structures as their basic field of study. Thus, Melucci's message might be interpreted as recommending that a social psychologist should be added to any interdisciplinary team studying a social movement, in order that the relevant variables be covered.

If, however, one takes seriously Melucci's message, then matters should not be so simple. Melucci's gap refers to the ways that meanings and collective identities are constructed in the course of social action. As he argues, the rise of social movements creates new ways of understanding the social world, and these conflict with previously accepted notions. Thus, Melucci was not envisaging the missing social psychological dimension to be a static, unproblematic entity, as if a new "belief system" suddenly drops ready-made into the social world.

Unfortunately, it can be argued that conventional social psychology is particularly ill equipped to explain the very issues to which Melucci draws attention. These issues refer, broadly speaking, to the social construction of meaning. Critics, especially those who identify themselves with the social constructionist school of thought, have claimed that orthodox approaches within social psychology ignore the extent to which social psychological phenomena are themselves socially constructed. For instance, the critics contend that orthodox social psychologists tend to treat "attitudinal systems" and cognitive processes as static, reified entities, which are assumed to determine the ways that atomized individuals process information (for social constructionist critiques, see Gergen 1989; Shotter and Gergen forthcoming; Shotter 1993b; Parker and Shotter 1990). According to such critics, the constructs and methods of orthodox social psychology would not satisfactorily fill Melucci's gap.

A hypothetical, and somewhat exaggerated, example can illustrate the point. A cognitive social psychologist might be recruited by an interdisciplinary research team in order to discover the "attitudinal frameworks" that are presumed to be possessed by the members of a particular social movement. By analyzing questionnaire responses from members and from a comparison group of nonmembers, the psychologist might produce a model of the "cognitive framework" of the "typical member." The framework might claim to illustrate how the typical member is likely to process incoming information. For instance, the model might predict that there will be a self-fulfilling bias in the interpretation of information: messages from movement leaders will be interpreted to confirm the belief system and its schemata, while the schemata will be employed to reject potentially disconfirming messages from opponents. Such a diagram of the hypothesized "belief system" will be essentially static: its categorical components will be treated as existing entities, that guide individual members' actions, thoughts, and categorizing of incoming information. Above all, such a diagram will not show how the elements of meaning used by members in their utterances and thoughts have themselves been socially constructed, and how these elements are themselves frequently matters of social contestation (for critiques of social cognition, see Billig 1985; Edwards 1991;

Edwards and Potter 1993a, 1993b; Lopes 1991; Sampson 1981, 1993; Shotter 1991). In short, such a model of cognitive schemata will take for granted many of the processes that, according to Melucci, should be studied directly by analysts of social movements. For these reasons, the social psychologies, emerging from the social constructionist school of thinking, should be taken seriously as possible contenders for filling Melucci's gap.

It might be argued that Melucci's questions about the identities and thinking of members of social movements cannot be answered by bracketing off members of social movements: their thought processes are not constituted of features uniquely different from the thinking of nonmembers. Instead, one needs to investigate the way that members of social movements think in relation to wider patterns of thinking within a society. This is because the ideologies of critique are marked by the more general ideologies of the society. In an obvious sense, the ideologies of critique are typically produced as arguments against prevailing patterns of common sense, which are presented as being "natural." For instance, feminism is an argument against commonsense notions about male and female "natural" capabilities; creationists question the "natural" common sense of teaching evolution as a scientific subject in schools. In both cases, the ideologies are formulated in contestation with common sense, and, in this sense, they are affected by the common sense. Moreover, the critics of the "natural" must use ordinary discourses of common sense, even as they construct their critiques, which argue against common sense. Thus, the critics cannot divest themselves of the ideological patterns of their times.

For these reasons, it is necessary to explore the nature of commonsense thinking in general if one wishes to understand the particularities of thinking that claims to contest common sense. It will be suggested that the rhetorical approach to social psychology stresses that social thinking, and by implication the thinking of a social movement's members, is a rhetorical, argumentative activity. By taking the rhetorical nature of thinking seriously, one can see that common sense, or widespread ideology, is much less systematic and unitary and more problematic than is often assumed. Indeed, commonsense reasoning often provides elements that can be incorporated into a social movement's ideology of critique. Thus, as will be suggested, the general ideology, which presents a society's particular version of common sense as being "natural," and which, in consequence, serves to "settle down" the members of that society into its orders of inequality, also contains the possibilities of argumentative critique.

Discourse and Social Views

The term *discursive/rhetorical psychology* has already been used. This rather cumbersome phrase is intended to cover both the "discursive psychology" proposed by Potter and Wetherell (1987) and Edwards and Potter (1993a) and the "rhetorical psychology" discussed by Billig (1987, 1991). Although it might be possible to make fine distinctions between these two approaches, and indeed between other discourse-based approaches to social psychology (Parker 1992), these two approaches share much in common.[1] The difference between the two might be expressed in the following way. "Discursive psychology" aims to produce a general account of how psychological phenomena are constituted within language. "Rhetorical psychology" concentrates on a particular form of language—rhetorical or argumentative discourses. In this sense, "rhetorical psychology" could be portrayed as a subsection of a more general discursive psychology.

I will mention a number of features of the more general discursive approach before outlining some of the specificities of rhetorical study. I will discuss briefly four aspects of discursive psychology: the importance of language, language as action, anticognitivism, and variability of interpretative repertoires.

The Importance of Language

Above all, the discursive approach underlines the importance of language in social interaction. It claims that most of the phenomena that social psychologists have traditionally taken as their objects of study are constituted in language. "Attitudes" are a case in point. Many social psychologists have considered that their discipline has been based on the analysis of attitudes (Jaspars and Fraser 1983). Typically, social psychologists have not treated "attitudes" as being essentially discursive phenomena. They have often seen "attitude statements" as the outward expression of more basic, internal, mental or emotional states, which are assumed to be essentially nonlinguistic. By contrast, Potter and Wetherell, in their book *Discourse and Social Psychology* (1987), argue strongly that what psychologists call "attitudes" are, in effect, language behaviors and, thus, social psychologists should be studying the details of discourse. In particular, they should be paying attention to what people are saying, and doing, when they offer their opinions (Lalljee, Brown, and Ginsberg 1984).

If psychologists emphasize the discourses themselves, rather than hypothetical but unobservable inner states, then they can more easily draw attention to the social nature of psychological phenomena. The act of speaking is itself a social act. If people speak their opinion, they are engaging in a social act of communication. Moreover, they will be repeating shared meanings. Individuals do not create their own languages: they repeat words, phrases and syntaxes that are socially shared. As Moscovici has written, "social and intellectual activity is, after all, a rehearsal or recital, yet most social psychologists treat it as if it were amnesic" (1983: 10). It is not surprising that discursive psychologists have treated remembering itself as a collective act, that also is constituted in language activities (Edwards and Potter 1993a, 1993b; Edwards, Middleton, and Potter 1992; Middleton and Edwards 1990).

Language as Action

Discursive psychologists view speech as a form of action, thereby disputing the common distinction between speech and action (Edwards and Potter 1993b; Potter, Edwards, and Wetherell 1993). When people speak, they are performing actions. Thus, the utterance "I do" at a Western wedding ceremony is a performative utterance. Similarly, acts of racist discrimination can be performed through discourse (see, for instance, Essed's 1988 analysis of a job interview involving a black woman applicant and a white male employee).

This position carries a methodological implication. Psychologists, wishing to understand what people "mean," should examine what people are doing with their words. People who are "giving their opinion" on an issue might be doing a number of things—trying to impress auditors, countering objections, exerting interpersonal power, and so on. In order to study these matters, analysts need to pay close attention to the dynamics of discourse and interaction. Discursive psychologists recommend that some of the techniques of conversation analysis should form a major part of social psychological methodology. Such discourse analysts place great emphasis on studying actual speech acts in their contexts. They do not seek to reconstruct, in the manner of some Foucauldians, abstracted patterns of discourses that are not based on actual, occasioned utterances. As Bakhtin wrote in his essay "The Problem of Speech Genres," "speech is always cast in the form of an utterance belonging to a particular subject, and outside this form it cannot exist" (1986: 71; for discussions of Bakhtin's importance for social constructionism, see Sampson 1993; Shotter 1993a, 1993b; Shotter and Gergen forthcoming; Wertsch 1991).

Anticognitivism

The methodological and theoretical commitment to studying discursive processes in context has a direct implication for Melucci's call to study the "cognitive frameworks" of social movement members. Discourse analysts are reluctant to use cognitivist constructs that imply that there are "systems" or "frameworks" located in the brain that control the stream of discursive action. Thus, discursive psychologists reject a theoretical move that cognitivist psychologists typically make: this move translates actual utterances and actions into hypothetical, hidden cognitive structures. According to discursive psychologists, the task of social psychology is not to infer the presence of hidden "attitudinal" or "cognitive" frameworks, but to make sense of discursive actions. Rather than using talk about the social world as evidence for the existence of internal processes or framework, the discursive psychologist would locate the utterances in their social context, examining what actions are being accomplished by the utterances.

Variability of Interpretative Repertoires

One of the major differences between the cognitivist and discursive approaches relates to the issue of variability. Cognitivists, by decontextualizing utterances and then relating them to hypothesized internal structures, tend to assume that individuals will produce fixed responses. For example, cognitivists assume that individuals possess attitudinal or belief systems and that these systems determine what attitudinal responses will be produced. Unless individuals alter their belief systems, or their cognitive frameworks, they will generally display consistent responses, for these responses are being generated by the same, substantially unchanged cognitive mechanism. By contrast, discursive and rhetorical psychologists do not expect such consistency, for no such generative mechanisms are being hypothesized.

By examining in detail what people actually say, discursive psychologists have claimed that people generally do not have a single "attitude," as social psychological theory has often assumed. For instance, people will use different "interpretative repertoires" to accomplish different actions (see Wetherell and Potter 1988; Potter and Wetherell 1988). Gilbert and Mulkay (1984) show how scientists use different repertoires of explanation. In discussing their own work, scientists tend to speak as if science were a matter of using precise techniques to "discover" elements of reality. By contrast, when scientists talk about the work of rival theorists, they offer very different accounts: they use psychological language that depicts the personal failings of fellow scientists. Similarly, white speakers have been shown to articulate both prejudiced and tolerant themes when discussing other "races" (Billig et al. 1988; Potter and Wetherell 1988; van Dijk 1987, 1992; Wetherell and Potter 1992). According to discourse analysts, this variability in talk in racist discourse is to be expected (Wetherell and Potter 1992). In different interactions, and at different junctures within the same interaction, speakers will be using different forms of talk to accomplish different sorts of task. To do this, speakers will need to vary their "repertoires of interpretation" (Potter and Wetherell 1987) and to switch between what Bakhtin (1981) called different "registers of voice." In fact, the switch can be accomplished within a single utterance, as Bakhtin recognized when he claimed that each utterance bears traces of heteroglossia. For instance, the phrase "I'm not prejudiced but . . ." is commonly used to preface the expression of prejudice. In so speaking, the speaker appears to use the discourse of tolerance (which is critical of the notion of "prejudice") in order to utter prejudiced criticisms of other groups (Billig, 1991; Wetherell and Potter 1992). To summarize all this as being the expression of an "attitude" or a "cognitive framework" is to undermine the rhetorical complexity of opinion giving. When characters on the historical stage—again, to borrow a phrase from Melucci (1989)—attempt to make sense of their social worlds, they are often engaged in complex rhetorical activity.

Rhetorical Dimensions of Thinking

So far, I have discussed general discursive aspects rather than specifically rhetorical dimensions. In the study of social thinking, and particularly the creation of new forms of social interpretations, not all instances of language action are equally revealing. The rhetorical approach draws particular attention to the argumentative aspects of language, for in discussions or arguments it is possible to observe thinking in operation.

This point can be illustrated in relation to the giving of opinions. People generally offer their views in a rhetorical context. This means that they seek to persuade auditors of the reasonableness of their views. Thus, persons who claim "I am not prejudiced but . . ." are seeking to convince hearers of the reasonableness of the statements that follow the "but." In order to achieve this, such speakers use the rhetorical tactic of ethos. The speakers are presenting themselves as persons of good character (i.e., unprejudiced), and are thus "credentialing" both their utterances and themselves (Hewitt and Stokes 1975). The utterance, however, does not reduce down to impression management or persuasive tactic. There is a further, basic element to the rhetorical situation. The utterance will be made to counter other possible utterances. Thus, the speakers are using prolepsis in order to counter in advance the possible criticism of prejudice. According to Ong (1989), most affirmations have negative elements, for they seek to exclude counterstatements. In general, thinking occurs through the countering and criticism of views. Thus, those taking part in arguing are doing more than presenting themselves in favorable ways or criticizing their fellow speakers: they are in a real sense exploring the social world.[2] As Julia Kristeva (1986) emphasized in her praise of "negation as affirmation," thinking, whether it is produced by individuals or by ideological groups, depends upon the faculty of negation. Agreement does not advance the argument.

This raises a general point about attitudes and opinions that tends to be overlooked by traditional attitude theorists. Expressions of attitudes are stances in matters of controversy. People are said to have attitudes about issues, on which there are recognized to be divergent stances. Thus, an attitude in favor of a position is always simultaneously a stance against the counterposition. Speakers will orient their utterances to this argumentative nature of opinion giving by using rhetorical or argumentative devices. In fact, the subject matter of classical rhetoric was considered to be opinion, rather than certain knowledge. Aristotle emphasized this in the opening sections of his *Rhetoric*. Rhetorical reasoning, he wrote, is used "only upon recognized subjects of debate"; these are matters that are uncertain, for "matters which admit of no ambiguity, past, present, or future, are debated by no one" (I, ii, 12).

The rhetorical aspect of opinions helps to account for the variability that discourse analysts have found. A speaker is not always confronted with the same rhetorical situation, with the same opposing views to be countered. Even speakers with strong views on an issue will find themselves in a variety of argumentative situations, wishing to fend off possible objections coming from various quarters. For instance, the same speaker might draw upon conservative rhetoric to counter possible radical objections and use radical rhetoric to counter conservatives. Again, this is not merely a matter of impression management, but the meaning of an utterance depends on its rhetorical context. Thus, a stance changes its meaning if the counterstance is changed.

By studying arguments in discussion groups, analysts can observe thinking in action. Speakers, in offering their opinions, do not repeat themselves, as if expressing a fixed cognitive framework. Even when arguments appear to go around in circles, speakers rarely repeat themselves word for word. Instead, they are engaged in a continually changing context of criticism and justification. New criticisms are offered and have to be considered. Thus, there is creative novelty in argument. In fact, one often discovers what one thinks by hearing oneself argue, for positions are tested and developed in argumentation.

This creativity is not only found in interpersonal discussions, as individuals argue face to face with each other. It also affects the ideologies of social movements. An ideology is an argument against another ideology. If the counterposition changes—or the point of argument alters—then the meaning of the ideology is changed and ideological developments may be produced to counter the changed situation. For example, in late-eighteenth-century Britain, criticism of the monarchy took on fresh force once the French Revolution occurred. The same antimonarchical utterances now implied a republican radicalism that they might have lacked hitherto. Some critics of George III, such as the cartoonist James Gillray, modified their rhetoric. This did not indicate a "change of attitude" in the simple sense of reversing previous opinions. It was a modification in the light of historical development and the changing rhetorical context, for new controversies demand new responses.

The Dilemmatic Nature of Common Sense

There is a paradox at the heart of rhetorical activity: it might involve creativity, but it is also based on repetition. Moreover, the repetition and the creativity are bound together, each simultaneously permitting the other. As I suggested earlier, the use of language and the expression of commonsense discourses involve repetition, for the speaker is not inventing the rhetorical and commonsensical resources that are being used. Even when a speaker is formulating a new utterance in a context whose precise conjunction of details has never before occurred, the speaker is also engaging in repetition. Barthes (1982) expressed this paradox when he wrote that the speaker is "both master and slave" of language. On the one hand, speech is an assertion by the self, and, thus, the speaker is the master of the moment. On the other hand, speech is a repetition of signs. Within each sign, Barthes suggested, there "sleeps that monster: a stereotype." As slave, the speaker must use the words of the language and, therefore, cannot but reawaken the sleeping monsters. Yet the speaker as master does more than repeat stereotypes: "I am not content to repeat what has been said, to settle comfortably in the servitude of signs: I speak, I affirm, I assert tellingly what I repeat" (460). And, Barthes could have added, I negate, especially when I assert so tellingly.

The rhetorical situation is not a simple one, and its complexity reveals something about the nature of common sense. Aristotle, in common with other classic theorists, offered a piece of advice to speakers. To maximize their chances of being persuasive, speakers should make an appeal to the *sensus communis,* or the shared common sense of the community, which includes speaker and hearers. Particularly useful are "commonplaces," as these are the sort of moral maxims that are laden with clichéd appeals to common values (Perelman and Olbrechts-Tyteca 1971). Thus, an orator's discourse that seeks to create new movements of opinion toward a minority position will often repeat, and claim to exemplify, the values of the majority. As Kenneth Burke (1969) suggested in *A Rhetoric of Motives,* the appeal to shared, traditional values can act as the fulcrum on which speakers seek to lever their audiences into new positions.

The classical textbooks of rhetoric give a clue that the *sensus communis* cannot represent a unitary system. The old textbooks used to present commonplaces the aspiring orator might care to use. For instance, courtroom orators acting for the defense would be advised to use commonplaces of mercy; prosecutors would be provided with handy themes advocating justice. In this way, the common sense would be assumed to contain the opposing themes that one should be merciful and that justice should be applied. Since both sides of the argument—defense and prosecution—were presumed to be appealing to the same audience, it was presumed that the individuals of the community valued both justice and mercy. The general point is not confined to courtroom rhetoric. Francis Bacon in *Of Dignity and Advancement of Learning* pointed out that for any proverb recommending a particular virtue, one can find an alternative proverb that recommends an equally valued but opposing virtue. Thus, maxims in favor of risk taking can be countered by those advocating prudence; "too many cooks spoil the broth" can be opposed by "many hands make light work" and so on.

Since the maxims are generally shared and can be called upon as rhetorical resources by all members of the community, there is an implication about the nature of the *sensus communis.* It will comprise contrary themes, or, to use the term of Billig et al. (1988), it will be "dilemmatic." Thus, members of the community, repeating the maxims of their society's common sense, will not find the social world depicted in a simple, nonproblematic manner. They do not possess a simple cognitive framework that provides a ready-made interpretation for every situation and that equips the thinker with a straightforward attitudinal position, obviating the necessity for further thought. Instead, the themes of common sense pull in contrary directions. As Billig et al. (1988) claimed, the themes of contemporary Western ideology set "ideological dilemmas." People, repeating the common themes of ideology, find their thinking being pulled simultaneously toward tolerance and prejudice; or toward valuing equality and toward respect for authority; or toward sympathizing with the poor and toward blaming them for their plight. In each case, ideological common sense provides the resources for moral dilemmas to think and argue about. The variability of opinion giving, which discourse analysts have demonstrated, is not merely a reflection of strategic considerations as speakers conduct their interpersonal and persuasive business with their auditors. It also reflects the dilemmatic nature of common sense: there is always more to say, more to argue about, more novel repetitions to be made.

The Example of British Monarchy

The dilemmatic nature of common sense can be illustrated with examples from a project that investigated the way that English families talk about the British monarchy. A fuller report on this project is presented in *Talking of the Royal Family* (Billig 1992). Although the topic of modern monarchy has tended to be ignored by social scientists, it is one of ideological significance, especially for understanding the contemporary ideology of nationalism. If a nation is an "imagined community" (Anderson 1991), then discourses about the royal family should provide clues about the ways that the British imagine their national community (Nairn 1988). Similarly, monarchy, as a symbol of inequality, might be thought to fulfill an ideological function: acceptance of monarchy would imply acceptance of social inequality in a highly visible form. If ideology is dilemmatic, however, then the discourses about such ideological themes should not be straightforward. The germs of critique might be present alongside the discourses of acceptance. Although there is no republican social movement in Britain, this would not mean that the ideological resources for republicanism are absent.

The research project was based on tape-recorded discussions of sixty-three families talking about royalty. An interviewer visited the families in their homes and raised topics in order to provoke discussion between family members. From a rhetorical perspective there are a number of advantages in studying discussion groups rather than responses to formal, or even semi-structured, individual interviews. In discussion groups it is possible to observe the patterns of argumentation, and thereby witness the processes of thinking in practice, as respondents engage in the cut and thrust of discussion.

The discussions yielded immensely rich, densely textured discourse, revealing that the British public can talk at length about its royal family. It was possible to observe ideological thinking in practice, for talk about the royal family involves more than merely talk about royalty. In speaking about a royal family, family members were talking about *family* and, hence, about themselves. In so doing, they were also conducting their own bits of family business. Moreover, because the ideological commonplaces expressed contrary themes, the discussants also explored argumentatively the moral order of society, for, in arguing about royal controversies, people were talking about key moral, ideological issues.

Because the ideological commonplaces expressed contrary themes, such discussions were possible. For instance, there was much debate about how royals should behave. Common sense, which was commonly accepted and commonly repeated, dictated that royals should be neither too ordinary nor too royal (or too "high and mighty"). For each commonplace ("they're just human, after all") there was an alternative and opposite commonplace ("they're quite different, really; they have to set standards"). The same was true for general truisms about the institution: monarchy represents the "priceless" heritage of the nation, versus monarchy as a money-making enterprise that attracts tourists. The tensions between commonplaces reproduce royalty as an object of interest and as a topic to be debated endlessly.

A further example of contrary themes is provided by the historical tales that were commonly told. As respondents talked about the royal family and about nationhood, they frequently gave commonsense accounts of history. Not only were these tales used to depict past time in the nation, but speakers, in claiming to depict in them the national past, were imagining the national community of the present. In particular, two different accounts were given, and these could be, and often were, brought into argumentative opposition. There was the story of decline and the contrasting story of progress

The account of history as national decline depicted the present as a decay from past standards, and, thus, the nation was imagined to be in decline. It was said that people are less respectful toward the royals today than in the past. In particular, the newspapers publish too much scandal and intrude upon the royal way of life. The royals themselves, especially the younger royals, are not behaving with the sort of reserved dignity that royalty used to display. The contrast between the present and the past depicted present times, marked by disrespect and disorder, as compared with a past age of respect and good behavior. The past society was depicted as some sort of gemeinschaft characterized by a sense of unity: people knew their place and shared a sense of unity. Life was more communal, more neighborly, and more authentic: it was experienced directly, not secondhand through television. In such demarcations of the present and the past, there is a narration of decline from better days; an essentially conservative history of the nation is being told.

A second narration imagined a story of national progress. Old aristocrats and regal tyrants have been defeated. The British today lead freer and materially better lives than their ancestors did in past times. The past was barbaric, whereas the present is civilized. One would not wish to go back to the old days of superstition, when ordinary people bowed down before their social superiors. In this account, there was a feeling that today people are more in control of their lives and are more socially equal than previously. Today, they can talk of themselves as being on a par with kings and queens, where previously a mute acceptance of authority was said to be required. Thus, the present was depicted as the climax of the past: old-fashioned evils and barbarism have been overcome. Modernity was celebrated in what was essentially a liberal account of national progress.

Both narrations of history—the conservative and the liberal—are part of common sense and are to be used by the same people. At one point a speaker might use the liberal, or populist, theme, particularly to qualify a conservative account produced by another speaker. On other occasions, even within the same conversation, the same person might switch to the conservative account (for examples, see Billig 1990a). Rhetorically, each theme seems to call forth its opposite.

The commonsense themes of monarchy, as ideological themes, also served to settle speakers into their own positions in a society whose inequalities are exemplified by monarchy itself. This settling down could be seen in the discursive phenomenon that can be called "double declaiming." As speakers were making claims about "them," the royals, so, implicitly (and sometimes explicitly), they were doubly making claims about "us," the commoners. There was a complex set of commonsense themes about whether "their" life was enviable. Respondents often expressed envy about specific elements of "their" life, particularly "their" money. The envy was typically tempered, however, by comments that "they" earned "their" money. These tempering comments would, in their turn, be qualified by criticisms of individual royals or a whole group of royal "hangers-on" who were said not to earn their money. There could be arguments about who exactly the hangers-on were and what exactly were their deficiencies. In addition, there was a truism, rarely challenged directly, that royals who were doing their job properly led a "hard life" and, therefore, deserved rich payment. "Their" life was hard, so it was said, because "they" enjoyed no privacy or freedom, living in the public (or in "our") eye.

The double declaiming operates because claims about "their" hard life imply claims, whether or not they are directly expressed, about the comparative benefits of "our" life. "We" have freedom to enjoy the cheap pleasures of life, which are denied to "them." Thus, the defense of "their" privilege rests on an implicit celebration of the ordinary, unprivileged, even in some cases impoverished, life: better to be poor and ordinary, so it was implied, than rich and royal. Part of this celebration included the sense that "we" are free to criticize "them," but "they" are not free to criticize "us." Royalists who firmly defended the institution of monarchy would often offer critical comments about individuals. They would enjoy joking at the royals' expense. It was a royalist mother and her younger son, rather than the critical older son, who swapped jokes about Prince Charles's baldness and the shape of his ears. The more that such royalists claim their freedom to mock and to criticize, the more they are celebrating the unprivileged life as the enviable national life. And, in this way, the truisms of common sense provide a discourse that settles down the speakers.

Although such ideological discourses might settle people into social orders of inequality, and although there might be an absence of any republican social movement, the seeds of critique exist. For instance, a populist history depicting the nation's past in terms of the struggle between the people and privileged tyranny is part of the cultural common sense. And this history can be drawn upon to make critical sense of the present. Billig (1990b) gives the example of a popular right-wing newspaper criticizing the queen, and drawing upon a populist history of the 1688 Glorious Revolution to do so.

In this way, ideological common sense is not unitary, but contains contrary themes. A similar point was expressed by Antonio Gramsci in his *Prison Notebooks*. He described the ordinary person, using the themes of commonsense thinking, as a "walking fossil," for the philosophies of past ages become sedimented in commonsense thinking. Gramsci wrote that common sense "contains Stone Age elements and principles of more advanced science, prejudices from all past phases of history at the local level and intuitions of a future philosophy which will be that of a human race united the world over" (1971: 324).

This implies that common sense retains the traces of past social movements. There might be no current republican movement in Britain, but antimonarchical movements of the past have left their mark in commonsense thinking. Perhaps these sedimented themes are articulated in discourses that accept contemporary monarchy and celebrate "our" national life. The acceptance is neither static nor unlimited, however, for the themes, in bearing the traces of their history and in claiming to recount that history, also contain the seeds of further critique. Thus, common sense, which at one level seems to act as a force for conservatism, also contains the ideological resources that could be rhetorically mobilized by future social movements of critique.

Social Movements and Ideological Dilemmas

Finally, I will sketch a few brief remarks about social movements and the dilemmatic nature of common sense. From what has been said about the importance of argumentation, social movements can be seen as conducting arguments against prevailing versions of common sense. Thus, the ideology of a social movement is affected by some of the same dilemmatic and para-doxical aspects of rhetoric that affect individual speakers.

An ideological common sense that appears to function in a conservative direction may include radical, potentially critical themes. Similarly, a move-ment's ideology of critique may also repeat the stereotypes of common sense as it reawakens the sleeping monsters for new argumentative purposes. The opening pages of *The German Ideology,* in which Marx and Engels first artic-ulated their materialist criticism of "ideology," illustrate this. These pages are withering in their sarcasm against "German professors" who know nothing about real life: a set of common, populist, anti-intellectual stereotypes was being mobilized by the intellectual, radical begetters of the new world.

A practical dilemma faces the ideologists of social movements whose ide-ology criticizes common sense but who seek to attract widespread support. In order to speak to potential recruits, the ideologists of the movement may need to use the language of common sense, including the parts that stand in opposition to their articulated ideology. For example, such a rhetorical dilem-ma faces conspiracy theorists, who are to be found at the core of many con-temporary fascist groups (Billig 1978, 1989; Graumann and Moscovici 1987). The ideology of conspiracy claims that many of the widespread beliefs of society have been deliberately spread by evil but powerful conspirators who wish to poison the minds of the masses in their pursuit of world power. Thus, the conspiracy theory is an argument against prevailing commonsensical interpretations of the social world. If fascist parties wish to recruit ordinary members for whom the anti-Semitism of the fascist conspiracy theory might be off-putting, however, they may have to mobilize their rhetoric from more general themes of common sense, including dilemmatic themes. For exam-ple, the National Front in Britain, in its recruiting propaganda, will try to draw upon shared themes of nationalism and racism. Moreover, it might draw upon, or attempt to co-opt rhetorically, the counterthemes of tolerance. Thus, it is possible to find racist propagandists using the discourses of tolerance in order to disclaim their own prejudice. In this way, the sedimented, common-sense discourses of liberalism are expressed within a fascist rhetoric that simultaneously seeks to argue against that commonsense liberalism and to promote an ideology that explicitly imagines the nation in terms of race.

A social movement of critique that engages in argument against aspects of common sense can affect the common sense in a number of ways. Its very ideology may represent the articulation of novel thoughts. In so doing it may formulate new words or phrases that become sedimented into common sense, thereby changing it. Thus, liberalism's argument against the aristocratic order produced new meanings for a word such as *prejudice,* and this philosophical term has been incorporated into common sense. Today, the feminist movement, in its argument with patriarchal language, is producing new phrases and words (such as *sexual harassment, sexism, ms*) that are slipping into common sense alongside older elements, which, as Gramsci ironically pointed out, appear to have been present since the Stone Age.

In addition, a social movement can have a less directly suasive effect on common sense. Individuals who support a majority position can be affected by hearing a minority position, which they reject. This has been demonstrated in laboratory studies (Moscovici, Mugny, and Van Avermaet 1985; Mugny and Perez 1991). A social movement may mount an original challenge against what had previously been accepted as "natural." In so doing, it may translate the "naturally obvious" into a matter of controversy and doubt, on which "attitudes" are to be taken. Thus, the issue will be talked about differently even by those who reject the minority position. The majority will be prompted to formulate new counterarguments, and, thus, their thinking is affected, and marked, by the minority position. This sort of process can be observed in discussions in which speakers can be forced to articulate new justifications when they are faced by new criticisms. On a more general level, a social movement, by its critique of common sense, can provoke a defense of common sense. Mannheim (1960) suggested that conservatism as a philosophy was articulated only in response to the challenge of liberalism. And this countercritique had its rhetorical effect upon liberalism. The elements of the countercritique need not leave common sense unchanged, for elements of critique and countercritique both become sedimented, adding to the dilemmatic nature of common sense. Thus, the stories of national decline and progress that the English can so readily use in their discourses about the nation have their own ideological history.

This suggests that it would be wrong to make a rigid separation between commonsense ideology and the ideology of social movements, as if they are distinctly different phenomena, based upon totally separate "cognitive frameworks." Nationalism again provides a case in point. Some theorists reserve the term *nationalism* for the ideology of social movements that seek to establish nations, or that attempt to base politics exclusively on the concept of the nation (Giddens 1985, 1987; Coakley 1992). In this account, nationalism is not the everyday ideology to be found in established, democratic nations. If ideology is seen as dilemmatic, however, then one should not expect an ideology to be completely either nationalist or nonnationalist. The everyday ideology of contemporary society will have its nationalist themes and myths, permitting the national community to be imagined in various ways. In this sense, the assumptions of nationalism will be used in commonplace discussions about politics, foreigners, and royal families.

There is a further point. An everyday ideology is not characterized only by the topics that are discussed and argued about. It will also be characterized by silences. To argue on one theme means to be silent on others. Thus, ideologies, by encouraging certain forms of argumentation, also silence other arguments and other possible critiques. In this respect, the topic of nationalism is instructive. Today, across the world, there is much dispute about national identity, about the borders between nations, about the place of foreigners, and on and on. All too consistently in the twentieth century, groups are willing to kill and die for their idea of the nature of nations. The backdrop for such disputes is an acceptance of the "naturalness" of a world of nations (Gellner 1983, 1987). Nationalist assumptions have become "natural" in contemporary political discourses (Billig 1993). As people dispute where and how particular nations should be constituted, so they accept that the world should naturally be divided into nation-states. In this world of today, nationhood is imagined to be as natural as rivers and mountain ranges.

Gramsci may have seen in commonsense thinking the intuitions of a future philosophy that would unite the human race across the world. In today's world of nations and national wars, however, these intuitions have become quieted. But, on the basis of past history, it might be presumed that they have not disappeared. As sleeping monsters within today's thoughts, they wait to be freshly awakened by a social movement of the future.

Notes

1. It should also be pointed out that many of the general points to be made about discursive/rhetorical approaches can also be made about the theory of social representations (Moscovici, 1983, 1987; but see Potter and Litton 1985 for criticisms of the theory of social representations from a discursive perspective; for a reply, see Moscovici 1985). Both approaches claim that the theoretical constructs of orthodox social psychology fail to recognize that their objects of study are socially created. Both take a critical approach to central concepts such as "attitudes": both seek to deconstruct the nature of "attitudes" rather than assume that attitudes "really" exist in a simple way that can be easily measured by standard questionnaire methodologies. As regards the issue of social movements, both approaches

are concerned with the way that beliefs are shared as "common sense" within a society. In consequence, both approaches deal with the basic ideological issue of analyzing the relations between shared commonsense beliefs—or the general ideology within a society—and the ideologies of critique that might emerge within that society.

2. Thus, rhetorical theorists, especially those involved in what Simons (1990) calls "the rhetorical turn," tend to celebrate rhetorical creativity. Billig (1987) praises the "spirit of contradiction" that permits exploration and thinking. If arguing is a form of thinking, then negation is crucial.

Part II

Cultural Processes in Mobilization

Chapter 5

Constructing Social Protest

William A. Gamson

Movement activists are media junkies. "Advocates of causes," Edelman reminds us, "are an avid audience for the political spectacle" (1988: 6). Along with other political actors, they eagerly monitor public discourse, using it along with other resources to construct meaning on issues they care about. Media discourse provides them with "weekly, daily, sometimes hourly triumphs and defeats, grounds for hope and for fear, a potpourri of happenings that mark trends and aberrations, some of them historic."

The more sophisticated among them recognize that many in their constituency—the potential challengers whom they would like to reach—are different from them. Hopes and defeats are defined by their everyday lives, not by public affairs, and their involvement with the political spectacle is more casual and haphazardly attentive. The trick for activists is to bridge public discourse and people's experiential knowledge, integrating them in a coherent frame that supports and sustains collective action.

General-audience media are only one forum for public discourse, but they are the central one for social movements. Activists may read a variety of movement publications and attend meetings and conferences where the issues that concern them are discussed. But they cannot assume that their constituency shares these other forums or is aware of this discourse. Only general-audience media provide a potentially shared public discourse.

Of course, one can assume more sharing than exists on many issues. Two people reading the same newspaper may end up with virtually no overlap in what they process from it. But on major events, the potential is often realized. Someone speaking on neglect of the cities and racial injustice in American society in the wake of the Rodney King verdict and the ensuing Los Angeles riot can reasonably assume media-based, shared images of these events. I do not mean to imply here that the *meanings* are shared, but one can draw on this public discourse to frame an issue with some assurance that potential challengers will understand the references and allusions.

This essay focuses on how the nature of media discourse influences the construction of collective action frames by social movements. Like Gitlin (1980), it asks how the media influence movements, but the focus is less on choice of mediagenic action strategies and the generation of media-based leadership and more on how this cultural tool affects the process of constructing meaning. It reverses the questions addressed by Gamson (1988) and Ryan (1991) on how movements attempt to influence media discourse as the central site of a symbolic struggle over which framing of an issue will prevail.

Media Discourse as a Framing Resource

Imagine a group of ordinary working people carrying on a conversation in which they are trying to figure out how they think about some complex public issue. The issue is a forest through which they must find their way—but not a virgin forest. The various frames in media discourse provide maps indicating useful points of entry, provide signposts at various crossroads, highlight the significant landmarks, and warn of the perils of other paths. Many people, however, do not stick to the pathways provided, frequently wandering off and making paths of their own.

From the standpoint of the wanderer, media discourse is a cultural resource to use in understanding and talking about an issue, but it is only one of several available. Nor is it necessarily the most important one on some issues, compared, for example, with their own experience and that of significant others in their lives. Frequently, they find their way through the forest with a combination of resources, including those they carry with them.

Elsewhere I describe conversations among about forty groups of non-college-educated people in the Boston area on four issues: troubled industry, affirmative action, nuclear power, and Arab-Israeli conflict. "Every group on every issue shows some awareness that there is a public discourse around them, even if they make minimal use of it and frequently apologize for not having better command of it" (Gamson 1992). On some issues, I found that media discourse was the main or even the exclusive resource used in constructing meaning, with experiential knowledge playing little role.

The public discourse on which people draw is much broader than the news. They quote advertising slogans and refer to movies. Nor do they confine the media discourse on which they draw to the issue under discussion but frequently bring in other related issues to make their point. They also make use of media discourse on the issue under discussion, employing catch-phrases, making references to the players featured in news accounts, and bringing in a variety of informational elements to support the frames that spotlight these facts.

Any single resource has its limits. A frame has a more solid foundation when it is based on a combination of cultural and personal resources. Let me concede that no resource is purely personal or cultural. Even our personal experience is filtered through a cultural lens. "Big Brother is you, watching" in Miller's (1988) clever phrase. We walk around with hyperreal images from movies and television and use them to code our own experiences. Media discourse is not merely something out there but also something inside our heads.

Similarly, people bring their own experiences and personal associations to their readings of cultural texts. Media images have no fixed meaning but involve a negotiation with a heterogeneous audience that may provide them with meanings quite different from the preferred reading. Oppositional and aberrant readings are common and, hence, media images are not purely cultural but infused with personal meanings as well.

Nevertheless, the mix of cultural and personal varies dramatically among different types of resources. Our experiences may have cultural elements but they are overwhelmingly our own private resources, not fully shared by others. People distinguish between knowing something from having experienced it and knowing something secondhand or more abstractly, and they generally give a privileged place to their own experiential knowledge. Experiential knowledge is valued precisely because it is so direct and relatively unmediated. While there is plenty of selectivity in the memory of experiences, it is our own selectivity, not someone else's.

Media discourse, at the other extreme, is a useful resource precisely because it is public. In spite of personal elements, it is possible to talk about the beating of Rodney King, for example, on the basis of assumed common images and factual knowledge. If everyone may not know the particular element of media discourse referred to, it is nonetheless a matter of public record, available to anyone who wants to know: you can look it up—unlike personal experience. Media discourse, then, is predominantly a cultural resource.

Iyengar and Kinder (1987) offer experimental evidence of the special impact of integrating the personal and cultural. First, they review a large number of studies that show that Americans sharply distinguish the quality of their personal lives from their judgments about public issues. For example, crime victims do not regard crime as a more serious problem for society as a whole than do those who are personally untouched by crime; people's assessments of economic conditions are largely unrelated to the economic setbacks and gains in their own lives; and the war in Vietnam was not rated as a more important problem among those who had close relatives serving there than among Americans without personal connections to the war.

The researchers then designed a series of experiments to test more subtle connections between media coverage and personal effects. One experiment concentrated on three issues—civil rights, unemployment, and Social Security. They showed edited television news broadcasts to their subjects, varying the amount of coverage of these issues systematically. (Stories on a variety of other issues were included as well.) In different conditions, subjects saw either no coverage, intermediate coverage, or extensive coverage of each of the three issues.

The subjects varied on whether they were in a category that was personally affected. Blacks were contrasted with whites on civil rights, those out of work with those currently working on the unemployment issue, and the elderly with the young on Social Security. All subjects were asked at the end to name the most important problems that the country faced.

The researchers found that on two of the three issues—civil rights and Social Security—members of the personally affected group were especially influenced by the amount of television coverage they watched. On the unemployment issue, they found no differences between the employed and the unemployed. Only this last result is consistent with the earlier studies showing the lack of relationship between people's personal lives and their views on public issues.

Iyengar and Kinder interpret their results in ways that suggest the integration of personal and cultural resources. "We suspect" they write, "that the key feature distinguishing civil rights and social security is that they are experienced psychologically both as personal predicaments and as *group* predicaments." Although they do not use the term, collective identity processes that do not operate on unemployment come into play. Presumably, being an African-American or a senior citizen engages individuals in a collective identity, but being unemployed does not. On civil rights and Social Security, then, it is not merely that "I" am affected, but also that "we" are affected. And "we" are especially sensitive and responsive to media coverage that suggests that "our" problem is an important problem for the country.

In sum, by failing to use media discourse and experiential knowledge together in constructing a frame, people are unable to bridge the personal and cultural and to anchor their understanding in both. When they fail to link their media-based understanding of an issue with experiential knowledge, their issue understanding is ad hoc and separated from their daily lives. Hence, there is a special robustness to frames that are held together with a full combination of resources.

Collective Action Frames

We know, of course, that collective action is more than just a matter of political consciousness. One may be completely convinced of the desirability of changing a situation while gravely doubting the possibility of changing it. Furthermore, we know from many studies of social movements how important social networks are for recruiting people and drawing them into political action with their friends. People sometimes act first and only through participating develop the political consciousness that supports the action.

Personal costs also deter people from participating, their agreement with a movement's political analysis notwithstanding. Action may be risky or, at a minimum, require forgoing other more pleasurable or profitable uses of time. Private life has its own legitimate demands, and caring for a sick child or an aging parent may take precedence over demonstrating for a cause in which one fully believes.

Finally, there is the matter of opportunity. Changes in the broader political structure and climate may open and close the chance for collective action to have an impact. External events and crises, broad shifts in public sentiment, and electoral changes and rhythms all have a heavy influence on whether political consciousness ever gets translated into action. In sum, the absence of a political consciousness that supports collective action can, at best, explain only one part of people's quiescence.

Lest we be too impressed by the inactivity of most people, the history of social movements is a reminder of those occasions when people do become mobilized and engage in various forms of collective action. In spite of all the obstacles, it occurs regularly and frequently surprises observers who were overly impressed by an earlier quiescence. These movements always offer one or more *collective action* frames.

Collective action frames, to quote Snow and Benford (1992), are "action oriented sets of beliefs and meanings that inspire and legitimate social movement activities and campaigns."[1] They offer ways of understanding that imply the need and desirability of some form of action. Movements may have internal battles over which particular frame will prevail or may offer several frames for different constituencies, but they will all have in common the implication that those who share the frame can and should take action.

Gamson (1992) suggests three components of these collective action frames: injustice, agency, and identity. The injustice component refers to the moral indignation expressed in this form of political consciousness. This is not merely a cognitive or intellectual judgment about what is equitable, but is what cognitive psychologists call a "hot cognition"—one that is laden with emotion (see, for example, Zajonc 1980). An injustice frame requires a consciousness of motivated human actors who carry some of the onus for bringing about harm and suffering.

The agency component refers to the consciousness that it is possible to alter conditions or policies through collective action. Collective action frames imply some sense of collective efficacy and deny the immutability of some undesirable situation. They empower people by defining them as potential agents of their own history. They suggest not merely that something can be done but that "we" can do something.

The identity component refers to the process of defining this "we," typically in opposition to some "they" who have different interests or values. Without an adversarial component, the potential target of collective action is likely to remain an abstraction—hunger, disease, poverty, or war, for example. Collective action requires a consciousness of human agents whose policies or practices must be changed and a "we" who will help to bring about change.

To understand the role of media discourse in nurturing or stifling collective action frames, I will examine how it affects each of the individual components. Since different aspects of media discourse are relevant for each, we must distinguish between the framing and salience of the issue and the movement. While there is some mutual influence of issue- and movement-framing activities, they can vary independently. One can frame the anti-Vietnam War movement negatively while embracing an antiwar frame. One can repudiate the actions of rioters in Los Angeles and elsewhere while endorsing a racial injustice frame on the condition of U.S. cities. It is always possible to accept the message and reject the messenger.

Injustice

For injustice frames, it is the framing and salience of the issue, not the movement, that is relevant. The media role in fostering or retarding injustice frames is complex and double-edged. Hardships and inequities can be presented in ways that stimulate many different emotions: compassion, cynicism, bemused irony, and resignation, for example. Injustice focuses on the kind of righteous anger that puts fire in the belly and iron in the soul. Injustice, as I argued earlier, is a hot cognition, not merely an abstract intellectual judgment about what is equitable.

The heat of a moral judgment is intimately related to beliefs about what acts or conditions have caused people to suffer undeserved hardship or loss. The critical dimension is the abstractness of the target. Vague and abstract sources of unfairness diffuse indignation and make it seem foolish. We may think it dreadfully unfair when it rains on our parade, but bad luck and nature are poor targets for an injustice frame. When impersonal and abstract forces are responsible for our suffering, we are taught to accept what cannot be changed and make the best of it. Anger is dampened by the unanswerable rhetorical question, Who says life is fair?

At the other extreme, if one attributes undeserved suffering to malicious or selfish acts by clearly identifiable persons or groups, the emotional component of an injustice frame will almost certainly be there. Concreteness in the target, even when it is misplaced and directed away from the real causes of hardship, is a necessary condition for an injustice frame. Hence, competition over defining targets is a crucial battleground in the development or containment of injustice frames.

More specifically, an injustice frame requires that motivated human actors carry some of the onus for bringing about harm and suffering. These actors may be corporations, government agencies, or specifiable groups rather than individuals. They may be presented as malicious, but selfishness, greed, and indifference may be sufficient to produce indignation.

An injustice frame does not require that the actors who are responsible for the condition be autonomous. They may be depicted as constrained by past actions of others and by more abstract forces, as long as they have some role as agents in bringing about or continuing the wrongful injury. From the standpoint of those who wish to control or discourage the development of injustice frames, symbolic strategies should emphasize abstract targets that render human agency as invisible as possible. Reification helps to accomplish this by blaming actorless entities such as "the system," "society," "life," and "human nature."

If reification does not prevent the development of an injustice frame, a second line of defense involves accepting human agency while diverting the focus toward external targets or internal opponents. Righteous anger cannot always be prevented, but it may still be channeled safely and perhaps even used to further one's purposes. Some sponsors of conservative frames claimed, for example, that the social welfare programs of the 1960s caused the 1992 Los Angeles riots.

For those who would encourage collective action, these strategies of social control provide a formidable dilemma. The conditions of people's daily lives are, in fact, determined by abstract sociocultural forces that are largely invisible to them. Critical views of "the system," however accurate, may still encourage reification just as much as benign ones as long as they lack a focus on human actors.

The antidote to excessive abstraction has its own problems. In concretizing the targets of an injustice frame, there is a danger that people will miss the underlying structural conditions that produce hardship and inequality. They may exaggerate the role of human actors, failing to understand broader structural constraints, and misdirect their anger at easy and inappropriate targets.

There is no easy path between the cold cognition of an overdetermined structural analysis and the hot cognition of misplaced concreteness. As long as human actors are not central in understanding the conditions that produce hardship and suffering, we can expect little righteous anger. Targets of collective action will remain unfocused. As long as moral indignation is narrowly focused on human actors without regard to the broader structure in which they operate, injustice frames will be a poor tool for collective action, leading to ineffectiveness and frustration, perhaps creating new victims of injustice.

To sustain collective action, the targets identified by the frame must successfully bridge the abstract and the concrete. By connecting broader sociocultural forces with human agents who are appropriate targets of collective action, one can get the heat into the cognition. By making sure that the concrete targets are linked to and can affect the broader forces, one can make sure that the heat is not misdirected in ways that will leave the underlying source of injustice untouched.

Media practices have a double-edged effect in both stimulating and discouraging injustice frames. The extent to which they do one or the other differs substantially from issue to issue. But some framing practices cut across issues and operate more generally.

Some encouragement of injustice frames is built into the narrative form that dominates news reporting. Most journalists understand that news writing is storytelling, but sometimes it is made explicit. Edward Epstein describes a memo that Reuven Frank sent to his staff at NBC News: "Every news story should, without any sacrifice of probity or responsibility, display the attributes of fiction, of drama" (1973, 241). Stories were to be organized around the triad of "conflict, problem, and denouement" with "rising action" building to a climax.

This dependence on the narrative form has implications for promoting an injustice frame. Narratives focus attention on motivated actors rather than structural causes of events. As new events unfold and changes appear in the conditions of people's daily lives, human agents are typically identified as causal agents in a morality play about good and evil or honesty and corruption. The more abstract analysis of sociocultural forces favored by social scientists is deemphasized if it enters the story at all.

Media emphasis on narrative form, then, tends to concretize targets in ways that would appear to abet injustice frames. Far from serving the social control needs of authorities in this instance, media coverage frequently gives people reasons to get angry at somebody. Of course, that "somebody" need not be the real source of grievance at all but merely a convenient surrogate. Nevertheless, however righteous indignation may get channeled, media discourse on many issues quite inadvertently helps to generate it by providing concrete targets. Hence it is an obstacle to social control strategies that diffuse a sense of injustice by moving the causes of undeserved hardship beyond human agency.

At the same time, the personalization of responsibility may have the effect of blurring broader power relations and the structural causes of a bad situation. Many writers have argued that the total media experience leads to the fragmentation of meaning. News comes in quotations with ever shorter sound bites. The preoccupation with immediacy results in a proliferation of fleeting, ephemeral images that have no ability to sustain any coherent organizing frame to provide meaning over time. The "action news" formula adopted by many local news programs packs thirty to forty short, fast items into a twenty-two-and-a-half-minute "newshole"—"one minute-thirty for World War III," as one critic described it (Diamond 1975).

Bennett analyzes the news product as a result of journalistic practices that combine to produce fragmentation and confusion. "The fragmentation of information begins," he argues, "by emphasizing individual actors over the political contexts in which they operate. Fragmentation is then heightened by the use of dramatic formats that turn events into self-contained, isolated happenings." The result is news that comes to us in "sketchy dramatic capsules that make it difficult to see the connections across issues or even to follow the development of a particular issue over time" (1988: 24). Hence the structure and operation of societal power relations remain obscure and invisible.

Iyengar (1991) provides experimental evidence on how the episodic nature of media reporting on most issues affects attributions of responsibility. He contrasts two forms of presentation—the "episodic" and the "thematic." The episodic form—by far the most common one—"takes the form of a case study or event-oriented report and depicts public issues in terms of concrete instances." In contrast, the much rarer thematic form emphasizes general outcomes, conditions, and statistical evidence.

By altering the format of television reports about several different political issues as presented to experimental and control groups, Iyengar shows how people's attributions of responsibility are affected. More specifically, he shows that exposure to the episodic format makes viewers less likely to hold public officials accountable for the existence of some problem and less likely to hold them responsible for alleviating it.

The implication of this line of argument is that if people simply relied on the media, it would be difficult to find any coherent frame at all, let alone an injustice frame. The metanarrative is frequently about the self-reforming nature of the system, operating to get rid of the rotten apples that the news media have exposed. If moral indignation is stimulated by fingering the bad guys, it is quickly and safely assuaged by their removal.

These complicated and offsetting characteristics force one to look closely at how media discourse treats the injustice theme on specific issues. Gamson (1992) found central and highly visible injustice frames in media discourse on affirmative action but very low visibility for injustice frames on nuclear power and Arab-Israeli conflict. Injustice frames were present in media discourse on the troubled steel industry, but the targets offered for indignation were selected ones, supporting some frames much more than others. Media-designated targets included the Japanese, for taking away the jobs of American workers, and the "Nader juggernaut," for forcing expensive health and safety regulations on American industry, but did not include the disinvestment decisions of U.S. steel companies.

Agency

What does it mean when demonstrators chant, "The whole world is watching"? It means that they matter—that they are making history. The media spotlight validates the fact that they are important players. Conversely, a demonstration with no media coverage at all is a nonevent, unlikely to have any positive influence on either mobilizing potential challengers or influencing any target. No news is bad news.

For this component of collective action frames, it is mainly attention that matters. How the issue is framed or even whether the movement is framed positively or negatively is irrelevant; the salience of the movement is the variable of interest. Potential challengers in the audience get the message that this group is taken seriously and must be dealt with in some way. Arrests and suppression only confirm the fact that they are important enough to be a threat to authorities. The content that matters with respect to agency is about the power of the movement and the ability of authorities to control it. The media role in this is, as usual, complicated.

The forces that discourage a sense of agency among ordinary citizens in most societies are overwhelming. Culture and social structure combine to induce collective helplessness. The vast majority seem condemned to remain subject to sociocultural forces that systematically remove from their consciousness any sense that they can collectively alter the conditions and terms of their daily lives.

Most of us, even those with political activist identities, spend most of our time and energy on sustaining our daily lives. Flacks points out that this includes not only meeting material needs but also "activity and experience designed to sustain one's self as a human being—to validate or fulfill the meaning of one's life, reinforce or enhance one's sense of self-worth, [and] achieve satisfaction and pleasure" (1988: 2). This daily activity typically takes for granted and reinforces the patterned daily life characteristic of a community or society; only very rarely do people have an opportunity to engage in activity that challenges or tries to change some aspect of this pattern—what Flacks calls "making history."

As long as history making is centralized and hierarchical, with very little opportunity for people to participate in any of the institutions that set the conditions of their daily lives, they will inevitably feel "that they themselves are objects of historical forces alien to themselves, that they themselves are without power" (Flacks 1988: 5). Everyday life and history are experienced as separate realms because we have a national political economy that is dominated by centralized, hierarchical, national corporations and a national state.

This structural impediment to collective agency is reinforced by a political culture that operates to produce quiescence and passivity. Merelman tells us:

> [A] loosely bounded culture prevents Americans from controlling their political and social destinies, for the world which loose boundedness portrays is not the world of political and social structures that actually exists. It is, instead, a shadowland, which gives Americans little real purchase on the massive, hierarchical political and economic structures that dominate their lives. (1984: 1)

He analyzes the role of television in particular in promoting a loosely bounded culture that backs people away from politics and directs them toward a private vision of the self in the world.

Edelman (1988) points to the powerful social control that is exercised, largely unconsciously, through the manipulation of symbolism used in "constructing the political spectacle." Problems, enemies, crises, and leaders are constantly being constructed and reconstructed to create a series of threats and reassurances. To take it in is to be taken in by it. "For most of the human race," he writes in his conclusion, "political history has been a record of the triumph of mystification over strategies to maximize well-being." Rebellious collective action can even buttress the dominant worldview by helping political elites in their construction of a stable enemy or threat that justifies their policies and provides a legitimation for political repression.

Bennett observes how the structure and culture of news production combine to limit popular participation:

> As long as the distribution of power is narrow and decision processes are closed, journalists will never be free of their dependence on the small group of public relations experts, official spokespersons, and powerful leaders whose self-serving pronouncements have become firmly established as the bulk of the daily news. (1988: xii)

Furthermore, these "advertisements for authority" are surrounded by other reports "that convey fearful images of violent crime, economic insecurity, and nuclear war. Such images reinforce public support for political authorities who promise order, security, and responsive political solutions." Granting that people take it all with a grain of salt, he argues that even minimal acceptance of basic assumptions about political reality is enough to discourage most people from participating actively in the political process.

It is no wonder, Bennett concludes, that few Americans become involved politically and "most cannot imagine how they could make a political difference." One can break out by reading specialized publications with a broader range of discourse, but "those who take the time to do so may find themselves unable to communicate with the majority who remain trapped on the other side of the wall of mass media imagery" (1988: xv). Gans, reviewing the many reasons for people to avoid political activities, is led to conclude that "it is surprising to find any citizen activity taking place at all" (1988: 70).

And yet it does. There are clearly moments when people do take it upon themselves to do more than evade or transcend the terms and conditions of their daily lives and behave as collective agents who can change them. At some level, they harbor a sense of potential agency. Are social scientists, in emphasizing how this culture of quiescence is produced and maintained, themselves promulgating yet another set of reasons for inaction, another discouragement to agency? Where are the cracks in which some idea of collective agency stays alive, ready to grow and prosper under the proper conditions, as it did so dramatically and to everyone's surprise in Eastern Europe, for example?

I accept the claim that American media discourse systematically discourages the idea that ordinary citizens can alter the conditions and terms of their daily lives through their own actions. But this message comes through more equivocally on some issues than on others, and in some special contexts a sense of collective agency is even nurtured.

Among the four issues (troubled industry, affirmative action, nuclear power, Arab-Israeli conflict) discussed in Gamson (1992), the generalization seems strongest for media discourse on problems in the steel industry. One media sample covered a moment of significant citizen action—a community effort by workers and other citizens in the Mahoning Valley area in Ohio to buy and run Youngstown Sheet and Tube Company. Sheet and Tube had been acquired in 1969 by a New Orleans-based conglomerate, the Lykes Corporation, which had used it as a "cash cow." Rather than modernizing the plant, Lykes used its cash flow to service the debt it had assumed in buying Sheet and Tube and to finance other new acquisitions.

By 1977, Lykes tried to sell the depleted company but found no buyers among other foreign and domestic steel companies; in September, it announced that it would permanently close its largest mill in the area and lay off 4,100 employees. An estimated 3,600 additional jobs would be lost through effects on local suppliers and retail businesses. Meanwhile, the United Steelworkers of America, with its primary weapon, the strike, rendered largely useless by changes in the worldwide steel industry, tried desperately to hold on to the gains it had won in the past, but seemed incapable of any initiative.

In response, a broad group of religious leaders formed the Ecumenical Coalition of the Mahoning Valley to search for a solution to the crisis. At the suggestion of local steelworkers, they began to explore the possibility of a combined worker-community buyout. Alperovitz and Faux describe the action as embodying "concerns for jobs rather than welfare, for self-help and widespread participation rather than dependence on absentee decision-makers" (1982, 355).

The new company was to be known as Community Steel, directed by a fifteen-member board with six members elected by the company's workers, six by stockholders, and three by a broadly based community corporation. Thousands of residents pledged savings to a fund that would purchase the factory, and the coalition received a grant from the Department of Housing and Urban Development (HUD) to conduct a feasibility study. Eventually, the plan faltered when the Carter administration failed to support the needed loan guarantees, but the two-year Youngstown effort was clearly the largest and most significant attempt to convert a plant to worker-community ownership.

Was it visible in national media discourse? When they are covering a continuing issue such as the decline of the troubled steel industry, journalists look for a topical peg on which they can hang their stories. The Carter administration provided one when it offered a six-point plan to deal with the problems of the steel industry in the late fall of 1977. If there was a story in the Youngstown effort begun a couple of months earlier, this was an excellent opportunity to include it. It was receiving extensive coverage in local media. Grassroots efforts of this sort are novel enough, and it was too soon to know what the outcome would be. HUD secretary Patricia Harris was calling for "new models of community involvement to solve these problems" (Alperovitz and Faux 1982: 355).One might expect that the normal assumption in media discourse that citizen action is irrelevant might well be suspended in such an instance.

A two-week sample of media commentary in fifty daily newspapers, three major television networks, and three major newsmagazines found no references or allusions to citizen action in the Mahoning Valley in the heart of the steel industry. Workers who appear in this commentary are passive; they are never the subject of what is happening, always its unfortunate object. Even their status as victims is sometimes challenged. Columnist James Reston thought they partly brought it on themselves; he chided American workers who "increasingly condemn the integrity of work and reject the authority of their managers" and quoted approvingly from a former Nixon administration Labor Department official who claimed that workers "no longer think that hard work pays off" and "increasingly resist authority in their companies, communities, churches, or governments" (*New York Times,* December 2, 1977).

On affirmative action, citizen action was visible when an administration sympathetic to the civil rights movement was in power and became largely invisible when official discourse turned unsympathetic. Official sympathy for citizen action, then, may alter its normal disparagement or invisibility and encourage journalists to treat collective actors as if they were relevant players in the policy arena.

On nuclear power, citizen action became and remained visible in spite of an official discourse that belittled it and attempted to diminish its importance. Apparently, there are circumstances in which media discourse will portray a movement as a significant actor even without official encouragement. On nuclear power, in particular, a strong case could be made that media discourse has been more help than hindrance to the antinuclear movement. It serves no official agenda to have antinuke protesters taken so seriously that they provide potential models for the next community targeted for construction of a nuclear reactor. Indeed, officials in industry and government who might consider commissioning a new nuclear reactor must certainly be deterred by the likely prospect of prolonged local protest with extensive media coverage.

Media-amplified images of successful citizen action on one issue can generalize and transfer to other issues. The repertoire of collective action presented on a broad range of political issues in media discourse—of boycotts, strikes, and demonstrations, for example—can easily be divorced from the particular context in which it is presented and adapted to other issues. Gamson (1992) concludes that "the media role in portraying collective agency seems, to a substantial degree, issue specific and variable rather than constant."

But none of this evidence contradicts Gitlin's (1980) observations on the type of collective action that will draw the media spotlight. Between the sustained but unspectacular citizen action of the Mahoning Valley coalition and the flames of burning buildings in the Los Angeles riot, there is no contest. The media may offer occasional models of collective action that make a difference, but they are highly selective ones.

Identity

Being a collective agent implies being part of a "we" who can do something. The identity component of collective action frames is about the process of defining this "we," typically in opposition to some "they" who have different interests or values. As Melucci (1989) suggests, social movements elaborate and negotiate this meaning over time, and some even make the question of "who we are" an important part of their internal discourse.

Here it is the media framing of the movement, not the issue, that is relevant. Media images of a movement, as Gitlin (1980: 3) argues, "become implicated in a movement's self-image," and frequently the quality of the media images do not present the movement's intended identity. Since there are many aspects to a collective identity, it is quite possible for media coverage to reinforce one part that a movement wishes to encourage at the same time that it contradicts or undercuts other parts.

It is useful to think of collective identities as three embedded layers: *organizational, movement,* and *solidary group.* The organizational layer refers to identities built around movement carriers—the union maid or the party loyalist, for example. This layer may or may not be embedded in a movement layer that is broader than any particular organization. The identity of peace activists, for example, rarely rests on one organization; people support different efforts at different moments while subordinating all organizations to their broader movement identity.

Finally, the movement layer may or may not be embedded in a larger solidary group identity constructed around people's social location—for example, as workers or as black women. That constituents may come from a common social location does not itself mean that this will be relevant for movement or organizational identities. Environmental activists, for example, may be largely white and professional-managerial class, but they are likely to decry the narrowness of their base. Their internal discourse often focuses on how they can activate more workers and people of color.

Sometimes these different layers are so closely integrated that they become a single amalgam: a movement arises out of a particular solidary group with widespread support from it, and one particular organization comes to embody the movement. Often, however, the different layers are separate. Many working-class Americans, for example, personally identify with "working people," but have no identification with their union and think of the "labor movement" as something that happened fifty years ago.

Note that the locus of collective identity—for all three layers—is at the sociocultural, not the individual, level. It is manifested through the language and symbols by which it is publicly expressed—in styles of dress, language, demeanor, and discourse. One learns about its content by asking people about the meaning of labels and other cultural symbols, not about their own personal identity.

All social movements have the task of bridging individual and sociocultural levels. This is accomplished by enlarging the personal identities of constituents to include the relevant collective identities as part of their definition of self. The most powerful and enduring collective identities link solidary, movement, and organizational layers in the participants' sense of self. The movement layer is especially critical because it is a necessary catalyst in fusing solidary and organizational identification in an integrated movement identity.

Some movements attempt to mobilize their constituents with an all-inclusive "we." "We" are the world, humankind, or, in the case of domestic issues, all good citizens. Such an *aggregate* frame turns the "we" into a pool of individuals rather than a potential collective actor. The call for action in such frames is personal—for example, to make peace, hunger, or the environment your personal responsibility.

There is no clear "they" in aggregate frames. The targets are not actors but abstractions—hunger, pollution, war, poverty, disease. These abstractions do not point to an external target whose actions or policies must be changed. If pollution is the problem and we are all polluters, then "we" are the target of action. "We" are the "they" in such frames, and neither agent nor target is a collective actor.

Collective action frames, in contrast, are adversarial; "we" stand in opposition or conflict to some "they." "They" are responsible for some objectionable situation and have the power to change it by acting differently in some fashion. We and they are differentiated rather than conflated.

Aggregate frames are central to what Lofland (1989) and McCarthy and Wolfson (1992) call "consensus movements." The latter define them as "organized movements for change that find *widespread support* for their goals and *little or no organized opposition* from the population of a geographic community." The movement against drunk driving provides an example. But widespread support for the broadest goals of a movement does not tell us much about whether there will be organized opposition. This depends on how a group translates its goals into action imperatives. Within the same movement, different social movement organizations will vary in how they frame the issue and in the form and targets of their action. The peace and environmental movements provide examples of a range of more consensual and more adversarial groups. It seems more useful to speak of consensus *frames* or consensus *strategies* rather than to treat this as a property of movements.

A blurry "they," by itself, does not imply an aggregate frame. It is quite possible to have a clear and collective "we" while the "they" remains vague because it is so elusive. This is especially likely to be true when the main targets of change are cultural more than political and economic. If one is attacking, for example, the dominant cultural code of what is normal, the decisions of governments and powerful corporate actors may be secondary. In the pursuit of cultural change, the target is often diffused through the whole civil society and the "they" being pursued is structurally elusive.

In such a situation, the mass media are likely to become the ambivalent target of action. To the extent that they reflect the cultural code that the group is challenging, they are necessarily an adversary. But since they also are capable of amplifying the challenge and expanding its audience, helping it to reach the many settings in which cultural codes operate, they are necessarily a potential ally as well. Hence the characteristic ambivalence with which so many movement organizations approach the mass media as both a means for changing society and a target that epitomizes the objectionable cultural practices being challenged.

In sum, frames with a clear "we" and an elusive "they" are quite capable of being fully collective and adversarial; unlike aggregate frames, agent and target of action are not conflated. These frames, then, are simply a more complicated type of adversarial frame.

In one respect, media discourse works to encourage adversarial frames. Collective action by movement organizations helps to define an issue as controversial, triggering the balance norm of presenting quotes from two conflicting sides. The process, with its simultaneous advantages and disadvantages from the standpoint of movements, is well illustrated by media coverage of the 1977 site occupation of the Seabrook, New Hampshire, nuclear reactor by the Clamshell Alliance.

The television story is about a dyadic conflict between Governor Meldrim Thomson and his allies and the Clamshell Alliance over whether the Seabrook reactor will be completed. The central question addressed is who will win and, hence, there is very little direct commentary about nuclear power as such. But the coverage does present images of the anti-nuclear-power movement as it implicitly addresses the question, What kind of people are against nuclear power?

For a deaf television viewer, the answer would seem to be people who wear backpacks and play Frisbee. All three networks feature these images in more than one segment. One sees beards and long hair, bandanas, "no nuke" buttons, people playing guitars and doing needlepoint. Outside the courthouse, after the demonstrators have been released, we see happy family reunions, with many children.

These visual images do not have a fixed meaning. One who believes that the experts know best may see frivolous flower children and environmental extremists who look as if they will not be happy until they turn the White House into a bird sanctuary. A more sympathetic viewer may see loving, caring, earthy young people who are socially integrated and concerned about our shared environment.

There are network differences in the words accompanying these images. The CBS and NBC coverage leaves the interpretive work to the viewer, but

ABC offers its own interpretation. We are told that these are the same kind of people who were involved in antiwar demonstrations, "demonstrators in search of a cause." The network allows two members of the Clam to speak for themselves, quoting their determination to win ("We have to stop it at any cost") while omitting any quotations dealing with their reasons for acting.

The demonstrators are presented relatively sympathetically in news-magazine coverage. Both *Time* and *Newsweek* mention their commitment to nonviolence, and *Newsweek* adds their exclusion of drugs, weapons, and fighting. The accompanying photographs reinforce the television images of backpackers; *Newsweek* calls them scruffy and mentions Frisbees, guitars, and reading Thoreau. *Time* also quotes the publisher of the *Manchester Union Leader,* William Loeb, who likened the Clam to "Nazi storm troopers under Hitler," but characterizes him in a discrediting way as an "abrasive conservative."

Some media frames invite the viewer to see the antinuclear movement in adversarial class terms. Opponents of nuclear power are presented as indulged children of the affluent who have everything they need. They have secure professional jobs in hand or awaiting them and can afford to ignore the imperatives of economic growth. These "coercive utopians" (McCracken 1977, 1979) are intent on imposing their antigrowth vision on others at the expense of the real interests of working people.

The adversarial frames offered by media discourse on nuclear power do not emphasize a collective movement identity that the movement would like to embrace. The movement's preferred identity cuts across racial and class lines. To the extent that it offers an adversarial frame at all, it is the people versus the nuclear industry and its allies in government. But when this adversarial frame appears in the media, it is in highly attenuated form, and it is often undercut by imagery that emphasizes the narrowness of the solidary group identities engaged by the movement.

On the issues discussed in Gamson (1992), media discourse is heavily adversarial only on affirmative action. Troubled industry and Arab-Israeli conflict are almost never framed as adversarial across solidary group cleavages in American society. And even on affirmative action, the adversarial framing is continually undercut by a discourse that assumes persons have rights as individuals. Although the term "equal rights," for example, could apply to the claims of a group as well, the discourse makes the articulation of collective claims problematic. The assertion of injustices based on social inequalities must contend with a culturally normative response that asserts that we are all individuals and implicitly denies the relevance of social location and group differences.

In spite of the tendency of media discourse to emphasize a fight, it narrows the basis of conflict, divorcing the movement level from the solidary group level. This works against the efforts of movements to integrate the different parts of a collective identity.

Conclusion

Qualifications and nuances notwithstanding, the overall role of media discourse is clear: it often obstructs and only rarely and unevenly contributes to the development of collective action frames. The good news for movement activists is that media discourse is only one resource. Selectively integrated with other resources—especially experiential knowledge—it remains a central component in the construction of collective action frames.

Using an integrated resource strategy is far from a sufficient condition for developing this political consciousness, but it helps. It is especially important in constructing the injustice component. Experiential knowledge helps to connect the abstract cognition of unfairness with the emotion of moral indignation. Media discourse is equally important in forging an injustice frame. Experiential knowledge of injustice in concrete form stimulates the emotions, but they may dissipate for lack of a clear target. Media discourse places the experienced injustice in context, making it a special case of a broader injustice. The experiential resource concretizes injustice; the media resource generalizes it and makes it shared and collective.

Relevant experiences, be they direct, vicarious, or the generalized sort embodied in popular wisdom, are not enough. They may be sufficient to guide people to some coherent frame on an issue but, if people are to become agents who influence the conditions that govern their daily lives, they must connect their understanding with a broader public discourse as well. Without an integrated understanding, relevant events and actors in the news will remain a sideshow—and a frequently bewildering one, having little to do with their daily lives.

The problem of linkage varies from issue to issue. Meaning on some issues is overly dependent on media discourse. The difficulty people face here is connecting their media-based understanding of the issue with their everyday lives. Understanding remains abstract and emotionally distant without the elements of collective identification and moral indignation that flow from experience. Integration does not happen spontaneously unless special conditions produce it—as they can, for example, when events in the news directly disrupt or threaten to disrupt their daily lives. More typically, the relevance is indirect and some cognitive leap is necessary to bridge the gap.

The organizer's task is more difficult on such issues. Abstract argument about complex indirect and future effects will not forge the emotional linkage even if people are convinced intellectually. Two alternative strategies seem more promising than presenting arguments about general causes and effects.

The first is to search for existing experiential knowledge that can be shown to be relevant for a broader collective action frame. It helps here if organizers share the life world of those who are being encouraged to make the linkage. Then they can draw on their own experience in pointing out connections with some confidence that others will have similar stories of their own. Some relevant experiences are universal enough to transcend a broad range of social backgrounds.

The second is to create situations where people can gain experiential knowledge of injustice. Public discourse facilitates knowledge through vicarious experience when it personalizes broader injustices by using exemplary cases to embody them. Hence, the concrete experience of Anne Frank conveys the meaning of the Holocaust in an experiential mode that no amount of factual information on the 6 million Jewish victims of Nazi death camps can convey. Social movement organizations frequently try to make the link by bringing potential participants in contact with witnesses whose firsthand accounts provide listeners with vicarious experiential knowledge.

There is a well-laid cultural trap into which movement activists sometimes fall. They frame their primary task as marketing a product for consumers through the mass media. The product is a cause in which they sincerely believe but that, for a variety of reasons, they must "sell" to others. The constituency for this mobilization effort is thought of as a set of potential buyers whose response of vote, donation, signature, or other token marks a successful sales effort. The logic of this approach leads one to look for a more effective marketing strategy, expressed through catchy symbols that will tap an emotional hot button and trigger the desired response.

Emotion is an important component of collective action frames, as I have emphasized. Perhaps it is quite possible to trigger a burst of moral indignation by finding the right photograph or clever slogan. The problem with the hot-button approach is not that it does not work, but that it directly undermines the goal of increasing people's sense of agency.

Collective agency can hardly be encouraged by treating potential participants as passive objects to be manipulated. This simply decreases any tendency toward the development of a collective identity and sympathy with some sustained effort at social change. It provides good reason to extend the pervasive cynicism about those who run the society to include those who supposedly challenge their domination.

To increase a sense of agency, symbolic strategies should attempt to draw out the latent sense of agency that people already carry around with them. Organizers need to assume that a sense of agency is, at least, dormant and capable of being awakened. Their task is to listen for it and to nurture it where it occurs spontaneously. One does not transform people who feel individually powerless into a group with a sense of collective agency by pushing hot buttons. Direct, rather than mass-mediated, relationships are necessary.

Notes

I wish to thank Mary Katzenstein and the editors of this volume for their helpful comments on an earlier draft.

1. They also define collective action frames as "emergent," but this seems an unwise inclusion. Changes in political consciousness can occur at various points, sometimes well in advance of mobilization. They may have already emerged by the time mobilization occurs, awaiting only some change in political opportunity to precipitate action. In other cases, they may emerge gradually, developing most fully after some initial collective action. Emergence should not be made a matter of definition.

Chapter 6

What's in a Name?
Nationalist Movements and Public Discourse

Jane Jenson

A notable theme of public discourse in Canada is the naming of nations. Denominating nations involves much more than the ethnic labeling familiar in polyethnic states like the United States, where Italian-Americans, Asian-Americans, and so on seek political recognition.[1] As in other multinational states, much of Canadian politics in the past three decades has involved competing assertions of nationhood, some of which reject the very label "Canadian."

As Benedict Anderson tells us, nations are "imagined communities" that claim sovereignty and recognize a limited number of people as members (1991: 6-7). They identify an "us," which can be distinguished from the "other." This discourse has meaning only to the extent that it is shared by members of the community, thereby constituting a collective identity. Therefore, nationalist movements are like other social movements; their politics includes the construction of a collective identity.

Since nations are the result of political action, there are a variety of ways, or styles, in which they can be imagined.[2] The identification of any nation can vary, depending upon the strategic choices made by the movement in light of the ends it seeks, the institutional constraints it faces, and the identity claims, national or not, made by others in the same community or state. National identities are no more "embodied" than are the collective identities of other social movements.[3]

One goal of nationalist movements, like other social movements, is to resist "outside naming" and to be "self-naming" (Chartrand 1991: 2). Therefore, movements struggle over names and seek recognition of the one they prefer, both within and outside the community. In competing for discursive space, communities are imagining more than their present and future; they also imagine their pasts. Therefore, social movements making national claims, like all other social movements, write and rewrite history in order to justify contemporary definitions of interests and strategies.[4] The imagined past is often as important a terrain of practice as the present.

Choices are never unconstrained, of course. They are made in particular structural and institutional contexts, traversed by relations of power. The power of dominant groups and institutions is a limit on the self-naming of subordinate communities. Yet the latter are never without power. The constitution of a shared collective identity involves the exercise of power. Moreover, during certain moments of economic and political turbulence long-standing social relations become more permeable to innovations and inventions, to the challenges mounted by subordinate groups seeking redress. And, as in any power relation, such an act of representing a community by name has real, material consequences; it is not simply a struggle over words.

The past three decades of Canadian politics provide an especially fertile terrain for examining the politics of naming. While Canadian public discourse by no means has been suffering from the violence and disintegration associated with nationalism in many parts of the world, it has been reorganized by the actions of nationalist movements demanding new rights and governmental powers. Nation-based claims have displaced the more familiar ones of polyethnic politics. They have done so, moreover, in a context of profound economic restructuring and political turbulence. This case will be examined, then, in order to unpack and explore the several propositions about social movement politics developed in this essay.

A Concise History of Naming Names

Contests over the collective identity of nations within Canada have long been at the heart of the country's politics. Canadian politics, like politics elsewhere, involves a dual process of representation, incorporating representation of interests via state institutions as well as those of civil society, *and* the constitution of the identities of the represented, through political mobilization and policy innovation (Jenson 1990: 662-64).[5] The formation of collective identities occurs as part of—and as central to—the definition of interests and elaboration of stategies of collective actors.

The terrain on which actors struggle over representation is the universe of political discourse, within which identities are socially constructed (Jenson 1987). Because actors with a variety of collective identities coexist in this universe, their practices and meaning systems jostle each other for attention and legitimacy (Jenson 1991: 52). It is by translating meanings into practice—

often within institutions—that actors create, sustain, or change representa-
tional arrangements.[6] The creation of meaning is, then, profoundly political.

Disputed representations of "Canada," as well as the groups imagined to
compose it, have a long political history, and have had a major impact on institutional arrangements. One long-standing and popular characterization of
Canada is of a society composed of two languages and cultures with equal
rights of recognition and cultural expression. Since 1867, minority language
(and some religious) rights have been protected by the Constitution and in
crucial institutions like schools. The collective rights thereby bestowed recognize this way of imagining the Canadian nation.

This "bilingual/bicultural" representation of Canada was central to the initial project of Confederation. In 1867 many people insisted that while a new
nation might be built, any "Canadian" identity must accommodate difference
because of the diversity of religions and "races" present in the new country
(Simeon and Robinson 1990: 22ff.).[7] While the goal was clearly to create a
new nation, with a common citizenship, the intent was not to extinguish the
collective rights of the diverse communities that Canada housed.

A redefinition of this project gained new support in the 1970s, reflected in
the federal government's legislation for bilingualism and biculturalism. This
was also a project of nation building, a "pan-Canadian" one designed to identify all Canadians. The identities that followed from it appeared at first glance to
be quite inclusive, designating all citizens according to language preference,
as either Anglophone or Francophone. This project was not particularly
accommodative of collective claims, however; rights belonged primarily to
individuals.

Therefore, contestation was intense as the Constitution was being rewrit-
ten in 1982-83. The proposed addition of a Charter of Rights and Freedoms
was the focus of debate because its originator, Prime Minister Pierre Tru-
deau, intended it to be a clear expression of liberal rights and protections.
Political mobilization by women, visible minorities, and Aboriginal peoples
forced modifications and compromises away from the original individualistic
charter. Collective rights were entrenched as Aboriginal peoples gained recognition and as affirmative action for gender equality was given constitutional sanction. Subsequent constitutional debate through the 1980s until the
1992 referendum centered in part on the Quebec provincial government's
opposition to the constitutional arrangements of 1982, from which it claimed
the province had been excluded because it had never accepted the package
agreed to by the other nine provinces and the federal government.

The demand of the provincial Liberal government for new constitutional arrangements rested on its version of Québécois nationalism, which has always provided an alternative to the pan-Canadian image of the country.[8] Since the rise of Québécois neonationalism in the 1960s, the community imagined by that movement has been centered in the province of Quebec, adopting its territory as the homeland of the people. The nation-building project is to arm that community with the resources necessary to allow the community to thrive. The Quebec state has always been identified by the nationalist movement as the instrument for orchestrating this nation building by empowering the Québécois (Balthazar 1986; Guindon 1988: 27-37; Gagnon and Montcalm 1990: chapter 3).

While all nationalists agree that Quebec is a nation, groups make different claims to rights and powers in the name of that nation. On the one hand, there is the call for sovereignty and the right to establish an independent state. The *indépendantiste* project has much support within the nationalist movement, forming a central tendency within it.[9] A federalist-nationalist wing also exists, however. Its demands are for alterations of existing institutions of federalism by redividing powers. In addition, there is an insistence on recognition of collective and societal difference, including demands for a constitutional clause stating that Quebec is a "distinct society."

The latter is, in other words, a strategy to realize national autonomy that identifies renewed federalism as an acceptable route to achieving it. Claims are directed toward the intergovernmental institutions of the Canadian state, most often expressed in the language of "federal-provincial relations." Indeed, they are styled as being "about" federalism.[10] The appropriate route to representation is through intergovernmental negotiations and elite bargaining.

In the 1980s, Quebec faced economic conditions that threatened its traditional resource and industrial bases. As a result, support spread for the nationalist demand for new powers for the provincial government to complete and expand the nation-building project. The goal was greater control over the levers of economic policy, so that the Quebec state could effectively influence, shape, and encourage economic restructuring. Despite many elements of neoliberal economic thinking present in the current government of the province, a commitment to state participation in the development of the province remains—a commitment that differentiated it from the neoliberal project of the federal government, led by the Progressive Conservatives until 1993 (Breton and Jenson 1991a: 84-85).

With this activist nationalist project and model, the imagery of the Quebec nation became hegemonic both in Quebec and in the rest of Canada. The pan-

Canadian idea of a single country defined around a linguistic duality has virtually disappeared. In its place there is now a clear representation of the Quebec nation, facing an "other." As the Québécois worked to create themselves as a nation, they perforce generated a mirror image of the other. This other is "English Canada," an other appropriate to a dualistic and language-based reading of Canadian history.

Nationalism in the rest of Canada is the least well defined of the three nationalisms (Bashevkin 1991). Indeed, it lacks a name for itself. Sometimes it is termed the nationalism of "English Canada," always in quotation marks (see, for example, Granatstein and McNaught 1991; McCall et al. 1992). This name has several problems. One is the association with English origin, totally inappropriate in the current polyethnic and multiracial society. Another is that it is sometimes the preferred term—of abuse—for angry Québécois nationalists. Recently, and with a certain irony, some people have begun to term it ROC. This name derives from the habit of federalists in Quebec of speaking of "Quebec and the rest of Canada" (whereas *indépendantistes* speak of "Quebec and Canada").

Neither name suits and both are examples of outside naming. There is, then, tremendous irony, but historical truth, in the realization that the group that objectively appears to hold the most resources in the current contest over naming nations is unable to identify itself.

The first manifestation of this nationalism, at a time when its promoters were self-named "economic nationalists," was in the mobilization against foreign investment and cultural domination by the United States in the late 1960s and through the 1970s (Resnick 1977). Concerns about the loss of sovereignty following from economic integration, via links of direct investment and other economic ties, fueled the movement. Since that time, these nationalists have been most comfortably housed within the social movements, especially the women's and labor movements.

The collective identity mobilized by this nationalist movement is one that recognizes distinctiveness by counterposing the Canadian experience to that of the United States, and more recently Mexico (Barlow and Campbell 1991). Nevertheless, because it is housed in the social movements of the popular sector, there is a strong tendency to represent the country in categorial terms and to mount a critique of the democratic deficit in liberal democratic politics with reference to its impact on particular categories of the population: women, the disabled, gays and lesbians, or the poor, for example.

Movements promoting these collective identities achieved a substantial place in the universe of political discourse in the 1980s. Visible minorities, women, immigrants, the labor movement, and church-based communities gained confidence, strength, and power from the nonparty politics of the popular sector. These social movements and interest groups often acted in coalition in the Action Canada network, bypassing the party system, whose capacity to present alternatives was at a new low in the 1980s (Clarke et al. 1991: chapter 1; Bleyer 1992). Opposition to the government's market-based economic restructuring, especially in the long run up to the 1988 "free trade election," and intervention in the constitutional debates of 1992 have been the major areas of action of these nationalists, who have argued for the impossibility of continuing with the old ways of the elite-designed, accommodational forms of postwar Canadian politics (Dobrowolsky and Jenson 1993: 49-50). They have been as critical of federal-provincial negotiations as a decision-making site as of the current party system.

The campaign against North American free trade, which began in the mid-1980s and continues as opposition to the North American Free Trade Agreement (NAFTA) was led by the Action Canada umbrella coalition of social movement organizations united around opposition to the neoliberal project of simply opening the North American market to the winds of trade (Bleyer 1992). Critics stress the loss of both sovereignty and democracy implied in establishing more open economies without a concomitant increase in mechanisms of political regulation. The major organization of the women's movement, the National Action Committee on the Status of Women (NAC), and the Canadian Labour Congress (CLC), both of which wear the mantle of economic nationalism, are major actors in Action Canada.

The third nationalist movement examined in this essay is that of Aboriginal peoples.[11] This is the name of choice—or self-reference—of the nations of indigenous peoples in Canada who have begun to deploy a nationalist discourse as a way of generating solidarity across many nations, peoples, and rural and urban areas (Chartrand 1992: 17). The common cultural markers of this movement are the colonial experience. Therefore, the Aboriginal national identity is an anticolonial one, based on a rejection of the names imposed by the colonizers. The movement incorporates groups who have been previously named by outsiders. One is the "Indians," so named by the federal government's Indian Act. Those with claims to "status" on a reserve are organized in the Assembly of First Nations (AFN), among other groups.[12] Because of the visibility of this social movement organization, as well as the clientele relationship status Indians have with the federal government, there is a tendency in public discourse to use the term "First Nation" to cover all Aboriginal peoples. Nevertheless, because of the presence of the Métis

Nation in the Aboriginal community, this name is not appropriate. The Métis Nation is formed by those who recognize a tie to the families originated, usually, by French-speaking men and Indian women and led in the 1860s and 1870s by Louis Riel (Chartrand 1991: 14).[13] A third major group is the Inuit, formerly named "Eskimo" by outsiders. There are also organizational representatives of off-reserve and "nonstatus" Aboriginal persons. The Constitution Act of 1982 recognized three Aboriginal peoples: the Indian, Inuit, and Métis Nations.

In the past decades, as part of their struggle to overcome the Fourth World conditions in which so many communities live, Aboriginal peoples have revitalized their own national discourse, which had fallen into disuse for several decades (Long 1992: 119; Jhappan 1993). The nation-to-nation discourse used through the nineteenth century had been deployed less as the consequences of political disempowerment and economic catastrophe devastated Aboriginal communities. Moreover, the "pan-Canadian" definition of citizenship after 1945 made collective claims difficult to mobilize. Only as that definition came under attack, including attacks from Aboriginal groups who refused the "individual rights" vision of assimilation sketched in a 1969 White Paper on Indian Affairs, did nationalism resurface as a powerful mobilizing option (Weaver 1981). Subsequently they have achieved recognition of their vision of history, in which indigenous peoples reappear and "founding" groups are styled as colonizers and invaders.

Aboriginal peoples, in demanding recognition of a new relationship with the Canadian state, have increasingly begun to base their claims on peoples' right to national self-determination as defined in international law (Jhappan 1993). This position leads directly to the demand for self-government and thus constitutes a challenge to existing state-society relations and the division of powers in federalism. In addition, they have used the courts extensively, for land claims especially. A major development has been their success in enlarging the negotiating table for the constitutional talks of 1991-92. Four Aboriginal organizations joined the ten provinces, the federal government, and the governments of the two territories (which were also included at that time). Nevertheless, demands for autonomy also implied demands for separate institutions; their participation in party politics, constitutional negotiations, and the other institutions of the state have been merely contingent.

From this rapid overview of the three nationalist movements currently playing an active role in Canadian politics, a number of observations emerge. One is that the movements do not share a common discourse. Indeed, they describe themselves and their significant "other" in quite different ways. In no case does a nationalist movement represent itself in the same terms as another movement represents it. A second observation is that the representations of each movement have changed over time, as they have confronted different circumstances. Third, they have quite different appreciations of the routes to achieving the representation they seek. Indeed, while they may all be involved in the same constitutional "game," they do not all operate in the same political opportunity structure.

With these observations in hand, it is worth exploring in more detail the impact that strategic choices about naming names, in this case nations, can have on social movement politics.

Social Movement Politics: Identities and Opportunities

The literature on social movements has frequently presented an analytic choice between a focus on the formation of collective identities and attention to institutional politics, especially the political opportunity structure. This essay refuses this choice and argues instead that the configuration of the political opportunity structure cannot be analyzed without first inquiring about who the actors are. The names with which movements represent themselves in seeking representation is one of the ways that opportunities can be made, and names may contribute to a reconfiguration of the political opportunity structure.

We know that movements "make opportunities," in part by framing codes of meaning, promoting ideological packages, and creating new models of collective action.[14] The next step is to couple this knowledge of the work of social movement organizations with the insight of analysts of collective identity that the process of forming an identity is itself an open one (for example, Melucci 1989: chapter 1). Such openness means that there will be variations across time and space in the way the "same" movement names itself.[15]

By making this link, my argument participates in the return to "culture," or "ideas," for understanding social movements.[16] Like the work of other analysts of social movements who share this perspective, it is more concerned with the how of collective action than with the why.[17] Therefore, it is concerned with the simultaneity of action and meaning production, treating the two as inseparable. Thus, this approach finds that social movements make their own history, albeit under constraint.

Yet this essay departs from the usual social movement analysis of collective identities by shifting the object of analysis. Instead of focusing on the processes by which collective identity are constructed—which is the usual "how" question of those using the collective-identity approach—it inquires into the consequences of particular collective identities *for* the structures and outcomes of politics. As a result, it shares the concerns of those who analyze the politics of protest and political repertoires of social movements.

Despite this shared concern, however, it does not treat the political structure and the environment as fixed entities *into which* social movements enter.[18] Rather, the structures themselves are understood as being created, recreated, and changed by actors struggling in the universe of political discourse. A crucial dimension of that action is their activity of self-naming.

This essay posits that collective actors are simultaneously subjects of ongoing social structures and acting subjects, carrying in their practices and meaning systems possibilities for not only system reproduction but also social change and transformation (Jenson 1989: 236-37). Politics, then, involves a struggle to be self-naming rather than outside-named, as well as to realize collective interests. Such struggle creates "winners" and "losers." Success in occupying space in the universe of political discourse limits the possibilities of others and may reconfigure the political opportunity structure. Thus, struggle over naming involves the exercise of power.

Yet everything is not possible. Collective actors are located in social relations organized in structured relations of power. These social relations set out the places within which action takes place (Jenson 1991: 54-56). Institutions, as well, materialize the power relations of these structures, reproducing them through time as well as providing a terrain for action. Therefore, representation to and within institutions also involves the exercise of power.

State institutions have a major role to play in establishing the terms of inclusion and exclusion for those seeking new rights and powers. Therefore, a social movement must not only mobilize a collective identity within the movement. It will also, if it is strategically appropriate, seek to compel recognition of that identity by public institutions. In doing so, movements make strategic decisions about routing their claims through institutions. Some state institutions may be more accommodative of a particular collective identity than others will be. The routing of claims does not depend only on the openness of state institutions, however. The availability of allies and the power of opponents will also affect opportunities for making claims. Thus, the choice of a name will configure the space available to the extent that it generates resources, identifies allies and opponents, and directs the routing of claims.

Finally, the power of social movements is affected by the moment of history in which they are acting. Moments of economic and political turbulence—

or crisis, as understood here—punctuate periods of greater stability, or regulation. The latter may be thought of as times in which a certain consensus exists around a commonsensical language of politics. Proponents of reform as well as supporters of the status quo *share* a language of politics, although their diagnoses of the present and their hopes for the future may vary widely. Included in this language are the names of the actors. Crises, in contrast, are moments of profound change in which the familiar is dying—but not yet dead—while the new struggles to be born. They are times of political agitation, of competition among worldviews, and of uncertainty about the meaning of things. At issue are not only distributional and power questions, but even definitions of actors and their interests (Jenson 1990, 1991). The space within the universe of political discourse for naming new names is enlarged at such moments.

The rest of this essay examines the ways in which decisions about self-naming affect social movements' strategies, by examining the three Canadian nationalist movements described earlier. It uncovers the ways in which choice of a name affects four aspects of strategy. First, a name generates strategic resources. Drawing boundaries around a community makes the resources of that community available to the movement as well as generating the solidarity necessary for successful action. Second, selecting one name over another sets discursive boundaries such that some claims become meaningful and others are less relevant. Third, any definition of one's own community locates it in relationship to others. Therefore, it presents possibilities for alliances as well as for identifying opponents. Likely conflicts and patterns of cooperation follow the borders delimiting the community. Fourth, any name has consequences for the routing of claims through state institutions. Routes to representation become available in accordance with the name selected.

Strategic decisions are made under constraints generated both by institutions and by time. Therefore, I also consider these constraints and the strategies developed to cope with them. I do so by focusing on the Canadian constitutional controversies of the 1980s and 1990s, particularly the period between the defeat of the Meech Lake Accord in June 1990 and the referendum of October 1993.

Constitutional Politics: Making and Losing Opportunities

The Meech Lake Accord was a package of constitutional reforms negotiated in 1987 by the federal government and the ten provinces. In essence, it involved constitutional recognition of Quebec as a distinct society and some rearrangement of powers between the two levels of government. Described as a "Quebec round" of constitutional negotiations, to bring Quebec "back into the constitutional family" after its 1982-83 exclusion, the accord provoked immense controversy. Of particular importance were the objections of Aboriginal peoples.[19] The process established in 1983 designed to achieve reform of Aboriginal peoples' constitutional standing had deadlocked in 1987. Yet the Meech Lake Accord was silent about them, in large part because the notion of a Quebec round implied a hierarchy of claims. Québécois nationalists asserted that only when their concerns were satisfactorily dealt with could others' be addressed. Social movement organizations too were chary, describing the accord negotiated behind closed doors as the work of "eleven white men in suits." The organizations' campaign against Meech Lake stressed both the lack of democracy and the decentralizing effects of the reallocation of powers, which would make it more difficult for the federal government to develop a response other than a market-driven one to the forces of economic restructuring.[20]

After three years, the accord, which had to pass eleven legislatures, ran out of time in June 1990 when Elijah Harper, a Cree member of the Manitoba provincial legislature, refused the unanimous consent necessary for its passage. The federal government then proposed to reopen negotiations in September 1991, this time by conducting a "Canada round" incorporating the demands of many more groups than Quebec.

These initiatives involved more participants. Aboriginal representatives were at the negotiating table. The government sponsored two commissions of inquiry to ascertain Canadians' position on constitutional change and to develop alternatives. Five weekend-long conferences brought together a wide range of representatives of interest groups and social movements as well as politicians and "ordinary Canadians" chosen by a countrywide lottery. After all this, the negotiating teams reached accord, signing the Charlottetown Agreement in August 1992. The agreement was put to a referendum in October 1992—and was rejected.[21]

The expansion of the agenda for the Canada round was a direct blow to Québécois nationalists, who had always argued that their needs, since they were one of the two founding peoples, took precedence over other matters. The Aboriginal peoples obviously argued from another perspective, based on their having been there first. Economic nationalists were determined to put their concerns about economic policy and escalating free trade onto the table too. In other words, decisions about process and about which and whose issues were on the agenda had serious implications for each nationalist movement, just as nationalist claims had implications for the very form and content of negotiations.

Québécois nationalists saw their resources dissipate in the 1991-92 round of constitutional politics.[22] In the past their strategy had been to reform the Canadian constitution so as to gain more powers for the Quebec government. A redistribution of responsibility for economic and social policy was sought in order to permit the Quebec state to create the conditions that would allow Québécois corporations to flourish and expand their activities beyond the border of both Quebec and Canada. This coalition of business and government also had the implicit support of the provincial labor movement, in what was essentially a corporatist-style tripartism dedicated to economic development.

Moreover, by the 1980s the national identity celebrated the proposition that Québécois corporations had overcome centuries-long aversion to business and capitalism to become the flying wedge of prosperity for the nation. The first wave of neonationalism after 1960 had struggled to banish the image of French-Canadians destined to be hewers of wood and drawers of water in a traditional Catholic society. By the 1980s the ideal-typical figure was an entrepreneurial hero, a capable capitalist who was the new voyageur prepared to conquer not just North American markets but those everywhere.[23] Support for the free trade agreements was an essential element of this strategy. Also banished was the social democratic discourse that the *indépendantiste* Parti Québécois had used in the 1970s and that had called for a strong state to realize social goals. Both federalists and *indépendantiste* nationalists espoused the discourse of "Québec, Inc."

Achieving their national goals required, according to the Québécois nationalists, control over the levers of economic power. Therefore, their nationalist claims centered on both the recognition of their distinctiveness and a reassignment of responsibilities for crucial economic powers from the federal government to Quebec. This demand could be realized in the arena of federal-provincial negotiations by a process of intergovernmental and elite bargaining.

The allies of Québécois nationalists were other governments, both the federal government, led by Prime Minister Brian Mulroney, who had committed himself to ending the constitutional deadlock in Quebec's favor, and some provinces. The latter were willing to support Quebec's demands for more powers if they received them too. There was, among these governments, less enthusiasm for either an asymmetrical federalism that would give Quebec

more powers than the others or recognition of its status as a "distinct society." Therefore, elite bargaining of this sort was likely to result in trade-offs
that might recognize a weak form of distinctiveness—thus bowing to the
national claims of Quebec—and that would make available to all provinces
any powers taken from the federal government.

Overall, then, the nationalist identity and claims of a Québécois movement
celebrating Québec, Inc., and seeking to use the national (i.e., provincial)
state to realize a nation-building project were most likely to be realized if the
federal-provincial division of powers could be changed in alliance with other
governments via negotiations. This was the nationalist movement's agenda—
and it lost control of this agenda after the collapse of the Meech Lake Accord.

The political opportunity structure was in rapid flux, as economic restructuring and constitutional crisis shattered the existing boundaries of the universe of political discourse around the Constitution. By the end of the 1980s
everything was on the constitutional agenda: strategies for competitiveness;
righting the historic wrongs of Aboriginal peoples; recognition of oppressed
social and economic minorities, including gays, lesbians, and the disabled;
redesigning national institutions, including the Senate; creating an economic
"union" and constitutionalizing a "social charter." The universe of political
discourse had exploded; no longer would constitutional reform be confined to
the division of powers. At the same time, the political opportunity structure
opened wide. Commissions, conferences, an enlarged negotiating table, and
the courts all gave new routes and new access to previously excluded actors.
Popular consultation rather than elite bargaining became the route to recognition and representation.

In all of this, Québécois nationalists were no longer able to dominate the
agenda. The debate took off and their concerns about federalism retreated
from view. Moreover, their former allies deserted them. Therefore, while the
Quebec government actually succeeded in gaining much of what it sought in
the Charlottetown Agreement, the political opportunity structure was so fluid,
in large part because of the successful insertion of other nationalist movements into it, that the victory was a hollow one; support for the agreement
both within and outside Quebec dissipated.

The political opportunity structure began to shift in the 1980s as Aboriginal peoples worked to widen the constitutional agenda and insisted that they
be recognized as nations within Canada. They learned from the nationalists in
Quebec that claims to nation building and national identity were powerful
tools in the Canadian universe of political discourse. Using these tools, they
rejected any notion that Aboriginal self-government was based on race or eth-

nicity; they were making a traditional national claim based on common culture (Chartrand 1993: 237-39).

Increasingly resorting to the principles of international law, as well as making use of the recognition of their national standing by crucial court cases, nationalists have followed two routes for realizing their claims (Chartrand 1992). The first is a "rights" approach that affirms that Aboriginal peoples are the bearers of historic rights and titles and that routes claims through the courts. Space for a third level of government, in this approach, is sought within the terms of existing institutions. The alternative approach is founded on peoples' right to self-determination recognized in international law and settled via politics. It provides a strong basis for the current call by Aboriginal peoples for constitutional recognition of their inherent right to self-government.[24]

To the extent that the politics of constitutional negotiations reinforced the second route to representation for Aboriginal nations, because the negotiating process in effect recognized the Aboriginal negotiators as embryonic governments (since the table was supposed to be one of governments, not "groups"), their identity as nations within Canada gained recognition. The constitutional conflicts became, among other things, a nation-to-nation-to-nations conflict as Canada, Quebec, and Aboriginal peoples faced off over the distribution of governmental powers.

Demands for a tripartite distribution of governmental powers obviously comes up against the competing claims of the Québécois nationalist movement to its own national rights. This encounter expresses itself in part in conflict over territory. Currently there are outstanding comprehensive claims to 85 percent of the lands of the province of Quebec. While these are now addressed to the federal government as well as to the province of Quebec, a change in Quebec's constitutional status would require a decision about the responsibility for these claims (Jhappan 1992: 145; Morantz 1992).

At the same time, there is a major dispute over the meaning of history. Recognition of Aboriginal nationhood challenges the historical vision of "two founding peoples" so crucial to Québécois nationalism. Just as significantly, it gainsays the vision of a progressive country embedded in the nationalism of the rest of Canada. Aboriginal nationalism demands from the rest of Canada that it rewrite its history and rethink its assumptions about fundamental political values, such as liberal rights and Canadian nation building.

As a result of these alterations in the universe of political discourse and political opportunity struggle, neither the federal government nor Québécois nationalists could bound the discourse of representation sufficiently to maintain a Quebec round. The boundaries shifted as public discourse opened to accommodate another understanding of Canadian history. As Aboriginal peoples pushed for recognition of their nationness, they effectively undid the representation of Canada as composed of two linguistic communities or two nations that had for so long defined the identity and interests of the Québécois nationalist movement. On the one hand, Aboriginal groups made claims as a collectivity in the terms of a rights discourse. This directly challenged the efforts of the Québécois to enshrine their definition of their unique collective rights—because of being a distinct society—in the Constitution. On the other hand, Aboriginal groups also made claims for access to governmental power, which if they were realized would fundamentally alter institutions of federalism upon which the Québécois claims have also always depended.

At issue in everyday public discourse is the matter of *who* has the right to name names. As Aboriginal peoples succeed in naming themselves as nations, they effectively undermine the system of recognition upon which the identities of the Québécois and the rest of Canada have long depended and the strategies that followed from them. Resources are, in the process, being redistributed. To the extent to which they succeed in naming themselves as a people with the right to self-determination they challenge the privileged access to the institutions of federalism enjoyed by existing actors, including provinces. To the extent that the Quebec government can be described as "unprogressive" on Aboriginal issues, it loses support within Quebec and the rest of Canada among those, including non-Aboriginal persons, for whom this is a crucial matter.

A crucial moment in this conflict came in summer 1990, just after the defeat of the Meech Lake Accord. Violence at Oka/Kanasatake, which pitted parts of the Mohawk Nation against the Quebec police, was represented in much of the rest of Canada as evidence that Quebec was unwilling to grant to Aboriginal peoples the same distinct status that it demanded for itself. Overall, the tendency of Québécois nationalists through those months was to postpone—or ignore—Aboriginal demands for constitutional standing (Breton and Jenson 1991b: 89).[25] Therefore, Quebec lost allies among popular-sector social movements in which the third nationalist movement, that of economic nationalism, was housed.

There were other important reasons these long-standing allies abandoned the Québécois nationalist movement. The alliance had, in the past, been based on a common economic and political commitment. Concerns for economic development and national sovereignty were shared by the social democratic Parti Québécois and the economic nationalists. While there was always a certain amount of studied ambiguity about the principle of national self-determination, which might lead to Quebec's separation, sufficient agreement existed to allow economic nationalists to support the Québécois nationalists' struggle. This support simply evaporated, however, when so many in Quebec used nationalist arguments to support the free trade agreement of 1988 and social democracy disappeared from the Parti Québécois's platform. A fundamental parting of the ways occurred.[26]

Therefore, the new identity of Québécois nationalism, centered on the entrepreneurial hero, reduced the common ground for an alliance with the left-leaning economic nationalism of the popular sector. Although in the constitutional politics of 1991-92 many popular-sector groups promoted the idea of asymmetrical federalism as a solution to the difficulty of recognizing Quebec without giving away the same powers to all provinces, and thereby disarming the federal government, their heart was not really in a long struggle. Other issues crowded their agenda.

An additional blow to the alliance came when, initially, the popular sector came out, as did many other progressive Canadians, in support of Aboriginal claims for recognition. To the extent that the government of Quebec dragged its feet on these issues, it lost allies.

Initially, in the constitutional politics of 1992-93, it appeared as if all progressive forces would line up behind the Aboriginal peoples' demand for self-government. Progressive intellectuals and many social movement organizations and networks began to speak of "three nations" (McCall et al. 1992, for example). This position imagined Quebec, "English Canada," and the Aboriginal peoples as nations. It was based on rewriting history by rejecting the imaginary "founding nations." At the same time it imagined a reconfigured (and also triangulated) map of Canada as a country stretching "from sea to sea to sea" (Jenson 1992: 214; McCall et al. 1992). This concept of three nations made it possible to recognize—simultaneously—the distinctiveness of Quebec within federal institutions, the Aboriginal peoples' inherent right to self-government, and the need for an active state to shape economic restructuring rather than simply accept market forces. Thus, it combined the agendas of the nationalist movements described here, including the themes that dominated the agenda of economic nationalists in the 1970s and 1980s.

This emerging alliance came to grief, however, in the referendum campaign. These events dramatically demonstrate the extent to which allies in the political opportunity structure depend upon the collective identities promoted and the routes to representation chosen to realize them. Throughout 1991-92 groups representing Aboriginal women complained that they were excluded from the negotiations. In particular, they were concerned that an agreement about Aboriginal self-government signed by the four organizations at the table would permit overrides of the gender equality rights of the Charter of Rights and Freedoms (Vickers 1993: 278-79; Krosenbrink-Gelissen 1993). Male leaders of Aboriginal communities in the past had claimed that national sovereignty exempted them, indeed required exemption, from the impositions of liberal equality rights. Women's groups mistrusted this position based on previous experiences, especially the opposition that some male leaders had expressed to women's claim to status under the Indian Act, even when they married non-Aboriginal men.[27] Therefore, these women's groups launched court cases designed to win them a place at the table, and to stop the referendum. This experience provides a good example of the differing routes to representation available even for groups using the same name.

Eventually, too, the organizations of Aboriginal women, which were members of the umbrella National Action Committee on the Status of Women (NAC), convinced that important organization to oppose the Charlottetown Agreement. NAC's championing of a No vote marked a crucial split among popular-sector groups. The Canadian Labour Congress (CLC), the other large organization active in Action Canada, supported a Yes vote, basically because of the social charter that was in the constitution and its evaluation of the positive aspects of the agreement on economic union, as well as the recognition of Quebec as a distinct society and of Aboriginal peoples' inherent right to self-government. In other words, one social movement organization, the CLC, decided to privilege its economic nationalism and recognize Aboriginal peoples' and Quebec's definition of their own nationalist identity. NAC, an equally important social movement organization, decided to privilege the less traditional identity promoted by Aboriginal women, which recognized the advantages of not only community autonomy but also the protections of liberal rights. Many observers saw NAC's decision to oppose Charlottetown as a turning point in the referendum campaign leading to the resounding No that eventually resulted.

These events highlight the fluidity in the universe of political discourse and of the political opportunity structure as traditional institutional actors, especially governments acting in federal-provincial institutions, lost control of both the agenda and the outcome. Their signature on a formal agreement, with all of the pomp and circumstance of constitutional formality, could not bound political discourse and action. Social movement organizations, especially nationalist movements, had become actors in their own right, insisting on being heard in the institutions and, indeed, on changing the institutional locale for such discussions. It was the national identities promoted by such groups, especially Aboriginal and economic nationalists, that required this shift in locale. On the one hand, as governments-in-becoming, Aboriginal groups claimed a seat at the table, thereby forcing open the negotiations in a dramatic way. On the other hand, economic nationalists lodged in specific social movement organizations were sufficiently strong to broaden the constitutional agenda to include their concerns about economic restructuring and governmental sovereignty, but insufficiently unified to form a united front behind the agreement. In all of this flux, of course, Québécois nationalists found themselves seated on the sidelines, both literally (because they refused to come to the negotiating table until late summer 1992) and symbolically, as the universe of political discourse about constitution making exploded.

Notes

1. The notion of multinational states and polyethnic states is from Kymlicka 1991. These two terms replace the highly problematic term *multicultural.*

2. As Anderson says, "All communities larger than primordial villages of face-to-face contact (and perhaps even these) are imagined. Communities are to be distinguished, not by their falsity/genuineness, but by the style in which they are imagined" (1991: 6).

3. Names are not embodied. The same individuals—and the movements that represent them—may take on a variety of names. One needs to think only of the struggles of women's movements since the 1960s to rescue the name "woman" from other forms of address, in order to constitute women as autonomous actors not defined, for example, in terms of family (as wives, sisters, etc.) or in class terms (as ladies, workers, housewives, etc.). For an analysis of the efforts of the French women's movement see Jenson 1987.

4. All social movements must write their own history, and thereby rewrite that of others. An obvious example comes from contemporary women's movements, which have explicitly undertaken to "make women visible" in history, to rewrite the story by placing themselves in history, and, in doing so, to recompose the discipline of History itself. For a discussion see, among others, Scott 1987.

5. This definition of politics departs somewhat from that utilized by, for example, Tarrow, who considers identity formation and "politics" in separate chapters (1989a: chapters 1 and 2). Yet he clearly sees the two as linked (see note 14).

6. As Raymond Breton says: "Those who are part of a society share its cultural assumptions and meaning, partake in the collective identity, and respond to common symbols. Relationships with institutions involve a symbolic/cultural exchange as well as an instrumental/material one" (1985: 27). The insight that relationships with institutions involve both symbolic and material interests is also the basis for the definition of politics given here, which derives from Jenson (1989: 237-38) and others. My formulation differs from Breton's, however, because it does not separate the two types of interests as sharply as he does. Following the passage quoted here he goes on to say, "In other words, people have symbolic as well as material interests" (1985: 27). I would argue, in contrast, that all interests involve *simultaneously* the symbolic and the "real," whether material or not (Jenson 1991: 51). The important point of commonality in these analyses is, however, the attribution of symbolic as well as material outputs to institutional arrangements.

7. In nineteenth-century discourse, *French, English, Scots,* and *Irish* were considered racial labels.

8. For the varieties of Québécois nationalism, see Balthazar 1986. Oliver 1991 discusses the first half of the twentieth century, and Coleman 1984 considers 1945 to 1980. For the situation of the past decade, see Gagnon and Montcalm 1990. It is not, strictly speaking, correct to speak of "Québécois" before the 1960s. That name was adopted as part of the shift, in the Quiet Revolution and after, toward a strongly territorial and statist definition of nationalism.

9. While it is very important, this project will not be elaborated here. The social movement organizations and political parties that represent it are not active participants in the politics of Canada, which is the focus of this paper. Their actions have been confined, for the most part, to Quebec.

10. See, for example, the choice *au comptoir de la cafétéria constitutionelle* described by Gérard Bergeron (1991: 55). Of the seven *plats du jour,* five involve changed federal forms, while two involve some form of sovereignty. See also François Rocher's (1992) discussion of Quebec's historical agenda, which is considered completely in terms of federalism.

11. Forming approximately 4 percent of the population of the country, there are—depending on estimates—thirty-five to fifty distinct Aboriginal peoples in Canada.

12. For a general discussion of the impact of the state on the identities of Aboriginal peoples, see Sawchuk 1992.

13. On the shifting definition of Métis, and particularly that nation's relationship to non-status Indians, see Sawchuk 1992.

14. As Tarrow says, "Political opportunities are expanded by the political imagination and initiative with which collective action is organised" (1989a: 36). By way of example he describes the opportunities generated by placing new frames of meaning, or discourses, on the agenda (36ff., 14-15).

15. There is obviously a problem in speaking of the "same" movement when its name is different. Nevertheless, if one considers, for example, women—that is, individuals embodied as female—they may name themselves in a variety of ways: as women, generating women's movements; as working women, acting in workers' movements; as ungendered persons, with the rights of universal citizenship; and so on. The variety of names available to the same "bodies" will become more apparent in the course of my discussion.

This point is not precisely the same as the notion of a plurality of identities now popular in the literature (see, for example, Burke 1992). There the notion is that any individual has many dimensions of experience and each may generate a different identity. I am arguing instead that the same dimension—sex, color, work—may generate a variety of identities. Once again, identities are social constructions and can only be read off the lived experience, including the discursive practices, of actors.

16. For a discussion of the attention to culture in the literature about new social movements and the links between that perspective and other critiques, especially among social historians, of structuralist perspectives, see Tarrow 1989a (13ff.) and Johnston 1991 (chapter 1). For a more general discussion of the return to "ideas" in social theory (including the contribution of feminism to this paradigm shift), see Jenson 1991 (43-49).

17. Johnston (1991: 5, 189) uses this distinction between why and how, which he draws from Alberto Melucci. See Melucci 1989, including the editors' preface, which elaborates these differences.

18. In this way it differs substantially from the argument of analysts who treat the shaping of social movement interests and identities as unidirectional with the causal arrows moving directly out of the political opportunity structure. See, for example, Kriesi 1991 (5).

19. The Meech Lake Accord was signed within weeks of the collapse of conferences with the Aboriginal groups mandated in the 1982 Constitution. The silence about Aboriginal concerns in the accord was a source of huge anger and frustration for these groups. As Tony

Hall says, "With sublime indifference to his special fiduciary obligations to aboriginal people, Brian Mulroney happily swapped away aboriginal interests to the ten premiers in the hopes of gaining a huge constitutional score" (1991: 125).

20. For a description of the women's movement's opposition to the Meech Lake Accord, see the essays in Swinton and Rogerson 1988 as well as Vickers 1993.

21. For a detailed discussion of this process, see Pal and Seidle 1993.

22. Again, the discussion in this section treats only the federalist wing of the nationalist movement. The experience of the *indépendantistes* is different.

23. The voyageurs were the traders who explored much of the continent in the seventeenth and eighteenth centuries in search of furs. Their engagement in the fur trade challenged the social relations of feudalism and the influence of the Catholic Church. Therefore, the free-moving voyageur has always been a figure in stark contrast to the *habitant* who stayed on the land, went to church, and kept his sights limited to Quebec. For a discussion, see van Schendel 1992.

24. The motive for self-government is to overthrow the power of the federal government, which "stands virtually *in loco parentis* in the exercise of powers delegated by the *Indian Act*" (Barsh and Henderson 1982: 56). The range of options for self-government is wide, from internationally recognized protectorates to a new province, with or without a territory, to institutional arrangements similar to municipal governments. Crucial to the concept is the insistence that the right is "inherent," always held, not delegated from any government and not limited (Jhappan 1992: 138ff.).

25. For important documentation of the creation of the representation of the Meech Lake debacle as a rejection of Quebec by English Canada—despite the role of Harper—see Nemni (1991: especially 185ff.). It was only in 1991-92, after the violence of Oka/Kanasatake and after the increasing pressure from Assembly of First Nations, in particular, to insist on Aboriginal peoples' right to "distinct society" status too, that relations really deteriorated.

26. This division is graphically captured by Philip Resnick in *Letters to a Québécois Friend* (1989).

27. This issue had festered until court cases in the 1970s reinstated Indian women's— and their children's—right to status. For more than a century, status, and the benefits and identity that came with it, were denied women and their children when they married non-status men (Krosenbrink-Gelissen 1993: 209-10). These important decisions also resulted in a number of important shifts in individual identity, as well as illustrating the power of the state to form both collective and individual identities. For example, Ovide Mercredi, the current grand chief of the Assembly of First Nations, representing status Indian bands, would not have been able to hold that position before his mother's status was won back. Prior to that he was self-identified as a Métis and active in Métis organizations.

Chapter 7

Public Narration and Group Culture: Discerning Discourse in Social Movements

Gary Alan Fine

Culture is a concept that, like mushrooms on a dewy summer morning, is now discovered everywhere. Suddenly it has emerged through the sociological underbrush, a reality to which this volume's theme pays heed. Social movements are, in several senses, cultural movements, underpinned by discursive practices.

The concept of culture is admittedly broad, useful both for macro- and microanalyses of social movements. From a "macro" perspective on culture, sociologists recognize that a social movement is not only politically and socially situated, but culturally situated as well (Eder 1982; Horowitz 1977; Marx and Holzner 1975). The proposals, tactics, and organization of a social movement are responsive to cultural pressures and themes. The culture (norms, values, traditions, artifacts, and expectations within a community) influences what social actors define as legitimate; it defines the framing of the movement (Snow et al. 1986; Snow and Benford 1992). One approach to culture is to treat it as an overarching macroconcept influencing the larger social system; in contrast, it can be observed on the micro-, interactional level, exemplified in relationships, emotions, and small groups.

Some social movements are explicitly cultural in that their instrumental goals are to influence the cultural order of the society in which they are embedded. They wish to alter not only the political and economic order, but also the cultural perspectives of the society. The feminist movement and the gay rights movement are compelling examples of movements that have a strong cultural component. Movements to curb the display of violence on television or obscenity in recordings are even more directly cultural, in that their agenda is to affect central cultural industries.

My emphasis in this chapter, however, grows from the "micro" cultural perspective: the internal culture within social movement organizations. I wish to examine, in particular, how cultural traditions and social cohesion are created, expressed, and made real through discourse. Treating social movements culturally allows for the investigation of the processes by which social movements are interpreted by members (Klandermans 1989). As Goffman notes, organizations can be understood technically, politically, structurally, culturally, and dramaturgically (1959: 240). It is his fourth approach—in light of the fifth—that I address. I believe that it is helpful to conceive of a social movement as a *bundle of narratives,* which when expressed within an interactional arena by participants strengthens the commitment of members to shared organizational goals and status-based identities (Nakagawa 1990), sometimes in the face of external opposition. In addition to the positive, binding functions of narratives, demands of audiences for assent and emotional response and for the production of comparable stories serve as forms of social control (Andrews 1987). Effective organizations are able to utilize culture to mobilize members both through the appropriation and personalization of established traditions and through the creation of indigenous traditions.

Every social movement organization (and, by extension, the broader social movement as a whole) develops through interaction, and, like all interaction, depends on members' recognition of a set of shared, repeated, and meaningful references that together lead to collective identity (Melucci 1989; Phillips 1990; Maxwell and Kraemer 1990; Taylor and Whittier 1992) and characterize members—a process that constitutes culture building. These cultural traditions call out affective responses in members that follow a set of emotion rules (Hochschild 1979). After describing the processes by which a collective group culture is established within a social movement, examining the movement as a social arena, I turn to how we can legitimately speak of *narrative* as a technique by which bonds are cemented within a social movement organization. To demonstrate the possibilities of this approach I present an example of the use of narratives within a social movement organization, Victims of Child Abuse Laws (VOCAL).

Group Culture and Social Movements

Every group—of whatever size and with whatever instrumental goals—develops a culture: a bounded set of images and traditions that come to characterize those individuals to themselves and often to outsiders. This *idioculture* (as described in Fine 1979, 1982) develops in interacting collectivities in which members share at least one trait (Dundes 1977; Oring 1992). An idioculture consists of a system of knowledge, beliefs, behaviors, and customs shared by members of an interacting group to which members can refer and which they can employ as the basis of further interaction. Members recognize that they share experiences, and these experiences can be referred to with the expectation that they will be understood by others, and will become tools by which to construct a social reality (McFeat 1974). By traditionalizing shared experiences, often through discourse, members are cohesively linked (Fine 1989; Shils 1985; Hobsbawm and Ranger 1983). This culture is a constitutive feature of the group, and it distinguishes insiders from those outside of the group's boundary. Cultural referents are, in Ann Swidler's (1986) powerful metaphor, a "tool kit" that is used to generate meaning, interaction, and, ultimately, structure.

The extent of a group's idioculture is connected to the length of time the group has been functioning, the social and psychological salience of the group to its members, the stability of the membership, and the intensity of the interaction (Fine 1982). Although families epitomize the power of group culture, social movement organizations, because of their self-consciousness, their emphasis on community building, and their intensity, frequently develop vigorous cultures as well (Fine and Stoecker 1985).

I do not allege that organizational culture is uniform; some social movements develop a more robust and vigorous culture than others—movement culture is variable, not constant (Benford and Hunt 1992). Lofland (1992) persuasively argues that social movements differ not just in the details of their cultures, but also in the elaboration, expressiveness, and compassion of their cultural traditions. Movement cultures can be differentiated from each other not just in their content, but also in their effect on the organization of the movement: their role in community building, division, or fragmentation (Martin 1992; Feldman 1990).

Social Movements as Staging Areas

In cultural terms it is useful to conceive of a social movement (or, for that matter, any group or organization) as a space in which actors interact; it is, in other words, a *staging area* for behavior (Fine 1981). The group provides a locus in which behaviors and forms of talk are judged to be appropriate and even encouraged. While culture can be understood on an analytic plane as a set of ideational images or cognitive schemata, culture only becomes meaningful through its public performance. Cultural forms are simultaneously a property of social actors, embedded within relationships, and also a property of the group or community: what Edward Shils, speaking of the development of ideology, labels an "ideological primary group" (1968: 70).

Through the public sharing of talk and behavior, culture becomes a resource. The group legitimates and implicitly endorses topics and styles of interaction that might not be either appropriate or meaningful elsewhere. This legitimation operates through two parallel processes of cultural contextualization. First, audience members through their reactions to performances and through their own performances reinforce the legitimacy and the significance of the presented texts. These texts, acceptable and significant in the group, might not be acceptable or significant in other behavior settings. In other words, culture is *situated.* Second, the individual actor perceives the movement as a locale in which certain types of talk—here, talk that articulates with the goals and themes of the movement—is legitimate and legitimated. This provides an *activated context* that demands a narrative discourse grounded in moral expression. The setting calls for the expression of public expectations and normative confirmation. Participants in the scene should reveal through their discursive practices that they share the perspective of the collectivity. Talk is ultimately a moral expression of the group. While many have recognized the moral context of social movements, few have emphasized that this morality depends on communication.

The group serves as a place of cultural enactment, where values take form and are invested with shared meaning. Groups, therefore, provide an organizing arena for processes involved in cultural work, including identification, ritual action, and resource mobilization.

Identification

Through collective enactment, culture serves a rhetorical purpose, promoting identification with speakers (Shils 1968: 70). Manning describes ideology, a key component of the culture of any social movement:

> A political ideology is intended, via action, to establish the identity of a body of persons who are thereafter to be understood to be related to one another in a particular way. The relationship is only one amongst many that each of the potential members of this group may, at a given time, have with a number of other persons, but it is the only relationship which ought, according to the ideology, to embrace them all. . . . Without commitment the group cannot hope to transform its circumstances with a view to eliminating or isolating relationships incompatible with the one deemed to be ideologically sound. (1976: 154-55)

Culture depends on identity and, to be shared, on identification (Feuer 1975). To be seriously immersed in a culture one must support a group espousing it (Manning 1980: 82; Shils 1968); one must belong to a "cultural community." As Robert Freed Bales comments about group cultures, "Most small groups develop a subculture that is protective for their members, and is allergic, in some respects, to the culture as a whole. . . . [The members] draw a boundary around themselves and resist intrusion" (1970: 153-54). But groups do more than retreat into a protective cocoon; they may also attempt to affect those outside of the group, through recruitment or calls for change. Culture provides a mechanism that facilitates or controls discourse with outsiders. Through cultural display a movement participant can try to influence or recruit others, transforming outsiders into insiders through a change in psychological affiliation and personal identification. An embraced culture both demarcates the boundaries of acceptable belief (Gieryn 1983) and inoculates members from being influenced by nonmembers.

Rituals

Above all, culture is a tool through which a group cements members to itself, legitimating requests for commitment and practical assistance. Moral and social discourse helps groups counteract the free rider problem. Culture becomes a central means by which the movement itself becomes valued to members, separate and apart from any material rewards that might be provided, mitigating economic or psychological costs. When culture is a salient feature of group life, personal relationships become salient as well, constituting a central process of attachment.

Talk, while powerful, is generally perceived to be somewhat less effective in cementing loyalty and a sense of community than is physical action:[1] putting words into deeds in a public domain. As a consequence, groups gird members to the group and to each other through ritual action (Collins 1981; Turner 1988; Fine 1989). Beliefs can become ritualized through the "meaning" of a secret handshake or blood brotherhood—one throws one's body into the breach, embodying one's commitment. Embodying the organization is a frequent goal of social movements, giving rise to the need for demonstrations to build loyalty as well as to promote change.

Rituals display in symbolic and behavioral space central elements of a culture: they provide the basis of attention and attitudes. Some groups, such as Alcoholics Anonymous, transform narrative occasions into ritual, making the very existence of stories central to the act of belonging (Denzin 1987).

Resources

Beyond the value of building an emotional attachment and discourse of community, culture both is a product of a resource base and contributes to the likelihood of gaining additional resources. The resources that are available to a social movement organization, as now is well known through the elaboration of resource mobilization theory, affect and constrain the presentation of group identity, cultural enactments, recruitment of supporters, and definition of the situation (d'Anjou 1990). The structure of behavior within social movements is in many ways a function of the central position of resources.

Yet the analysis of resources should focus not only on the material utility of resources, but also on the centrality of resources as symbolic goods. In transcending traditional resource mobilization approaches, Zurcher and Snow, presenting an approach to ideology that melds symbolic analysis and resource mobilization, suggest that ideology (read: culture) "is probably the best example of a resource that functions in a symbolic fashion and that is importantly related to a movement's mobilization efforts and organizational viability" (1981: 470). Cultural expressions, slogans, and patterns of rhetoric are vital resources—manipulated consciously or emergent spontaneously— that symbolize the causes of discontent for movement actors and serve to energize and justify their actions. Zurcher and Snow believe that the concept of resources needs to be extended to incorporate *symbolism,* and that the concept of mobilization should include *symbolization*—the process by which objects acquire meaning and, hence, value (1981: 471).

The presentation and enactment of culture involve mobilizing symbolic and material resources necessary to organize or counter an injustice frame (Gamson, Fireman, and Rytina 1982). In order for culture to have an effect, participants must believe that others feel or can be induced to feel similarly. Merely recognizing the existence of a like-minded community, however, is a necessary but not a sufficient condition for mobilization. In addition, a communications network must coordinate action; a consensual authority system is required to permit social control and routinization. Finally, material resources enable public performances. These four features: *public support, communications, authority and social control,* and *material resources* facilitate cultural expression.

Each "movement community" depends upon a network of social relations, and each network has access to a set of resources. Social movements are internally organized as communications networks (Tarrow 1988), which consist of both elites (movement entrepreneurs) and adherents (members). The network facilitates the organization of actions, cultural diffusion, and the framing and reframing of movement ideology and demands (d'Anjou 1990: 8; Snow et al. 1986). Those who share a set of cultural images and metaphors are potentially a "quasi group" (Mayer 1966) that can be activated under certain conditions that can be specified (Johnston 1991).

When groups meet regularly, and members are frequently activated, the meetings serve as arenas for the staging of culture. The tighter the organization, the more that culture will be routinely emergent, transformed, and discussed. Although cultural images always have the potential for sparking collective action, some self-conscious groups are more likely to see that activation as among their goals (see McAdam 1988).

Worlds of Narrative

In a cohesive organization each member is expected to provide a sympathetic and supportive hearing to colleagues who present discourse that is defined as being motivated by sympathy to the group perspective. A text presented by "supporters" is given more leeway than those presented by strangers and outsiders. By virtue of public allegiance, members have established idiosyncracy credit (Hollander 1958) that permits them to "get away" with remarks that might provoke criticism if they came from outsiders. Potentially ambiguous statements are defined as supportive rather than critical.

It is now customary to conceive of any string of action or talk as constituting a "text"—a coordinated set of meanings aimed at specific or generic audiences. Within the construct "text," speakers intentionally create symbolic productions, primarily, but not exclusively, verbal, that we describe as discourse. Each form of discourse, situated within a context, has certain practices (norms or expectations) associated with its presentation. Within discourse, some talk is described as narrative, typically because of its storylike characteristics (presenting a string of events in overt or implicit chronological order, connected to a set of dramatic personae).

Narrative is a crucial cultural domain in constructing shared meaning and group cohesion, and it contributes to organizational identity (Hardesty and Geist 1987; Martin et al. 1983). Yet it has barely been explored by social movement researchers. Indeed, only recently is any form of talk defined as important in social movement life (e.g., Gamson 1992b): typically talk is recognized only when participants present their personal life histories and experiences to researchers (Johnston 1991; McAdam 1988; Viney and Bousfield 1991). Despite this recent interest, however, the talk is rarely described *in the context* of the social movement itself. Talk is not examined as situated within collective action, an approach that would require ethnographic investigation. Hank Johnston's insightful examination of the ideological and biographical grounding of participation in Catalonian nationalist movements examines discourse, but only in the context of the participant's describing a life history to the researcher, without analyzing the role of talk within the movement. Similarly, McAdam's magisterial examination of participants in the Mississippi Freedom Summer (1988: 69, 71) cites stories that activists told the researcher well after the fact, which perhaps mirrored some of the stories shared that summer, as well as the experiences about which the researcher inquired.

With increased attention to the "framing" of social movements (Snow et al. 1986), the talk that embeds "master frames" should become central to analysis. Snow and Benford (1992) suggest that some frames have greater resonance for movement success and more "narrative fidelity." However, Snow and his colleagues have not addressed how frames are expressed and made concrete. I argue that the process of exemplifying a frame occurs through the stories that members share, through the collective bundle of narratives that are treated as relevant to the movement ideology. The dramatic images provided by these stories, incorporated into group culture, provide a legitimated basis of community and collective action. A group with a shared narrative tradition may be better able to mobilize its members in that the stories provide models for appropriate behaviors, as well as identification with the key actors in the movement.

Ethnographically grounded analyses of movement culture, as distinct from descriptions of that culture gathered through in-depth interviews, has largely addressed the domain of ritual, linking members of social movements— notably secret societies—behaviorally. Ritual presupposes that group members engage in a common behavior that has a central focus (Collins 1981, 1989). Narrative, as a connection tethering group members, has a different quality. It is not communal, but by its nature is asymmetrical, presupposing a performer and an audience.[2] Narrative production, however, often assumes some turn-taking mechanism by which members of the group share their stories sequentially. The experience of sharing personal accounts cements the underlying frames by which members understand the world.

We narrate stories to help us process our experiences. As a result of our conversations, we build shared identification and rely on common emotional reactions that are easily called out. My fundamental claim is that a social movement is not only a set of beliefs, actions, and actors, but also a *bundle of stories*. Movement allegiance depends on personal accounts, which concretely clarify that extended effort is worthwhile and that others have similar experiences and feelings. Central group members are expected to have a stock of personal experience narratives that they can share with colleagues (Stahl

1989). These narratives constitute the informal history of the group: memory is stored through the set of stories. With the decline of more collective, traditional discursive practices such as the legend or epic, personal accounts have come to dominate narrative discourse. These accounts are typically told about oneself (Goffman 1974: 503-16), but may be expanded to include episodes depicting others as well—and include such related, subsidiary forms as gossip or anecdotes. The emphasis on personal storytelling, and its blending into performed life history by groups such as Alcoholics Anonymous and other self-help groups, is one characteristic of movements aimed at the reconstruction of individual identities and, perhaps, of new social movements in general. The so-called twelve-step groups place special emphasis on the development of narrative facility as a means of coming to terms with one's besmirched past self and one's changed future self.[3]

Narrative Types

Although no one set of topics characterizes every movement, movement stories do routinely fall within a few broad, inclusive categories. These stories revolve around such fundamental issues as (1) affronts to the movement actor (horror stories), often promoting active involvement with the movement; (2) collective experiences within the movement (war stories) that speak to the value of community; and (3) stories that reaffirm the value of the movement in achieving material or personal ends (happy endings). Each class of stories plays upon the emotions of participants, drawing out a set of emotions deemed suitable for the staging area in which the narrative is embedded, and permitting audiences to share the affective state—what Orrin Klapp (1991: 78), in a slightly different context, labels *emotional hitchhiking.*

The first category of narratives, *horror stories,* justifies involvement in the movement. Some negative experience is made dramatic, compelling, and persuasive in the telling, particularly when it is presented, as movement narratives typically are, to a sympathetic audience (Rice 1992). These stories, sad and angry in turn, are an archetypal example of the way in which individuals address their public "stigma," transforming it from a public deficit to a subcultural advantage. Examples of such weepy tales are those narrated by Mothers Against Drunk Driving (Weed 1990) and accounts of rape survivors and incest victims. These narratives produce both sympathy, leading to tightened identification, and anger, leading to motivation to induce change in the face of personal costs. While these may be presented individually to inquiring investigators, they are particularly effective when they are shared in the context of a set of sympathetic others, aiming at an agenda of social change. Similarly, coming out stories of participants in the gay rights movement may have the emotional tenor of a horror story. Crime victims' stories also have the texture of a horror story (Wachs 1988; Kalcik 1975). These are narratives that postulate a bad time, which is only now being overcome, often with the aid of one's colleagues within the movement. These bad times are transformed into entertaining episodes, which, if not comic, are appropriate for sharing. The horrors provide justification for these movements: their existence reveals a "social problem" to be confronted and overcome.

A second class of stories is *war stories.* These narratives recount experiences that members of the movement have experienced within the context of their participation. Such experiences may include hostile public responses from counterdemonstrators (and both sides, as in the abortion battle, may create war stories from the same incidents), strangers, or agents of social control. The speaker will recount a "tough time," but one that has as its underlying message that the movement is just and that the participants are moral actors (e.g., McAdam 1988: 69). Like soldiers after a battle, members may be exhilarated by the accounts of comrades-in-arms. In some of these tales, participants triumph, and in others they emerge temporarily bested but prepared to fight another day with commitment strengthened. In each of these texts they have shared meaningful events; the telling of the tale ratifies this experience. In the telling of the war story the event is *processed* and is incorporated into the culture of the group.

The third set of stories is *happy endings.*[4] In these narratives the speaker surprisingly benefits from movement participation, or changes occur for the better. They provide a morale boost and directly reinforce movement involvement. Someone or something seen as a likely hostile force suddenly turns out to be supportive or can be persuaded, or a situation that appears at first to be threatening is found to be rewarding. Such stories bolster the beliefs of movement participants that they have more support than might first appear, as when participants within gay rights movements tell about how some seemingly stereotypical "straight" (an older woman, for instance) is actually supportive of the movement or a member. Public activity, these stories assert, is filled with surprises, and collectively these surprises will lead to triumph. Members are comforted by the thought that there is more support than appears on the surface.

Ultimately each narrative type supports the organizational and instrumental goals of the group, promoting cohesion (war stories and horror stories) or alleging that victory is ultimately possible.

Movement and Narratives

The same extent or pattern of narrative will not apply to all social movements. Obviously, a certain degree of variability is attributable to the articulateness of the participants and the emphasis that their background cultures place on narrative fluency. Other differences depend on the amount of time that members spend together and what is achieved during that time. It is reasonable to expect that in movements in which members spend time together, are articulate, and value narrative fluency, narratives are used more frequently and have a more prominent and central role.

In addition, the content of the movement ideology affects narratives. I expect that more narratives are performed in social movements in which attacks on participants' identity and behaviors are a source of complaint than in movements in which alterations in social policy are the primary goal. We should find narratives that are more frequently expressed and more prominent in *rights movements* than in *policy movements*. Personal and immanent threats are more effective in producing narrative than are generalized threats. For instance, personal narratives should be more common in movements such as the gay rights movement and the civil rights movement than in the antiwar or antinuclear movement. One expects stories in circumstances in which one is fighting directly for oneself, rather than others, in which one is fighting personal stigma or control of one's behavior. Narratives flow most effectively from self-involvement. From this view, personal narratives are more likely in the abortion rights movement than in the pro-life movement.[5] These are, of course, empirical questions that require systematic research.

As noted, most of these stories fall within the discursive rubric of personal experience narrative, in which the teller is the primary actor within the account, a genre that has recently been emphasized within the discipline of folkloristics (Stahl 1989; Robinson 1981). These stories gain their power through their discursive immediacy and from the power of the personal connection between narrator and audience. In presenting the self, we find accounts that reveal demands for either *acceptance* or for *denial.* The accounts of participants in Alcoholics Anonymous and similar organizations serve as archetypal instances of stories of acceptance. These accounts present the self as *blemished,* along with dramatic, grotesque, and pathetic instances of that failure. The more dramatic the failure, the more effective the account—the more it is powerful internal propaganda for the movement. In these stories the social movement is the savior of the self. Religious narratives are similar: the self is lost, and the sinner eventually sees the light (gaining communal moral stature) with the help of the movement ("I once was lost, but now I'm saved"). The alternative approach, common in "stigma-deflecting" social movements—movements that attempt to justify or valorize participants or those for whom the participants stand—uses narrative to deflect the stigma that would otherwise adhere. Here the main figure, typically the narrator, is shown to have been mistreated by a source of power or authority, and has, in terms of the story, an *unblemished* self. In movements that contend with injustices, heroic narratives are common.

Victims of Child Abuse Laws

In order to examine the role of narrative and narrative bundles in social movements, I provide a case study from a social movement that a student and I examined. The project did not develop into a full ethnography, but over several months in 1985 and 1986 we obtained sufficient data to provide a basis for this preliminary analysis. We collected information at a national convention with representatives from thirty states, at local meetings, and through phone conversations.

During the 1980s, the mass media routinely depicted horrific activities of parents and day-care providers—media "horror stories" (Johnson 1989)[6] —and legislators responded to public demand, intensified by the media, with tough laws and provided additional authority to family social workers (Elshtain 1985; Carlson 1986). The emergence of the "epidemic of child abuse" was a dramatic and compelling instance of the "construction of social problems" (Spector and Kitsuse 1977; Schneider 1985). Of course, in such a heated circumstance, many, even most, of the charges were not justified; yet the publicized accusation could be as damaging as a conviction (Wexler 1985; Goldstein 1987). In the mid-1980s, in response to this "epidemic," a small group of parents and providers accused of abuse organized in defense, claiming that social workers had too much power.

Specifically, I examined Victims of Child Abuse Laws (VOCAL), a social movement organization founded in Minnesota in 1984 in response to a series of well-publicized cases involving parents who had been charged with abusing their children. In 1992 the organization had approximately 10,000 members nationwide in more than 150 local chapters. Most members of the organization had been accused, either by social workers or by the legal system, of abusing or neglecting a child. As a consequence of the attacks on their core identities, group members became adept at narrating their own stories to persuade others of their moral virtue, as well as at calling for a series of policy changes that would affect how the state investigates incidents of suspected child abuse. While this organization emphasizes narrative accounts more than most, the emphasis on narrative may suggest the power of stories in other movements as well.

In my observation of VOCAL, participants shared horror stories about their experiences, and I was impressed that they were prepared to detail to complete strangers their life tragedies, leaving themselves open for possible moral condemnation.[7] Given the communal nature of the movement gathering, sympathetic ratification was expected, whatever the audience member's private judgments. Speakers could reasonably assume that their audience had also been the target of similar charges. Stories were the medium of exchange among these strangers. On occasion participants shared their stories with humor, as did two men who joked with each other about being arrested by the police, recognizing that the commonality of their horror story provided a basis for fellowship.

I never observed any story publicly questioned, surely an act of bad faith among people committed to each other. People shared their experiences with social workers and the courts, explaining what one called his "crawl through hell" as a result of abuses of "the system." Indeed, a frequent conversation starter was some variant on "What happened to you? What are you doing at VOCAL?" The proper response to this question is a story that makes sense given the culture, values, and ideology of the group: a story that is shaped as it gets told again and again. It is symbolic that the organization's acronym is VOCAL, for members believe that it is essential that they present their side of the case—a perspective to which they contend the public has not been sufficiently exposed—vocally. The public assumption in such cases is that an accusation is equivalent to a conviction, and stories often address the concern that neighbors, relatives, friends, and co-workers suddenly become hostile. As a means of deflecting their stigma, members vehemently recount instances in which the governmental organization treated them in an irrational, dishonest, or vicious manner, assuring each other that they are presenting "common stories."

Members describe children who engaged in mutual masturbation being labeled "homosexuals," provide accounts of social workers who mistakenly (and negligently) accused a father rather than a son with the same name of sexual play with a younger child, and claim that divorce proceedings frequently generate abuse allegations. Accounts of manipulative questioners and biased professionals abound and in some prominent cases have in fact lent doubt to some accusations of abuse.

The mystery, irony, and horror of sudden infant death syndrome (SIDS) is

frequently invoked in horror stories by doubly battered parents. One participant narrates an account of a case in which a father walked into the bedroom
of his six-month-old child to discover that the baby was dead. Three months
earlier the child had suffered a fractured rib when the three-year-old sister
pulled the baby from a table: "A fractured rib three months ago and now a
dead baby, it had to be child abuse. . . . They buried that baby on Friday at
two o'clock and at four o'clock [the three-year-old] was taken from the home."
After twelve days the child was returned to the home without charges being
filed, but the narrator suggested that the three-year-old lived in terror that
her parents might try to kill her next (field notes). The misdiagnosis of SIDS
provides a publicly acceptable defense for the parent in a mysterious child
death, whereas homicide by the parent is often a diagnosis of first choice,
according to some governmental agents.

Organizational members imply that their willingness to present their stories publicly, without shame, is central to their coping strategy. Implicit is the
belief that only innocent narrators would be willing to put themselves on the
line. Willingness to go public addresses the justice of their claims, particularly when it is often necessary to explain what pieces of evidence originally led
to the charges. One speaker tells the plenary session in a frequently heard
refrain: "There's a lot of horror stories out there. I'm honored to be with so
many brave people. We're not at all unlike people in Nazi Germany in 1939. I
mean that literally. We're not unlike people in South Africa. We remember
the McCarthy era" (field notes).

Horror stories, in addition to justifying the speaker's stigmatized self, also
make the case that changes in the law are necessary, and that the social
movement is the appropriate place to begin the process of collective action.
Dramatization is a key ingredient relied upon by the successful social movement in making a case for legislative change (see Hilgartner and Bosk 1988;
Best 1989).

An outsider to the group might be surprised to learn that not all horror stories within the community are tragic: explicitly humorous stories—"mock"
horror stories that play off expectations of that genre—are also narrated.
These accounts satirize how individuals might be mistreated by the system.
For example, one speaker described how he was "almost reported for spouse
abuse." His wife was cleaning under their refrigerator, and he opened the
door and a ketchup bottle broke on her face. He relates: "She worked in a hos-
pital and she spent the next week telling people that her husband didn't beat
her. [The audience laughs.] I think most people believed her, but people who
know me didn't. [The audience laughs again.] My wife will tell you this, and if

she doesn't, I'll hit her. [The audience laughs again.]" In this supportive context, the speaker can play the part of a spouse abuser without offending the audience. Perhaps the reason that I did not hear similar joking about child abuse was that the charge hit too close to home.[8]

Ultimately, narratives play off expectations of how the hostile world—the world that needs changing—operates. Social psychological research (for example, Martin and Powers 1980) has demonstrated that a concrete example has more persuasive appeal than a set of statistical tables. For social movement activism, local narrative accounts weigh heavily. This weight is useful internally to cement members in shared understanding and externally to convince outsiders through example that the cause is just. Along with the mobilization of bodies, narratives are the greatest assets of any social movement to create change. When these narratives are "bundled" into a set of stories, the movement is seen as having greater justice (Gamson 1992b).

Conclusions

A movement culture can be a powerful force promoting internal cohesion and group satisfaction, ultimately facilitating the conditions of action. An organizational idioculture provides a set of nonmaterial resources and rewards that allows movements to overcome the free rider problem. Culture can, at least potentially, be an effective tool by which social movements achieve their instrumental ends, while ostensibly serving expressive needs. In this chapter I emphasize the power of narrative to make concrete the shared assumptions and personal relations among members, and the role of the movement as a *staging area* in which group traditions can be performed.

Narrative creates social spaces in which audiences are encouraged to identify with the situations, problems, and concerns of others. Through its discursive process, narrative exemplifies C. Wright Mills's (1959) sociological imagination by transforming biography into history. The experience of one has become the identifying mode of the many (Burke 1969). By making experiences immediate, concrete, and dramatic, narrative by its expression provides unarguable proof of the claims of movements.

Behind the argument of this chapter is the belief that narrative structure aids in the process of mobilization. Admittedly, the ethnographic evidence presented did not address that critical question, and additional empirical evidence is necessary to judge this claim. To understand narratives and movement culture generally as increasing identification implies that it may be a short step to understanding how they promote action. If this can be demonstrated, and I believe that the claim is a plausible one, then the position of narrative becomes powerful. The model presented here suggests that shared experience produces narrative, which in turn promotes identification, in turn facilitating collective action. Beyond this, we might inquire whether different forms of narratives (horror stories, war stories, and happy endings) operate differently. Is one type more likely to produce effective mobilization? Similarly, we should examine how the emotion produced by talk (anger, sorrow, amusement, joy) produces community. Clearly, the examination of the effects of narrative on social movement is in its infancy.

I aim for this chapter to justify the connection between the sociology of culture and the analysis of social movements. This can be a powerful linkage. The resource mobilization metaphor has greatly benefited the conceptualization of social movement organizations, but often has seemed to downplay the content of the movement or what it is that the movement is about: the why behind the how (Melucci 1989). A cultural analysis emphasizes that content and its situated quality. To think of a movement that does not *mean* anything, a movement in which members do not share, a movement in which tradition and talk is absent, is impossible. Movement actors are awash in talk. The goal of those who wish to blend the sociology of culture and social movement analysis must be to provide the analytical infrastructure to make these ties explicit. This is our charter: to build a vision of social movements that includes the self, the organization, the resources, and the culture.

Notes

The author wishes to thank Hank Johnston and Bert Klandermans for their comments on an earlier draft of this paper.

1. Talk is, of course, action of a sort, but the distinction between the two realms remains a common one.

2. In practice, many narratives are created collaboratively, although typically there is at any given time a primary teller to whose stories others contribute.

3. The argument that I put forth extends well beyond social movements and those organizations (like Alcoholics Anonymous) that are on the boundaries of social movements. It also applies to all organizations with a common focus and goal direction. In my research among mushroom collectors (Fine 1987) I found that personal experience narratives were crucial for establishing the similarity of members in the face of centrifugal tendencies.

4. In some realms one also finds "tragic narratives"—instances in which the possibility of success is thwarted. Jacobs (1987) notes the prevalence of such accounts among perpetually frustrated probation officers.

5. The pro-life movement does generate horror stories about symbolic others, and a few of those who enter the movement have experienced the trauma of unwanted pregnancy themselves.

6. Media reports about child abuse did not begin in the 1980s; the problem was discovered in the 1960s after the publication by Drs. C. Henry Kempe and Ray Helfer of their now-

classic article, "The Battered-Child Syndrome," in the *Journal of the American Medical Association*. However, the mid-1980s seemed to reveal a revival of interest in the problem (Best 1990).

7. Some, though not all, are even willing to provide accounts of their traumas to the mass media; often their names are changed. Typically these are particularly active members and people with compelling or dramatic stories. Perhaps as a function of the newness of the organization, I heard fewer "war stories," but one state executive director did indicate that there were cases in which merely belonging to VOCAL led to negative treatment from the system, a proto–war story. Individuals present "happy endings" for themselves or others, although horror stories are the most dramatic texts.

8. Nonstigmatized parents do joke to their friends about child abuse in tones of mock exasperation. They can get away with such jollity because the self-directed charge is seen as so implausible.

Chapter 8

Culture in Rebellion:
The Appropriation and Transformation of the
Veil in the Algerian Revolution

Rick Fantasia and Eric L. Hirsch

Social Movement Havens and Cultural Production

Theorists recently have made strides in answering key questions about social movement dynamics—why they begin when they do, why people join them, how they are organized, why they succeed or fail—by taking account of the subjective dimension of movement mobilization (Ferree and Miller 1985; Friedman and McAdam 1992; Gamson 1992a; Johnston 1991; Klandermans 1992; Melucci 1989; Morris 1984; Snow et al. 1986; Snow and Benford 1992; Tarrow 1992a; Taylor and Whittier 1992). The attention to culture and the subjective experience of movement participation fills a theoretical need resulting from the influence of resource mobilization theory, a perspective that largely eschews subjective and cultural concerns in favor of an emphasis on the structurally based institutional resources available to collective actors (McCarthy and Zald 1987). Because of an emphasis on material resources, the continuity between social movements and institutional forces, and the notion of the rational actor derived from a utilitarian economic model, resource mobilization has not been of much use in understanding the subjectivity and intersubjectivity of movement participants or the cultural dynamics of movement processes.

The contributions in this volume are evidence of the range of insights that can flow when culture is placed into the mix of concerns by which we consider collective action and social movements. For students of social movements, the conception of culture must be linked closely to social structure to be able to adequately reflect the creative adaptation to structural inequalities that generates most social movement activity, yet it must be fluid enough to allow us to be able to visualize culture as a dynamic process of creation, even in the most unlikely settings. That is, if an emphasis on culture is to yield real insights for sociologists studying collective action and social movements, we cannot rely on the classical anthropological conception of culture as a seamless, integrated whole, an overarching web of meaning that minimizes or disregards discontinuity and rupture (Malinowski 1944; Benedict 1961; Kroeber 1963). We do better, as Bahktin has suggested, when we view culture as "an open-ended creative dialogue of sub-cultures, of insiders and outsiders, of diverse factions" (quoted in Clifford 1988: 46). We favor a concept like that employed by Raymond Williams, who focused on the emergent properties of culture and who emphasized those forms of "countercultural," "counterhegemonic," or "oppositional" cultural expression that arise within the wider cultural framework, but that are emergent in their embodiment of new practices and meanings (Williams 1977: 114). Culture is not simply a static field, providing opportunities and constraints for a movement; it is contested terrain.

From this perspective, culture would seem to be more than just a "tool kit" of custom, ritual, and tradition from which strategies are chosen during "unsettled periods," and cultural forms more than resources to be "borrowed" from other times and places (Swidler 1986; Newman 1987). While it is important to understand the strategic employment of cultural objects in social movement activity, we want to understand the social processes (interactional dynamics, spatial forms, organizational encasements) through which cultural objects are actively transformed in collective action. For if social conflict creates genuinely oppositional cultural formations, as we have argued elsewhere (Fantasia 1988; Hirsch 1990a, 1990b), then cultural traditions and objects are not only resources to be wielded in their original state, but can be seen as having been actively transformed in and by collective action (Tarrow 1992b).

We believe that the analysis of the relationship between culture and social movements will be facilitated if theorists focus attention on what takes place in the interactive struggle for power between elites and movement participants. To be sure, cultural practices, beliefs, and ideologies reflect and sustain existing power arrangements. But those excluded from power often adapt to their subordination by creating cultural forms that express oppositional practices, values, and beliefs. The very subordinate position of outsider groups means that their oppositional cultural expression cannot be cultivated openly (Scott 1990). Thus, subordinate groups must operate in private, isolated from the surveillance and rule governance of elites. These "havens," or "free social spaces," are relatively isolated social settings where subordinate groups may question the rationalizing ideologies of the dominant order, develop alternative meanings, iron out their differences, and, particularly in times of acute social struggle, transform traditional cultural meanings and construct emergent cultural forms. On the most basic level, they are meeting places where communication can be facilitated without deference to those in power, representing "liberated zones" to which people can retreat, spatial "preserves" where oppositional culture and group solidarity can be nourished, tested, and protected (Evans and Boyte 1986; Fantasia 1988; Flacks 1988; Hirsch 1990b; Thompson 1963). It is in such relatively "free" social spaces that members of subordinate groups discover their common problems, construct a collective definition of the sources of their oppression, and note the limits of routine means of redressing grievances, where collective identity and solidarity are cultivated in practices, values, and social relations. Examples are many: block clubs, tenant associations, bars, union halls, work shifts, and departments in working-class communities and workplaces (Fantasia 1988; Hirsch 1986, 1990a); student lounges and hangouts (Hirsch 1990b); within the families of nationalist militants (Johnston 1991); in women's consciousness-raising groups (Evans 1980); lesbian feminist communities (Taylor and Whittier 1992); black churches and colleges in the civil rights movement (Morris 1984). Often, these "havens" exist as traditional cultural spaces until group conflict and the demands of social movement activity give them an oppositional character, paradoxically recommending the potential for radicalism that lies dormant in tradition (Calhoun 1983).

And so we often find, constructed beyond the sight and earshot of the powerful, socially structured "havens" that, in the context of acute social struggle, serve as a social encasement for oppositional cultural creation, providing a spatial and social-organizational basis for cultural transformation. As we will demonstrate here, we believe that the understanding of such sites of cultural production can be extremely useful for a cultural approach to social movement analyses, but we want to emphasize at the outset that while the spatial/organizational vehicle for cultural change is important, it is the context of acute social and political crisis that provides the key fulcrum for the transformation of traditional cultural forms.

In what follows, we will consider the process by which such bedrock traditional cultural expressions were transformed, in the context of collective action, into oppositional cultural forms. We choose as an empirical case the changing role of women in the Algerian revolt against French colonialism in the 1950s, with particular attention to the politics of the veil over the course of that revolt. We draw upon this case because of the widespread belief in the cultural centrality and durability of gender relations generally and within Islamic societies specifically, and because of the symbolic significance of the veil for understanding gender relations in Algerian society through a traditional and identifiable cultural object (Fanon 1967; D. Gordon 1968). Most importantly, we seek an empirical case far afield from our previous research on collective action and the U.S. working class so that we might have a comparative touchstone from which to consider social movement "havens" in the interplay between acute social struggle and cultural transformations.

Cultural and Historical Background to the Revolt

France invaded Algeria in 1830, then colonized it in 1840, seizing land from native Algerians and distributing it among European settlers known as *colons* (Wolf 1969: 212). This eliminated a complex system of peasant land use rights, quickly displacing a large proportion of the native Algerian people. By the end of the nineteenth century, many native Algerians had become low-level employees of the *colons* in the cities or day laborers in Algerian vineyards owned by the French.

From the beginning, the French administrators sought to eliminate the cultural basis of Algerian resistance, which they defined as Islam. As missionary Charles Foucauld stated: "If we cannot succeed in making Frenchmen of these people, they will drive us out. The only way to make them into Frenchmen is to make them Christians" (Knauss 1987: 19). The colonists sought to strip the Algerian people of their existing culture in order to be able to deposit French culture on a blank slate. Early French tactics included the destruction of Islamic mosques and schools as well as the *zawiyas,* religious lodges that distributed aid to the poor and hungry (Knauss 1987: 18-19). French schools were founded in order to proselytize for the superiority of French culture. The Native Code, which forced Muslims to acquire permits to celebrate religious feasts and prohibited pilgrimages to Mecca, was introduced. Muslims were even conscripted into French military service, which violated the Koranic law against fighting for a non-Islamic army (Knauss 1987: 20).

The French attempt to break down Algerian culture was largely successful if one considers only the formal organizations of Islam. For example, by 1862 in Algiers, the French had destroyed nine of thirteen grand mosques, one hundred one of one hundred nine small mosques, twenty-three of thirty-two chapels, and all twelve *zawiyas* (Knauss 1987: 18-19). But destroying the formal organizational basis of Islam only tended to strengthen its ideological importance to the Algerian people. As Frantz Fanon noted, "It is the action, the plans of the occupier which determine the centers of resistance around which a people's will to survive becomes organized" (1967: 47).

The virtual outlawing of Islam turned many Algerians inward, toward the adoption of a distinct attitude of reserve directed against foreign encroachment. This stance is known as *kitman,* a Koranic term meaning hiding place or a tendency to turn inward (Wolf 1969: 225). Increasingly, resistance to colonialism became synonymous with the faith and the practice of Islam. Colonial repression created a polarized cultural crisis, forcing native Algerians into hiding where Islam became a "language of refusal" (Bourdieu 1972: 27). Clearly, this was a world of competing cultural systems and not a monocultural field from which movements draw resources and opponents set constraints.

In the 1920s and 1930s nationalist Islam developed an organizational expression in a reform movement called the Association of the 'Ulama, led by Sheik Abdelhamid Ben Badis. Antagonistic to those local religious lodges that had accommodated themselves to the French authorities, the Badissia movement established its own schools, *medersas,* and other religious institutions such as Islamic Boy Scouts, under the slogan "Arabic is my language, Algeria is my country, Islam is my religion" (Wolf 1969: 228).

Despite these developments, the opportunities for open public resistance were few. Most formal religious institutions had been destroyed and native Algerians had lost nearly all power in economic, political, and social institutions. Expressions of open resistance were met with overwhelming military force, and often torture and death for those who participated. Though there had been revolts against French rule in the 1830s and 1840s led by Abd el Kader, and in the 1870s led by El Moqrani, they were ruthlessly suppressed, so that between 1871 and 1954 opposition tended to be "covert rather than overt, quiescent rather than emphatic" (Wolf 1969: 225). As the only autonomous social spaces left, traditional Islamic community and family life became a form of sanctuary to which many Algerians retreated, a traditional preserve from which colonial occupation could be endured.

The retreat into traditional Islamic family life meant the potential reinforcement of traditional gender practices and beliefs. From the Western vantage point, Islam has often been simplistically regarded as the root of the social degradation of women, but there are wide variations in how the Koran and other Islamic texts are interpreted with relation to gender. Many traditional gender practices actually antedate Islam, and there are certain Islamic principles that provide advantages to women, while others are clearly disadvantageous (Tillion 1966; D. Gordon 1968). But, certainly, early Arab societies were rigidly patriarchal. It was common practice to commit female infanticide; a father could marry his daughters to whomever he chose; husbands could divorce any one of their multiple wives for any reason; and women generally did not inherit from their fathers or husbands (Fernea and Bezirgan 1977: xxii). In the context of these early gender practices, the seventh-century teachings of Mohammed in the Koran can be viewed as actually progressive:

> Infanticide was prohibited; the number of legal wives which a man could take at one time was reduced to four; legal machinery was set up by which women could protest injustice and ill treatment, institute divorce in certain situations, and sue if their share of inheritance (half a man's share) was denied them. The Koran gave women the right to inherit property for the first time and also granted them inalienable rights to their own inherited wealth, to their personal jewelry, and to their own earnings. (Fernea and Bezirgan 1977: xxiii)

The Koran did not, however, change the basic principle that women were subordinate to men; women were still viewed as men's property, to be protected from possession by other men. And what may be viewed as progressive for women in the seventh century would not be viewed the same way in the twentieth. The fact that resistance to the French took the form of a return to traditional Islam meant the reinforcement of traditional gender practices such as the veiling and cloistering of women. The traditional status of women was further reinforced by the loss of power across all social institutions that Algerian men experienced under the French. As their power in the public arena was stolen, Algerian men tended to assert power more strongly in the private sphere, in that institution where they still retained control, the family. As Peter Knauss has stated: "The family thus became the only real arena in which men, deprived of most external sources of self-esteem, power, and achievement, could act as sovereigns and masters. There they often exerted a heavily authoritarian role and influence regardless of their social class" (1987: 24).

Parodoxically, then, the position of Algerian women was weakened in reaction to contact with modern (albeit French colonial) society. Women, as the last inviolate property of men, had to be protected from interaction with, even from the gaze of, European men. There was increased use of the haik, the large square veil worn by Arab women to cover the face and the body. And women were cloistered, restricted to the home, the garden, the fountain, where they carried out their traditional child-care and housework roles; they were not allowed to be physically present in the world of men—the mosque, the cafe, the business world. A common expression was "Let the women make the cous cous; we'll take care of politics" (Knauss 1987: 5).

Like most native Algerians in occupied Algeria, women had little if any formal power. But segregation also granted women their own social spaces (havens within a haven), in which they could exercise their own informal means of resistance (Abu-Lughod, 1985). A woman could respond to the unacceptable behavior of her husband by seeking aid through alliances with her mother-in-law, other female relatives, her children, or the mobilization of her uncles; she could draw on weapons like silence, gossip, withdrawal of sexual attention, and so on (Abu-Lughod 1985; Knauss 1987).

The French, too, viewed the Islamic household as the last haven for the cultivation of a native Algerian culture, a bastion of resistance to French rule. The veil in particular represented a powerful symbol of defiance to the French: "The nonreciprocity involved in the wearing of the veil, the 'seeing but not being seen' aspect, presumably represented to the settler an inviolable core of native resistance outside his or her control" (Knauss 1987: 26). In the view of Frantz Fanon, the veil came to symbolize for the French the obstinance of Algerian society and culture, and colonial doctrine held that to thoroughly conquer Algerian society and delimit its capacity to resist the colonial administration, Algerian women would have to be unveiled: "If we want to destroy the structure of Algerian society, its capacity for resistance, we must first of all conquer the women; we must go and find them behind the veil where they hide themselves and in the houses where the men keep them out of sight" (1967: 37-38).

As in all colonial societies, the occupiers rationalized their rule as the "modernization" of a backward culture. Thus, colonial propaganda was devoted to "defending" the Algerian woman, who was "pictured as humiliated, sequestered, cloistered . . . unfortunately transformed by the Algerian man into an inert, demonetized, indeed dehumanized object" (Fanon 1967: 37-38). French mutual aid societies, charitable organizations, and social workers promoted "solidarity" with Algerian women and descended on the Arab quarters to lecture against the barbarism and backwardness of Algerian men. Moral proscriptions against the veil and the sequestering of women were distributed along with food to the poor. According to Fanon, the colonial effort to convert the Algerian woman to European values was not an act of liberation but an exertion of power by those with the power to shame: "Every new Algerian woman unveiled announced to the occupier an Algerian society whose systems of defense were in the process of dislocation, open and breached" (42).

While employing a language of liberation, the actions of the French in unveiling Algerian women embodied, in wresting control of native Algerian women from native Algerian men, a symbolic rape and defilement. Fanon, a psychoanalyst, reported a close interaction in the common fantasies and dreams of Europeans of unveiling and rape (1967: 45-46). And Knauss reports a brisk European trade in the sale and circulation of pornographic picture postcards of unveiled Algerian women (1987: 26-27). According to Fanon, the colonial relationship was inscribed in the everyday encounters between Europeans and Arabs. He offers the example of the European employer who summons his Arab employee to his office to invite him and his wife to a social affair, thus forcing the Arab to decide whether to "prostitute his wife" by exhibiting her to the European and making her a "possible object of possession" or go to the affair alone, thus refusing satisfaction to the boss and putting his job at risk (1967: 39-40).

As the veil became symbolically central to colonial goals, it resulted in the revival of the cult of the veil, source of symbolic resistance to French authority (43). Traditional Islamic life was contrasted with the libertine, immoral life of European women. Women who rejected the veil were labeled traitors (*renegate* or *M'Tournis)*, were threatened with ostracism, and were considered unfit to marry a Muslim or to inherit from one (Knauss 1987: 55).

The Struggle for the Veil in the Anticolonial Struggle

A variety of factors made revolution possible in the 1950s. Many Algerians had emigrated to France during World War I, so that by 1950 there were in French cities 600,000 Algerians who had created a strong movement to support anticolonial resistance (Wolf 1969: 233). Moreover, France, beset by social divisions resulting from the Nazi occupation, stubbornly resisted all efforts to reform the colonial system, even after it suffered a humiliating defeat at the hands of the Vietnamese in 1954 (Quandt 1969: 2, 88). The colonial relationship was emphasized dramatically at the close of the war as 15,000 Muslims were massacred by the French in a suppression of rioting that followed a celebration of the Allied victory in Europe (Wolf 1969: 235-36). Yet many Algerians who had fought for France during the war returned with both valuable military experience and a strong belief in their equality with the French (Wolf 1969: 235). As the war came to an end, resistance took the form of an underground armed militia within the National Liberation Front (FLN). On November 1, 1954, 500 FLN insurgents struck seventy French military, police, and communications facilities. And by 1956, 15,000 to 20,000 Algerians had been recruited into the National Liberation Army (ALN).

Until 1955, the revolution was fought exclusively by men. Women volunteers were assigned traditional female roles as cooks, laundresses, and nurses, while others provided food, clothing, and shelter to militants and their families. The leadership of the FLN and the ALN was completely dominated by men (Quandt 1969). The decision to involve women as fighters was made in response to the ferocity of the war waged by the French, which made it necessary as a practical matter to consider all forms of combat, including the use of women, a tactic that would not have been considered in another context (Fanon 1967: 48).

At first, the FLN segregated women and men into separate political cells and military units to maintain traditional social distance between men and women, and the FLN leadership preserved traditional patriarchal authority by usurping the father's traditional right to approve marriages and divorces (Knauss 1987: 83-84). At the outset, only the wives of male militants were recruited; later, widows and divorced women were employed. Since traditional households would not typically allow an unmarried young woman to walk the streets unaccompanied, and because the consequences were considered too great a threat to traditional family life, young women were not recruited until later, when the sheer number of unmarried volunteers and the demands of the revolution caused the leaders to open the ranks to all women (Fanon 1967: 51).

Though only a small percentage of women served in military roles (Amrane 1982), the decision to incorporate women into direct revolutionary activity had great symbolic importance for Algerian culture and society. Djamila Bouhired, Djamila Boupacha, Zohra Drif Bitat, and other women militants who suffered arrest and torture at the hands of the French were widely admired as fearless patriots and later received a prominent place in the pantheon of revolutionary heroes (D. Gordon 1968: 53-56; Fernea and Bezirgan 1977).

For women who were accustomed to a cloistered life and strictly regulated mobility, involvement in the revolution led to a radical transformation. In the initial stages of women's involvement, women would serve as couriers or scouts, wearing the veil and walking ahead of a male "protector." In response to the massacre of Algerian civilians, aerial bombardment of villages, the systematic use of torture, and the growing numbers of prisoners "shot and killed while trying to escape," the focus of revolutionary strategy shifted in 1956 to the European city that surrounded the Casbah as an "almost organic curtain of safety" (Fanon 1967: 51).

Because Algerian men were harassed, searched, and arrested, women were now sent, unveiled, into the protected preserve of the colonist (Fernea and Bezirgan 1977: 251-62). Often donning Western clothing, makeup, and hairstyles, and learning to smile flirtatiously at the French patrols as she carried false identity papers, pistols, and grenades, this "new" Algerian woman had to learn to display and literally to embody a Western "self"—to thrust her shoulders back and walk with a graceful, measured stride, to bare her legs (Fanon 1967: 58-59). This transformation, according to Fanon, was not based on an ideological imperative, but was a response to practical problems: "The doctrine of the Revolution, the strategy of combat never postulated the necessity for a revision of forms of belief with respect to the veil" (47).

The use of the veil, which was strictly enforced in reaction to French attempts to unveil women in the colonial situation, was being transformed in the context of anticolonial collective action. The traditional gender roles that assigned confinement to the prerevolutionary Algerian woman were challenged, and the beliefs that reproduced it were shaken as well. Increasingly convinced of the importance of the role of women in the revolution, fathers, husbands, and brothers were forced to release themselves from traditional conceptions of women. Fanon observed that "the Algerian's age-old jealousy, his 'congenital' suspiciousness have melted on contact with the Revolution. . . . The husband or the father learns to look upon the relations between the sexes in a new light" (59-60). Similarly, Sheila Rowbotham noted the extent to which the Algerian woman's relationship to her family was transformed by revolutionary activity:

> She was forced to travel to other towns, sleep in strange places. It was only because of the urgency of the political situation that fathers and husbands were not overcome with shame. They knew that their acquaintances were sharing a similar experience. Young girls started to admire the women who suffered death and who were imprisoned for the liberation movement. They not only took off their veils and put on make-up, they joined the maquis living in the mountains with the men. They returned with new identities, full of ideas and arguments; and as for their virginity, how could their fathers question them about that when their very lives were in danger and they risked more than he did. Gradually, during the war the father's control slipped. Marriages were no longer arranged. A new mode of women's liberation evolved out of the national liberation front. This was not imposed like the colonizers' emancipation; it came out of a situation which men and women made together and in which they needed and depended upon one another in new ways. (1972: 239-40)

While these accounts might be considered overly optimistic with respect to the long-term durability of such changes, there is little argument on the changes in gender roles that were occurring during the revolutionary process itself (D. Gordon 1968: 57-60). The family, citadel of tradition, became, in the context of the struggle, a social encasement, a movement "haven" within which gender roles were debated, challenged, and tested. For many militants, the family became the crucial site of cultural transformation as "the traditional patriarchal authoritarian family structure tended to collapse" (59). Moreover, as the heroism of women militants became increasingly popularized, the veil was discarded by many more Algerian women, including those not directly involved in the struggle (Fanon 1967: 61).

Using segregation to their advantage, small revolutionary cells hidden deep within the Casbah planned and carried out guerrilla actions. By definition, the revolutionary cell represents an intended haven, protected from the surveillance and disruption of the authorities, an autonomous place in which strategies, alliances, and decisions are forged or carried out. In response to massacres of civilians, cell members increasingly ventured into the European quarter to assassinate French soldiers and officials and bomb cafés and other public facilities frequented by *colons* and French troops. The French responded to the escalation and the discarding of the veil by FLN militants by arresting and torturing several women activists, and they began to challenge those with a European appearance, searching their bags as they entered the European quarter (Fanon 1967: 61). Evidently, the French had correctly read the relationship between the veil and the changing role of women in the struggle.

But this prompted a further tactical shift within the movement, as women militants again donned the haik, learning to conceal weapons and bombs while reembodying the traditional Algerian self: "to carry a rather heavy object dangerous to handle under the veil and still give the impression of having one's hands free, that there was nothing under this haik except a poor woman or an insignificant young girl" (Fanon 1967: 61). Beneath this visual representation of "insignificance" was a woman whose actions were clearly significant for the success of the revolution. Her body, which had had to conform to European proportions at an earlier stage, now had to be "swelled," "made shapeless and even ridiculous" in order to be able to carry a bomb or a parcel of grenades bound to her body by straps and strings while exhibiting free hands and an appearance of insignificance (62).

As the French realized the new use and meaning of the veil, all Algerian women were now deemed suspect, as were their children and their men, and this was reflected in the actions of the patrols who searched everyone without discrimination. In reaction to this new phase (in which the effort to unveil Algerian women took a more aggressive turn as servants, poor women, and prostitutes were forced into public squares and symbolically unveiled by mobs of colonists), "spontaneously and without being told, the Algerian women who had long since dropped the veil once again donned the haik, thus affirming that it was not true that woman liberated herself at the invitation of France and of General de Gaulle" (Fanon 1967: 62). Almost unanimously,

Fanon reported, the values of the occupier were rejected, and though the use of the veil was resumed, it was "stripped once and for all of its exclusively traditional dimensions" (63).

While David Gordon (1968) and Peter Knauss (1987) dispute Fanon's assertions that the revolution changed all of Algerian society to the same degree that it changed the active participants, what is significant is that the patriarchal structures that governed the lives of militants were clearly changed by the struggle. As Gordon wrote:

> The father could no longer give orders to a daughter he knew to be working for the national cause; women fighting by the side of men could no longer be regarded as passive objects; heroines now appeared as models for other women; independent feminine revolutionary cells stood in refutation of the idea that women could only be complements to men; the husband might have to remain at home when his wife was called out on a mission. . . . For all these reasons the emancipation of women became a dimension and a principle of the revolution. (1968: 59)

While traditional gender relations were not completely overturned in Algeria (or any other society, for that matter), and certainly not for all time, the experience of women in the revolution placed the issue of gender roles squarely onto the public agenda, where it has remained. The formation, after the revolution, of the Union Nationale des Femmes Algériennes, with roots in the women's revolutionary cells and led by former militants in the anticolonial struggle, provided an organizational counterweight to traditionalists and fundamentalists who would seek to return women to their prerevolutionary status (D. Gordon 1968: 66-67).

After the revolution, the principle of equality for women was established as a central ideological stricture (Rowbotham 1972: 241). The speeches of the socialist Ben Bella who led the first postrevolutionary government were punctuated with the affirmation of the new status of women, a principle repeated by all official newspapers and journals; the Tripoli Program, prepared and adopted as the charter for the new Algerian nation, asserted the right of women to participation in all spheres of social life and called for removal of the "negative mentality" that considered women inferior to men (D. Gordon 1968: 62). When Ben Bella was overthrown by Boumedienne in 1964, La Charte d' Alger was issued, repeating the principles surrounding gender that were laid down earlier. As Gordon recounted: "It describes the traditional 'degradation' of women as the result of 'retrograde and erroneous interpretations of Islam' and of colonialism which led traditional society, out of self-defense, to turn in upon itself (and so become, this implies, more conservative than it would otherwise have been)" (63). While such ideological pronouncements did not in themselves constitute social reforms, they provided an important symbolic counterweight to traditional ideologies upholding women's subjugation.

Though the dismal state of the economy and the reaction of traditionalists slowed potential gains for women in the labor market, tangible social reforms were enacted on behalf of women, particularly in education, where women made significant immediate gains that have been directly attributed to the rise of women during the struggle (Knauss 1987: 78-80). And though Knauss sees little change for women in Algeria since the 1960s, he concedes the presence of a significant modern women's movement that has fought for the interests of women for over three decades (131-32). Indeed, it is worth noting that in recent years Palestinian women's organizations have explicitly pointed to the Algerian experience as an exemplar of the importance of women's involvement in revolutionary movements, both for the movement and for women. However, Algeria has also served as a warning that over the longer term, the status of women can easily be eroded without the proper vigilance (Hiltermann 1991: 53).

The emergent role of women in the revolution created a sphere of cultural space in Algeria that would have seemed impossible in a previous period. Commentators report that after the revolution, an ideological battle of the sexes ensued, fought out on the radio airwaves and in letters to editors of newspapers and journals (D. Gordon 1968: 67-68). A compilation of women's grievances was published in a widely read book entitled *La femme algérienne*, written by a celebrated radio personality and feminist (M'Rabet 1964). Questions about the role of women in the family and the workplace became public issues to a degree that they could not have been prior to the struggle (D. Gordon 1968; MacLeod 1991: 11).

Conclusions

We have considered the relationship between culture and social movements through an analysis of an acute social conflict, through the interplay of power relations within the context of that conflict, and with attention to the ways and the settings within which cultural meaning was constructed and transformed by the interaction of contending groups. In social movement analysis, culture is not simply a storehouse of useful goods nor an overarching web of constraints (though it is indeed both of those things). We contend that oppositional culture is generated in and by social movements, specifically within protected havens that are relatively isolated from the surveillance, the ideas, and the repression of elites.

Algeria provides a useful example of the relationship between cultural transformation and movement havens. In the colonial period, any open expression of dissent was punished by arrest, torture or death, and Islam was repressed with the intention of imposing French culture upon the Algerian people. The French colonial regime successfully quelled open rebellion, but its attack on Islam had an effect that was the opposite of what was intended. Islamic beliefs and religious practices became oppositional, serving as a "language of refusal." Paradoxically, the retreat into traditional community, home, and religion created the social-organizational bases for revolutionary activity and cultural change, and the traditional practices of the veil and the cloistering of women became symbolic of resistance to cultural imperialism. Not only did traditional religious practices, family life, and community represent a threat to French domination in symbolic terms, but the family, the mosque, and the Casbah also served as critical loci of resistance to French rule and were targeted by the colonial administration as sites of oppositional culture. These "free" social spaces or "havens" have had counterparts wherever dominant and subordinate groups have coexisted, and their importance can be shown by the attempts of strategically perceptive elites to destroy them, from the attempt as part of the U.S. temperance movement to eliminate taverns and saloons, crucial gathering places of the labor movement, to assaults by white supremacists on black churches during the civil rights struggle (Hirsch 1990a; Morris 1984).

Though havens can serve as the locus of cultural transformation in the context of acute social struggle, they also provide the organizational basis for traditional cultural transmission. That is, as the products of structural inequalities, havens are a means of adaptation to an unequal social order, serving as bearers of the traditional forms that such adaptation takes. It must be remembered that it was in the context of anticolonial revolt that the family, the mosque, and the Casbah were transformed from traditional social spaces (spaces relatively free of colonial dominance) into vehicles of cultural and revolutionary change.

Whereas colonial domination depended on the eradication of Algerian culture in the case that we have described, in other situations subcultural "worlds" (and their havens) may exist relatively peacefully amid the folds of the parent culture. In the context of acute social conflict, however, subcultural havens may become oppositional or countercultural social spaces that are capable of being mobilized by movements, thus posing a direct threat to elites.

We would emphasize that the extent to which culture is transformed in collective action depends not only on the availability of social and spatial "preserves" within which traditional forms may be collectively renegotiated but also, and more importantly, on a level of social conflict that forces participants outside the daily round of everyday activity. When people are confronted by an immediate crisis—in an uprising, a rebellion, or a revolutionary mobilization—conditions are created for the remapping of cultural practices, meanings, valuations, and institutional configurations in order to navigate the shifting terrain. When the world is turned upside down the balance of forces that have structured everyday life are (by definition) upset, and the crisis necessitates a level of cultural transformation and production that previously might have seemed impossible.

This would seem to provide support for Ann Swidler's emphasis (chapter 2 in this volume) that the power of culture is more clearly revealed in certain *contexts* (particularly those relatively ephemeral periods in which social movements emerge as central actors) than in others (when culture may appear to be "deep"). But to her emphasis on the temporal, we would want to add (or specify further) the sociospatial context of cultural transformation represented by subcultural preserves that, in the context of acute social conflict, become social movement "havens." Similarly, the question of the appropriation and transformation of the veil as a cultural symbol speaks directly to Swidler's point about cultural *codes* and the cultural "recoding" that social movements facilitate and that may redefine the interpretative terms through which groups interact. Our analysis from a social movement perspective highlights this process with respect to the veil as a cultural symbol, emphasizing the enabling rather than the constraining aspects of codes.

And while we are in general agreement with Swidler's suggestions about institutions as rule-governed patterns that generate cultural consistency and that shape the nature and direction of movements in broad and deep ways, our focus is less on the institutional or more stable patterns of colonial rule and how it might have shaped the movement and the role of women within it than on the *process of struggle* between the contending groups, an approach that emphasizes contingency and interaction in the unfolding of a process of conflict.

In the dialogue between culture and social movements, cultural transformation is not proactive, but is an interactive process. Whether women would be veiled or unveiled was not determined on an abstract ideological scale (in terms of neither revolutionary ideology nor Islamic law) but was made as a series of strategic decisions that were determined as much by the actions of the opponent as by the movement itself. As the pragmatic needs of the movement shifted, women's involvement shifted, all the while bringing women militants closer to the status of equals. Though women's initial involvement tended to reproduce their traditional place in Algerian society, the demands of the struggle forced the male leadership of the FLN to break with tradition and bring women into direct combat against the French. As even minor combatants, women had entered a role that directly challenged traditional precepts. As the requirements of an escalating conflict demanded penetration of the European quarter of the city, women militants adopted European styles of dress and demeanor, inspiring other Algerian women (those not involved in combat) to do the same.

When the colonial administration responded by arresting, torturing, and searching Algerians on a wide scale, the veil was *readopted*, not only by militants, but by most Algerian women. A traditional cultural form had become, in a real sense, an oppositional cultural form, to the extent that it was employed in opposition both to the French administration and to women's traditional position in Algerian society. These reveiled women militants had actually risen to almost coequal position with men in terms of their role in the struggle. They had not simply adopted traditional ways of dress and demeanor, but had used traditional forms to represent this new status. In essence, their new traditionalism reflected a practical rejection of their traditional roles.

The family, bedrock of traditionalism, was clearly shaken by the militant participation of women in the struggle. Moreover, within the ranks of the militants the family served as a virtual social movement haven in which the emergence of new, oppositional cultural forms was debated, tested, and challenged. Thus, we see a social movement haven serving as the site of cultural transformation, a site that may itself be transformed in collective action. That is, as spatial and cultural expressions of the outsider status of subordinate groups, havens serve as sites of oppositional cultural formation and may themselves be transformed by the process of collective action. Though we do not have the evidence to make a definitive argument on this issue, we would suggest that the availability and nature of such "free" spaces play a key role in the success of a variety of movement mobilization efforts *and* in the process of cultural transformation and that there is a need to look further at this phenomenon, including the relationship between their organizational structures and movement success and failure across a wide range of cases. Such an inquiry is likely to be fruitful for our understanding of culture, our understanding of social movements, and our understanding of the dynamics of their interpenetration.

Part III

Cultural Analysis of Social Movements

Chapter 9

Analytical Approaches to Social Movement Culture: The Culture of the Women's Movement

Verta Taylor and Nancy Whittier

All social movements, to varying degrees, produce culture. Scholars who have studied the processes that make it possible for individuals and groups to come together to mount a concerted campaign for social change recognize that those who challenge the status quo face a formidable task. Most analysts agree that the mobilization of protest is facilitated by a group's ability to develop and maintain a set of beliefs and loyalties that contradict those of dominant groups. Scholars have referred to the spheres of cultural autonomy necessary to the rise of social movements as "cultures of solidarity" (Fantasia 1988), "social movement communities" (Buechler 1990), "submerged networks" (Melucci 1989), "oppositional subcultures" (Johnston 1991), "cultural havens" (Hirsch 1992), and "abeyance structures" (Taylor 1989). What all of these concepts share is attention to the ideas and beliefs—or the collectively shared grievances and unique frames of understanding—that drive protest.

Recent interest among social movement scholars in the relationship between culture and social movements is part of a larger trend in which sociologists from a variety of specialties, criticizing the structuralist bias of American sociology that privileges mechanistic explanations over subjectivist and cultural interpretations, are calling for the reintegration of symbolic factors in social analysis (Lamont and Wuthnow 1990; Alexander 1990). Yet, although culture has been a core concept in the field of sociology, its definition and impact remain the subject of considerable controversy (Wuthnow 1987; Swidler 1986; Wuthnow and Witten 1988; Alexander 1990; Alexander and Seidman 1990; Lamont and Wuthnow 1990).

Major approaches to the analysis of culture advance different concepts, based on distinct epistemological frameworks, for analyzing the relationship between symbolic forms and the structure of social relations. For functionalists, culture is conceived as values and norms, while Marxists and neo-Marxists analyze culture as ideology and class consciousness. Symbolic interactionists emphasize intersubjective meaning, focusing on the subjective dimensions—beliefs, goals, normative expectations, states, and motivations —that underlie social interaction, while dramaturgical approaches think of culture as ritual. A new generation of cultural theorists, influenced by post-structuralism and postmodernism, construe culture as discourse.

In the analysis that follows, we draw from contemporary social movement theory to delineate and illustrate four conceptual frameworks that draw on these different theoretical traditions to relate culture to collective action. These are the concepts of emergent norms and collective action frames, collective identity, ritual, and discourse. To illustrate the explanatory potential of each of these concepts, we use our research on different factions of the women's movement and the lesbian and gay movement. First, we discuss the significance of *emergent norms and interpretive frameworks* for resistance cultures. This dimension grows from the symbolic interactionist tradition and is suggested by the classical emergent norm approach of Turner and Killian (1987) and further developed in the contemporary work of Snow, Benford, and Hunt, who view social movement culture as the distinct interpretive frames defined in the course of mobilizing collective action (Snow et al. 1986; Snow and Benford 1992; Benford and Hunt 1992). Second, new social movement theorists Cohen (1985), Melucci (1985), and Touraine (1985) point to the concept of *collective identity*, which is a more general term than *class consciousness* and is applicable to a wider range of contemporary challenges directed toward life politics as well as emancipatory politics (Giddens 1991). Collective identity arises out of a challenging group's structural position, challenges dominant representations of the group, and valorizes the group's essential differences through actions in everyday life (Taylor and Whittier 1992). Third, although less explored than the two foregoing dimensions, dramaturgical approaches to culture emphasize the significance of *ritual* for expressing solidarity and evoking widely shared feelings among dominated groups. We describe ritual as a site for analyzing the emotions that mobilize activists. Fourth, the most recent work focuses on the new symbolic codes created by challenging groups that are expressed through a variety of forms of public *discourse*, including speeches and textual materials, myths, stories, and nonlinguistic modes of expression. It is important to recognize that the four cultural dimensions that we lay out in this essay overlap considerably, because they are not so much separate and independent elements of social movement culture as they are alternative ways to approach the analysis of culture that reflect different theoretical positions and epistemological stances.

Our research, separately and together, on the liberal women's rights, lesbian feminist, and radical feminist branches of the American women's movement points to the significance of oppositional culture for mobilization. This research began with Taylor's research with Leila Rupp on the women's rights movement after World War II (Rupp and Taylor 1987; Taylor 1989). That work, based in a resource mobilization framework, documented the centrality of a tight-knit women's community sustained by intimate bonds among activists to the survival of a feminist challenge during the hostile postwar period. The rich oppositional culture within the National Woman's Party and participants' deeply held collective identity sustained the movement and allowed it to survive and pass a legacy to the resurging women's movement of the 1960s.

As we began to work together on the lesbian feminist movement, we expanded our examination of women's movement culture to the extensive lesbian feminist communities that flowered in the 1980s (Taylor and Whittier 1992; Taylor and Rupp 1993). Rooted in the radical feminist movement of the early 1970s, lesbian feminists built an extensive network of alternative institutions such as bookstores, music festivals, self-defense and martial arts schools, rape crisis centers, publishing houses, and travel agencies. The communities nourished a complex oppositional culture in which participants politicized the actions of daily life. We became convinced by this that collective identity, or the enduring self-definition that a group constructs in the process of collective action, is central to the forms that mobilization takes. We found that in the hostile climate of the 1980s, the culture of lesbian feminist communities not only served to comfort, protect, and console activists in retreat, but also nourished women involved in myriad protests, both within and outside the women's movement (Taylor and Rupp 1993).

Building on this work, we each began separate projects. Both of these new projects point to the ways that the culture and collective identity associated with the women's movement have filtered into other challenges and arenas (see also Meyer and Whittier 1994). Whittier (1995) examined the evolution of radical feminism from its origins in the late 1960s into the 1990s by tracing the lives of longtime activists and the trajectories of radical feminist organizations in Columbus, Ohio. Veterans of the 1970s radical feminist movement constructed and internalized an enduring sense of themselves as "radical feminists." As a result, they continue to interpret their interactions and surroundings in a feminist light and pursue feminist social change through their employment and daily lives. Cultural strategies have been important to the survival of radical feminism in a variety of venues. In addition to centralized national organizations that operate in the traditional political arena, such as the National Organization for Women, the National Abortion Rights Action League, and the Women's Equity Action League, feminist individuals and groups have continued the struggle in local communities, in workplaces, and in the rhythms of daily life, ensuring the continuity of a radical feminist challenge. In order to understand this challenge, and thus to understand the course of the women's movement, we find it necessary to view political participation and social movements through a broad lens. Collective efforts for social change occur in the realms of culture, identity, and everyday life as well as in direct engagement with the state.

The fourth project on which this chapter is based is a study of a national postpartum depression self-help movement that emerged in the mid-1980s (Taylor forthcoming). Women's self-help movements, which have proliferated around issues ranging from battering and incest to breast-feeding and codependency, illustrate the kind of "life politics" concentrated on the collective definition of self that dominates the social movement sector in late modern societies (Giddens 1991). As the mass women's movement of the early 1970s receded, diverse constituencies of women began to apply feminist ideas and the distinctive strategies of the women's movement to a host of new problems that had not been central to the early second wave of feminism. The tactics of self-help movements are heavily cultural and revolve around disputed meanings: they establish new boundaries, deconstruct group definitions, and apply new labels. In the case of the postpartum depression movement, women are challenging dominant representations of motherhood and women's nurturant and caring roles by calling attention to emotions that deviate from the maternal ideal. But the postpartum depression movement embodies the contradictory nature of a great number of contemporary women's self-help movements. It incorporates feminist ideals of gender equality, on the one hand, by challenging both the meaning of motherhood in contemporary American society and the imperative that women be defined principally in terms of motherhood. On the other hand, like so many self-help movements, the postpartum depression movement has a tendency to depoliticize women's emancipatory struggle by advancing a medical model that locates and classifies women's experience as a "disease process" (Simonds 1992; Haaken 1993). In order to understand the burgeoning feminist self-help industry and its mobilization of culture as both subversive and supportive of the gender status quo, we have found it necessary to turn to conceptualizations of collective action that accentuate culture and the interrelation of meaning and power.

In sum, we have documented a distinct feminist culture in the United States that contributed to: (1) the survival of the women's rights movement during a period of intense antifeminist opposition from 1945 to the mid-1960s; (2) the persistence of activism among women who participated in the 1970s radical feminist branch of the movement; (3) the adoption of strategies of everyday resistance by women in contemporary lesbian feminist communities; and (4) the proliferation through the 1980s of women's self-help movements that confront a host of women's problems, ranging from battering and rape to breast cancer and postpartum depression. Our aim is to generalize from this case to outline potential frameworks that can be used to analyze the cultural dimensions of any social movement.

Emergent Norms and Interpretive Frames

Collective behavior theorists distinguished social movements from conventional political action on the basis of the new and noninstitutionalized norms that emerge in the course of collective challenges (Smelser 1962; Turner and Killian 1972; Weller and Quarantelli 1974). Resource mobilization and political process approaches, in contrast, accentuated the similarities between social movements and institutionalized politics. If movements consist of both new normative frameworks and new relationships, as Weller and Quarantelli (1974) suggest, then resource mobilization theory has focused on the social movement organizations that are the new relationships to the neglect of emergent norms. It is not surprising that contemporary researchers interested in studying the interpretive frameworks that give meaning to collective action have introduced concepts, such as collective action frames (Snow et al. 1986), that draw on earlier collective behavior approaches to spell out a model of meaning construction in social movements.

The "emergent norm" approach, as formulated by Turner and Killian, drew from symbolic interactionist assumptions to emphasize the process by which collectivities construct "an emergent (revised) definition of the situation" (Turner and Killian 1987: 33). The emergent norm approach highlights the way that challenging groups redefine normative frameworks to justify and promote mobilization for change. Building on the work of Turner and Killian, Snow et al. (1986) proposed the concept of "frame alignment" to explain how movements bring potential recruits' individual viewpoints into congruence with the movements' emergent and collective perspectives. The frame alignment approach is based on a recognition of the importance of cultural factors to recruitment and mobilization and offers an explanation of the role of meaning in collective action that can be integrated with the structural concerns of resource mobilization theory (Capek 1993; Gerhards and Rucht 1992).

The notion of frame, drawn from Goffman, refers to the "interpretive schemata" developed by collectivities for understanding the world (Snow et al. 1986). Snow and Benford identify three functions of collective action frames: punctuation, or calling attention to the injustice suffered by a collectivity; attribution, or explaining the causes of and proposed remedies for the injustice; and articulation, or connecting diverse experiences into a coherent outlook (1992: 137). In a similar vein, Klandermans (1988) proposes the concept of consensus mobilization to describe how movements use persuasive communication to produce consensus or frame alignment among potential supporters. In this view, frames are not only meaning systems but also strategic tools for recruiting participants.

As Snow et al. (1986) have pointed out, collective action frames do not exist a priori, but are defined in the course of collective action through frame alignment processes. Snow, Benford, and their colleagues hold that movements' interpretive schemata both draw from and modify elements of the dominant culture, through processes they term frame bridging, frame amplification, frame extension, or frame transformation. Thus, collective action frames incorporate preexisting beliefs and symbols as well as oppositional values that emerge in the course of a group's struggle. The carryover from preexisting values and understandings illustrates the importance of what Bourdieu (1984, 1990) considers "cultural capital." Factors such as participants' education, gender, race, ethnicity, and class background, generally viewed as structural, provide groups with distinct sets of beliefs and skills, or cultural resources, that shape the contours of their resistance (Alexander 1990; Lichterman 1992). In Bourdieu's (1984, 1990) terms, this is "habitus," which is "cultural know-how"; in Swidler's (1986) terms, it is the cultural "tool kit" from which movements borrow.

Snow and Benford (1992) hold that influential social movements construct master frames that shape how subsequent challengers interpret and package their causes. Widely adopted master frames are successful because they resonate with the experiences of potential supporters and incorporate prevalent beliefs and concerns. The concept of master frames links the beliefs and ideas of protest groups to political opportunity structures because it is, after all, the political and structural viability of a master frame that permits an idea to spread and gain adherents. In fact, Snow and Benford view the emergence of a generalizable "master frame" as a major determinant of larger cycles of protest that give way to multiple and related social movement organizations.

The women's movement illustrates the significance of emergent norms and interpretive frames for mobilization. The feminist frame that views gender as a central organizing feature of the social world, celebrates women, and criticizes dominant masculinity might even be considered a master frame, since it has been influential in mobilizing a range of women's movements, including groups as diverse as women of the Ku Klux Klan in the 1920s (Blee 1991), the battered women's movement (Gagne unpublished), Afrocentric feminists (Hill Collins 1990), and adult children of alcoholics (Simonds 1992).

Scholars of the women's movement generally agree that one of the major results of more than a century of feminist activism in the United States has been the flourishing of a distinct "women's culture." It is important, however, to distinguish between the emergent feminist cultures that grow out of women's resistance and the "dominant women's culture" based on traditional domesticity, which might hinder as well as facilitate feminist organizing. While feminist cultures often reflect elements from the dominant women's culture—notably, an emphasis on nurturance and caring—they nevertheless extend them to new arenas. Even though feminists have for the most part contested biological explanations of gender differences, the belief that there are fundamental differences between female and male values has nevertheless permeated the feminist movement throughout its history (Buechler 1990).

A large body of scholarly and popular writing valorizes egalitarianism, collectivism, altruism, pacifism, and cooperation as female traits derived from an ethic of caring (Gilligan 1982; Chodorow 1978; Tronto 1987; Fisher and Tronto 1990; Morgen unpublished). In contrast, an emphasis on hierarchy and oppressive individualism, an ethic of individual rights, violence, and competition are denounced as male values. Most feminist organizations make explicit claims to an "ethic of care" that defines collective organizational structure and consensus decision making as more "feminist" than bureaucratic structure and hierarchical decision making, which are seen as promoting self-interested behavior and undermining ties among women (Freeman 1975; Cassell 1977; Buechler 1990; P. Martin 1990). While some feminists hold essentialist views and link female values to women's biological capacity to reproduce, others take a social constructionist position and attribute the differences to socialization and prescribed gender roles.

Whether a movement emphasizes social constructionist or essentialist explanations of its distinctiveness influences mobilization patterns. Social constructionist accounts minimize differences between challenging and dominant groups, open up the possibility for coalition with a broad range of challengers, and suggest strategies aimed at deconstructing the categories into which individuals are placed, rather than elevating the position of a given category. Essentialist accounts, on the other hand, view group membership as real, reify difference, and promote organizing around shared identity to improve the position of group members (S. Epstein 1987).

When lesbians in the women's movement began organizing around 1970, the nascent movement made explicit use of a feminist frame that cast lesbianism as the end of a continuum of "woman loving," or as a strategy that allowed women to place their primary focus and "energy" on other women while simultaneously withdrawing from male-dominated relationships and institutions. In contrast, the mixed-sex gay liberation movement justified same-sex relations on the basis of sexual freedom. In the early 1970s, the feminist master frame that packaged lesbianism as an act of political resistance and lesbians as the vanguard of the movement resonated with the already widespread valuation of women's experiences and female bonding that dominated feminist discourse in the period (Ransdell forthcoming).

Throughout the 1980s, as the mass women's movement receded and the AIDS epidemic took its toll on the gay male community, lesbians were drawn increasingly into a mixed-sex gay and lesbian movement. Conflict between essentialists and social constructionists in the lesbian and gay movement illustrates the significance of differing frames for mobilization. The radical branch of the gay and lesbian movement, including the early Gay Liberation Front and newer groups such as Queer Nation, has sought to deconstruct the categories of homosexual and heterosexual and make sexuality more fluid and open, arguing that sexual and romantic relationships are a matter of choice rather than biological dictate (Adam 1987; S. Epstein 1987). In academia, this radical approach is represented by the development of so-called queer theory, a discourse that deconstructs the separate identities of lesbian and gay to recognize a shared queer experience and identity (Plummer and Stein forthcoming). Gay and lesbian groups working within the mainstream political arena, on the other hand, have defined gay men and lesbians as a minority group and portrayed sexual orientation not as a choice but as a biologically determined characteristic (S. Epstein 1987).

One consequence of the social constructionist approach of Queer Nation is that the group includes participants who identify as lesbian, gay, and bisexual and members of other "sexual minorities" such as celibate, asexual, transgendered, or sadomasochist. Lesbian feminist groups, in contrast, include some heterosexual women but are closed to men of any sexual orientation, because they tend to be driven by radical feminist frames that give primacy to gender. For instance, during the 1970s, members of the radical feminist Women's Action Collective of Columbus, Ohio, barred men from access to all areas of a collectively owned house except the room occupied by a bookstore, in order to create "women's space" (Whittier 1995). The interpretive frames that groups employ, in short, affect organizational structure, membership, and strategy.

Although Snow and his colleagues view frames as guides to collective action, frame alignment theory does not focus on the ongoing process of meaning construction that takes place once a movement is under way. Framing theory instead turns our attention to the processes movements use to recruit participants, namely, by the construction of congruence between the movement's collective and political frames and the individual meanings systems already present in everyday life (Capek 1993). Frame alignment approaches also attend to the origins and development of the ideas and beliefs of social movements, especially as they arise from the beliefs and frameworks of prior social movements or earlier cycles of protest (Tarrow 1989b). For an approach that highlights the significance of a social movement's distinct interpretive schema for its ongoing actions and strategic choices, we turn to a discussion of collective identity.

Collective Identity

Collective behavior theorists emphasized the relationship between group grievances and collective action (Davies 1969; Smelser 1962; Gurr 1970), while initial advocates of the resource mobilization and political process models, arguing for the rational calculus of collective action, deemphasized discontent and instead explained movement emergence primarily in terms of organizational and political variables (McCarthy and Zald 1973, 1987; Oberschall 1973; Tilly 1978; McAdam 1982). Recently, however, the relationship between group consciousness and collective action has again become a focus of research by scholars working both within and outside the resource mobilization perspective (Fantasia 1988; Fireman and Gamson 1979; Ferree and Miller 1985; Ferree 1992; Gamson 1992a; Klandermans 1984, 1992; Klandermans and Tarrow 1988; Klein 1984; McAdam 1988; Morris and Mueller 1992).

Analysts of contemporary social movements, especially a group of scholars grouped together under the label of "new social movement theorists," suggest that collective identity is a key concept for understanding the means by which structural inequality becomes subjectively experienced discontent (Pizzorno 1978; Boggs 1986; Cohen 1985; Melucci 1985, 1989; Touraine 1985; B. Epstein 1990b; Taylor 1989; Taylor and Whittier 1992). Building on the Marxist tradition that defines class consciousness as the cultural mechanism of conflict movements, scholars who take the construction of collective identity to be the critical cultural dynamic emphasize the larger structures of power and inequality that shape the cultural meanings, consciousness, and group loyalties of contenders (Mueller 1992). For some new social movement theorists, political organizing around a common identity is what distinguishes recent social movements in Europe and the United States from the more class-based movements of the past (Klandermans and Tarrow 1988). In this view, cultural and expressive elements of mobilization—sometimes referred to as "identity politics"—are unique to recent American and European movements (Cohen 1985; Touraine 1985; Melucci 1989; B. Epstein 1990b; Kauffman 1990). A substantial amount of research suggests, however, that identity construction processes are crucial to grievance interpretation in all forms of collective action, not just in the so-called new movements (Friedman and McAdam 1992; Fantasia 1988; Mueller 1994). The "newness" of recent movements is not to be found in their cultural processes, but in the fact that in late modern societies, participation in collective action is becoming a key factor in the ongoing social constitution of personal identities and biographies (Giddens 1991).

Collective identity is the shared definition of a group that derives from members' common interests, experiences, and solidarity (Taylor 1989). For Melucci (1988) as well as for other social movements analysts, collective identity is not to be confused with the social psychological concept of social identity (Weigert, Teitge, and Teitge 1986; Skevington 1989). Rather, collective identity is seen as constructed, activated, and sustained only through interaction in social movement communities (or submerged networks, in Melucci's [1989] terms) and as shaped by factors such as political opportunity structures, the availability of resources, and organizational strength—in other words, matters of resources and power. In this respect, collective identity is analogous to ideology. Both are activated by individuals who ultimately are the agents of change; as a cultural mechanism of collective action, collective identity is an emergent socially constructed property that cannot be reduced simply to subjective individual attitudes. In light of the politicization of identity and everyday life associated with recent social movements, however, we find the broader notion of collective identity preferable to the term *ide-*

ology, which has its origins in the more class-based struggles of the nineteenth century.

Collective identities are rooted in social movement communities. But they can also become disembedded from the context of their creation so they are recognizable by outsiders and widely available for adoption. For example, the growth of lesbian and gay communities, made possible by economic and social changes that allowed individuals to live outside heterosexual family relationships, the concentration of gay men and lesbians in urban port cities, and shifts in gender roles permitted the concept of homosexuality to develop as an identity rather than simply as a behavior (D'Emilio 1983). Even individuals who are not engaged in same-sex relationships can identify as gay, and some do. Although probably there have always been individuals in every society who had same-sex relationships, to be gay or lesbian in the contemporary context is not simply to state an individual sexual preference. Rather, it is a collective identity that conveys a distinct set of statuses and roles, relationships, and meanings.

The concept of collective identity can be made amenable to empirical study by directing attention to the observable practices (e.g., gestures, acts, dress, and appearances) and the discourses (talk, words, speeches, symbols, and texts) through which movement participants enact their activist identities (Hunt and Benford unpublished). Social movement participants construct identity narratives that connect their experiences and explain their lives in terms of frames of meaning that are historically and contextually situated in social movement communities (Hunt and Benford unpublished; Giddens 1991). Making claims about the characteristics of the group is central to the process of identity construction (Benford unpublished).

Elsewhere, we have conceptualized collective identity as consisting of three interrelated processes: the construction of group *boundaries* that establish differences between a challenging group and dominant groups; *consciousness,* or interpretive frameworks that emerge out of a challenging group's struggle to define and realize its interests; and the *politicization of everyday life* through the use of symbols and everyday actions to resist and restructure existing systems of domination (Taylor and Whittier 1992). This model is an attempt to theorize so-called identity politics, which makes the individual a site of political activity.

Interactions and meaning systems in contemporary American lesbian feminist communities illustrate the processes of identity construction. Within such communities, a complex symbolic system affirms the existence of differences between women and men and between heterosexual and lesbian women, idealizing the female while vilifying the male. Radical feminist ideology also provides an interpretive framework for defining lesbianism as a political strategy rather than—or as well as—a sexual choice (Taylor and Rupp 1993). And the politicization of everyday life is, in many respects, the hallmark of lesbian feminism. Every aspect of life—where one lives, what one eats, how one dresses—can become an expression of politics. As one member of the radical feminist Women's Action Collective in Columbus, Ohio, put it, members of the community learned to "examine everything you do for political consistency" (Whittier 1995).

The most significant displays challenge conventional standards of gender behavior that subordinate women and are an arena for intense conflict. For example, radical and lesbian feminists in the early 1970s emphasized comfortable, practical, nonfeminine styles of dress and strictly egalitarian relationships as a way of challenging expectations that women present themselves as sexual objects and subordinate themselves in relationships. Activists sought to restructure every aspect of daily life, including language, eliminating disparaging terms such as *bitch, cunt,* and *girl,* substituting *herstory* for *history,* and spelling *women* as *womyn* or *womoon* in order to omit *men.* The breast cancer movement provides another example of the politicization of everyday life. Some activists refuse to wear a breast prosthesis in order to challenge the cultural emphasis on the breast; some display photographs of beautiful, tattooed mastectomy scars (van Willigen unpublished).

The self-definitions that groups construct are by no means static. Klandermans has demonstrated how changing perceptions of the Dutch peace movement altered its composition and focus (Klandermans 1994). As activists have long taken for granted, coming of political age at different times gives people different perspectives. What it means to call oneself feminist varies greatly over time and is often a source of conflict over movement goals, values, ideology, strategy, or individual behavior. For example, groups of women who entered the radical feminist movement at various times during its peak saw themselves as distinct "microcohorts" within the larger movement (Whittier 1995). Radical feminists in the late 1960s, socialized in the male-dominated movements of the period, drew on New Left terminology to describe themselves as "women's liberationists" and evoked military imagery to urge women in their daily lives to "put their bodies on the line." In contrast, radical feminists in the mid-1970s emphasized their connections to other women by referring to themselves as "woman-identified," talking about the importance of "women-only space" and constructing identity narratives that cast close relationships with women lovers, friends, and relatives as central to personal fulfillment and political freedom (Whittier 1995). On a larger scale, some veterans of the 1970s women's movement who had consciously rejected traditional feminine attire were appalled when young lesbian feminists in the 1990s expressed their sexuality by wearing miniskirts or lacy lingerie and criticized narrow standards of "politically correct" appearance. The intensity of such conflicts over cultural expression is itself an indication of its significance for distinguishing who is and is not a feminist.

The politicization of group membership may be more or less explicit and more or less linked with being a particular kind of person, as opposed to a person involved in a particular kind of activity. Movements made up of people who see themselves as a distinct type of person tend to politicize a greater range of everyday activities than do movements that organize around a more limited shared interest (Lichterman 1992). Participants in the radical feminist movement of the 1970s, for example, politicized their everyday activities to such an extent that even twenty years later participants' lives remain organized around feminist concerns. For example, many have chosen employment that focuses on improving women's status—providing direct services to rape survivors, battered women, or women subjected to sexual harassment; working for political organizations that engage in lobbying or protest; teaching women's studies—or engage in feminist activism in the workplace (Whittier 1995).

In effect, the concept of collective identity recognizes that the self-understandings around which groups organize are central to the transformation of hegemonic meanings and loyalties. By bringing the concept of collective identity into the mainstream of social movement analysis, we can begin to focus on the processes that challengers use to construct symbolic support for resistance to enduring patterns of dominance. To link the study of social movement culture to the construction of collective identity allows us to focus on cultural practices that challenge not only large-scale structures of domination but also the everyday interactions that sustain inequality.

Ritual

For Durkheim, the key cultural element was ritual; religion was the consummate ritual. Durkheim stressed the autonomy and internal structure of cultural systems; division into the sacred and the profane, oppositions conceived of as emotionally and morally charged, formed the basis for organized communities. To the extent that ritual is seen as mediating between these symbolic divisions to produce social solidarity and maintain group equilibrium,

Durkheimian cultural theory has been faulted for ignoring power, conflict, and change. It is not surprising, therefore, that there have been few analyses of collective action as ritual.

There are, of course, some exceptions. In an extended treatment of ritual, Hobsbawm (1959) argued that ritual was central to "primitive" social movements prior to the late nineteenth century, including early trade union societies and secret brotherhoods growing from the Masons. In such groups, rituals of initiation, ceremonials of periodic meeting, practical rituals such as secret passwords, and extensive symbolism served to create solidarity and evoke emotional response. Hobsbawm, however, viewed the prevalence of ritual as a feature of such movements' "primitivism," arguing that modern challenges, although not devoid of ritual, center on more rational and utilitarian practices.

More recent work suggests, on the contrary, that ritual, broadly defined, remains pervasive in twentieth-century social movements. We may view ritual, in Wuthnow's (1987) definition, as symbolic expressive events that communicate something about social relations in a relatively dramatic way. Contemporary approaches to ritual are best illustrated in work that builds on dramaturgical analysis, as defined by Goffman (1959, 1967) and Garfinkel (1967), to analyze how symbolic performances express conflict. Rituals of collective action have been analyzed by Snow and Benford (1992) as framing devices. Mueller (1987) draws parallels between Tilly's characterization of collective actions such as strikes, marches, and demonstrations as "performances" and Goffman's dramaturgical theory. Snow, Zurcher, and Peters (1981) and more recently Benford and Hunt (1992) apply the dramaturgical perspective to demonstrate how challenging groups use performance and ritual to define the terms of conflict and communicate power.

A primary reason for making ritual central to the study of collective action is that rituals are the cultural mechanisms through which collective actors express the emotions—that is, the enthusiasm, pride, anger, hatred, fear, and sorrow—that mobilize and sustain conflict. Since Durkheim, rituals generally have been thought of as intensely emotional and dramatic symbols that are distinguishable from purely instrumental kinds of actions. There is wide agreement that ritual functions to produce moral solidarity principally by evoking emotion (Hobsbawm 1959; Durkheim 1961; R. Turner 1969; Collins 1975; Kemper 1981; Wuthnow 1987). Emotions are, as Collins puts it, "the glue of solidarity" (1990: 28). While we agree with scholars who suggest that ritual can communicate other meanings as well (Benford and Hunt 1992), our aim here is to highlight the emotional significance of ritual. We view ritual as part of what Gordon (1981) has termed the "emotion culture" of a group. The rituals of challenging groups—whether they are marches and rallies, riots and rebellions, styles of dress and consumptive patterns, or twelve-step programs and "bibliotherapy" (Steinem 1992)—are an important site for the analysis of the emotions that drive protest. Further, the study of ritual practices makes the emotional dimensions of social movements more observable than subjectivist approaches that treat emotions as motives.

Recent approaches to the sociological study of emotions suggest two directions for articulating the links between structural arrangements, culture, and feelings (Hochschild 1990). First is work that ties emotions such as anger, fear/anxiety, guilt, shame, hate, depression, love, pride, satisfaction, and happiness to structural inequalities in power and status (Kemper 1978). For example, Scheff (1990) views shame and pride as being at the heart of conflict between groups and even nations. Depression, according to Mirowsky and Ross (1989), is linked to women's low social and economic status, and women's high rates of depression have been the backdrop against which a booming women's therapeutic self-help industry has appeared (Taylor forthcoming).

While structural factors can give rise to any number of emotions, the expression and management of emotions is ultimately a social matter governed by cultural and interactional processes. A second strand of work provides tools for analyzing the distinctive "emotion cultures" that specify "feeling rules" and "expression rules" governing even the most basic of emotions (Hochschild 1983). Challenging groups, to varying degrees, develop rituals to create and legitimize new emotion norms that include expectations about how members should feel about themselves and about dominant groups, as well as how they should manage and express the feelings evoked by their day-to-day encounters with dominant groups.

In the social movement communities and feminist organizations that are the heart of the contemporary women's movement, ritual is an important mechanism for challenging dominant gender norms for the content and expression of emotion. This is accomplished through an elaborate set of alternative institutions and a network of national and local feminist cultural events that attract participants. Central to most feminist organizations is a distinctive emotion culture that both draws upon and challenges the dominant ideal of women as nurturers. Based on our research on the women's movement, we propose that ritual is a cultural mechanism through which challenging groups express and transform the emotions that arise from subordination, redefine dominant feeling and expression rules to reflect more desirable identities or self-conceptions, and express group solidarity.

To take up the first point, being a woman in a male-dominated and misogynist society evokes a wide range of feelings (Taylor 1994). Through consciousness-raising and a host of other practices, feminist groups aim to channel women's fear, shame, and depression into feelings conducive to protest and activism rather than resignation and withdrawal. Ritual is an important component of this process. At demonstrations, marches, and cultural events such as conferences, films, plays, and music festivals, ritual is used to evoke and express emotion, dramatize inequality and injustice, and emphasize the way that women's individual experiences are connected to their disadvantaged status as a group (Eder, Staggenborg, and Sudderth unpublished). Rituals in such settings include testimonials, healing circles, song, and chants such as "Out of the houses and into the streets, we won't be raped, we won't be beat," heard at Take Back the Night marches.

Militant and dramatic tactics are also used to signify anger. For instance, in the early 1980s in Columbus, Ohio, after an unpopular judge dropped charges of rape against a local man on the grounds that his four-year-old victim was a "promiscuous young lady," members of a feminist group expressed their anger by sending pig testicles to the judge. In Seattle, activists dramatized the problem of bulimia in a demonstration in which they simulated vomiting into a toilet decorated with Barbie dolls and diet books (Colvin 1993).

A second characteristic of feminist emotion cultures is the redefinition of feeling and expression rules that apply to women. Women have generally been deemed—largely as a result of gender inequality—more emotional, subjective, and relational than men. Among feminists emotion is, therefore, both a basis for defining oneself and a tool for change. To resist patriarchy means resisting gender norms for the expression of emotion inside feminist communities as well as in everyday interactions in the outside world.

Anger, for example, is an emotion that it is less acceptable for women to express than for men. Feminist organizations such as Sisters of the Yam, an African-American women's recovery network, encourage women to trade fear and shame for anger and pride (hooks 1993). For example, testimony by women who have had illegal abortions, been raped, undergone forced sterilization, experienced psychotic disorders following childbirth, or survived incest reframe feelings of shame over past events into pride over having survived such ordeals. The antirape movement relies heavily on rituals that downplay the fear, guilt, and depression women experience following victimization, emphasizing instead emotions that empower women (Matthews

1992). The ritual of "taking back the night" by marching in all-female groups through urban areas and the use of the term *survivor* to refer to victims of rape, incest, or battering explicitly legitimate women's experiences and encourage participants to recognize women's collective strength.

A third aspect of feminist rituals is their symbolic emphasis on caring, dramatizing the primacy of relationships between individual women and promoting female bonding. In defining an Afrocentric feminist epistemology, Hill Collins states that "a central component of the ethic of caring concerns the appropriateness of emotions in dialogues" (1990: 216). The feminist emphasis on caring is conveyed through women's references to each other as sisters and the open expressions of love and affection that are typical among women who have participated in a common struggle. To take a historical example, the upper-middle-class members of the National Woman's Party who carried the torch of women's rights from the end of the suffrage campaign until the resurgence of the women's movement expressed strong bonds of friendship and joy over participating in the campaign for an equal rights amendment, leading one woman to exclaim that "it is as thrilling as a love affair, and lasts longer!!!!" (Rupp and Taylor 1987: 97).

Feminist practices reinforce new expression rules that dictate open displays of emotion and empathy and legitimate extensive attention to participants' emotions and personal histories (Morgen unpublished). Undoubtedly this contributes to the kind of interpersonal conflict that plagues so many feminist organizations and communities, described both by activists and by scholars of the women's movement (Freeman 1972-73; B. Ryan 1992). On the other hand, the open expression of emotion is a central component of the support function performed by feminist self-help groups. For example, the annual board meeting of Depression After Delivery, one of the major organizations spearheading the postpartum depression movement, begins with a two-hour session in which members share personal feelings and experiences. In effect, the way emotions are dealt with in the women's movement is meant to serve as an example of the new feeling rules and expression norms advocated by feminism; in other words, the women's movement practices emotional prefigurative politics (Breines 1982).

The women's movement is not unique in its use of ritual to express new emotional frames that link challengers' feelings to social injustice and the actions of dominant groups. But, to be fair, social movement scholars have neglected emotion partly in order to avoid depicting social movement actors as irrational. There is a general tendency in sociology to view reason and emotion as opposites (Morgen 1983, unpublished; Jaggar 1983; Turner and

Killian 1987), and early collective behavior theorists used irrationality to distinguish participants in social movements from those who participate in routine social action (LeBon 1960; Smelser 1962; Blumer 1955; Lang and Lang 1961). Yet, as Turner and Killian (1987) point out, emotion and reason are not irreconcilable, and social movement participants, like all other social actors, are not only thinking but also feeling actors (Ferree 1992; Morgen unpublished). By drawing on the sociology of emotions to suggest ritual as a site for observing the emotion culture of protest, we aim to begin bringing emotions back into the study of collective action.

Discourse

Collective behavior theorists have long emphasized the socially constructed nature of social problems and pointed to the significance of social movements for the cultural interpretation of experience (Blumer 1955; Turner and Killian 1972; Brown and Goldin 1973; Aguirre, Quarantelli, and Mendoza 1988). Recently, resource mobilization theorists such as Morris (1984), Gamson (1990), and McCarthy (1994) have joined scholars such as Gitlin (1980), Gusfield (1989), Johnston (1991), and Hunt and Benford (unpublished) to explore how social movements affect and are affected by the discourse—or the language, ideas, interpretations, and symbols—of conflict. This work views any political or social conflict as developing its "own culture," so to speak, reflected in a set of discourses between challenging groups and dominant groups that form what Gamson terms a general "issue culture" and Gusfield calls a "social problems" culture.

Recent attention to the discourse of protest does not represent simply a renewed interest in subjectivist models but is a reflection of a larger theoretical trend toward cultural analysis. The current rethinking of the concept of culture in sociology focuses on its observable features, namely, discourse and the symbolic-expressive acts or practices, including ritual, in which discourse is embedded (Swidler 1986; Wuthnow 1987, 1989). For Wuthnow, "discourse subsumes the written as well as the verbal, the formal as well as the informal, the gestural or ritual as well as the conceptual" (1989: 16). Language and the discourses of science, technology, and medicine—among others—are central to the ideological practices that maintain domination (Smith 1990). When we conceive of culture in this way, it is possible to separate the analysis of culture from social structure and to understand its relative influence on action. The fact that newer approaches view cultural change as linked to culture-producing actors and organizations suggests, as Wuthnow (1989) contends, that social movements can be viewed as "communities of discourse" engaged in the enunciation of new cultural codes that very often contest dominant representations.

Cultural analysis highlights the economic, political, and institutional features of late modern societies linked to the distinctive character of recent social movements. Various attempts to theorize postmodernity share the assumption that the postindustrial age—ushered in by the end of the Second World War—brought a new type of society in which the exercise of power is fragmented so that political and economic institutions are not the only sites, nor class the only relations, of domination. Postmodernist sociologists call attention to other systems of human domination—mainly gender, race, ethnicity, and sexuality—and poststructuralists highlight the complex institutional contexts through which inequality is maintained—schools, the workplace, medicine, religion, law, and science (Smith 1987, 1990; Richardson 1991; Fraser 1989; Agger 1991; Denzin 1991). Postmodernity is characterized by an explosion in communication, information, and new technologies associated with what Thompson (1990) terms the "mediazation of modern culture"; the rise of increasingly rationalized and abstract professional discourses of medicine, science, education, and therapy that frame and monopolize issues (Smith 1990); the ascendance of massive and reflexively monitored organizations that coordinate and control social relations across indefinite time and spaces; and the increasing commercialization of life experience.

These developments open more domains of life as contested terrain, changing the sites or focus of collective action (Cohen 1985). As a result, new social movements target not only the state but civil society, specifically institutions specializing in the transmission of cultural codes such as schools, families, religion, medicine, and the therapy industry. Class-based collective action, or what Giddens (1991) terms "emancipatory politics," is no longer the driving force for change: the focus of newer movements is on "life politics." As participants in the new movements—the majority of whom are drawn from the ranks of the new middle class and are well educated—struggle for the right to choose their own kind of life and identity, the production of knowledge and new normative guidelines, or the enunciation of new discursive frameworks that contest dominant cultural codes, takes center stage (Lichterman 1992). By underscoring the transformations of late modernity that create a new space within which dissenting discourses can flourish, cultural theory points to the study of public discourse for understanding how social movements are agents of cultural change.

Discourse analysis uses the production and interpretation of naturally occuring speech acts, symbolic codes, textual materials, and visual materials as a means of understanding how culture is produced or shaped within social situations. A great deal of discourse analysis, tracing its roots to sociolinguistic research, semiotics, the French structuralists, and the poststructuralism or deconstructionism of scholars such as Foucault (1977, 1978), Barthes (1970, 1975), Baudrillard (1975), Bourdieu (1984), and Lyotard (1984), is highly technical. Sociologists of social movements have been less likely to embrace deconstructionist methods that assume the primacy of language or the text (Palmer 1990). Instead, they have been interested in ideas and symbols as vehicles of the social meanings that underlie collective action (Gamson and Modigliani 1989; Klandermans 1992; Moaddel 1992). In his analysis of Catalan nationalism in Spain, Johnston (1991), for example, applies discursive analysis to the speeches of militants to analyze the "oppositional subculture" of Catalonia. Hunt and Benford (unpublished) examine "identity talk" in peace movement organizations to understand how activists use discourse to align their personal biographies with the collective identities constructed by challenging groups. Other social movement analysts equate discourse with ideology but prefer the concept of discourse because it escapes the pejorative implications associated with both Marxist and Mannheimian conceptions of ideology as misleading and illusory (Moaddel 1992). In an examination of the discourse of the Iranian revolution, Moaddel (1992), for example, defines discourse as the set of principles, concepts, symbols, and rituals used by actors to fabricate strategies of action.

The most explicit recognition of discourse as a social movement strategy appears in Katzenstein's (unpublished) analysis of feminist politics in the Catholic Church. Katzenstein draws from the work of postmodernist feminist scholars (Smith 1987; Scott 1988; Richardson 1991; Nicholson 1990; Harding 1991) who hold not only that women and other groups have been excluded from the dominant culture but also that the practices of male domination are to a large extent inscribed in texts and discourses that represent men's standpoint as universal. Underscoring the significance of cultural resistance, Katzenstein distinguishes two types of activism that have been central to feminism: interest group activism or strategies designed to influence political elites and legislative and policy decisions; and discursive politics, or efforts expressed primarily through speech and print to reinterpret, reformulate, rethink, and rewrite the androcentric masculinist norms and practices of society and the state.

Our own research confirms that discursive strategies have been employed by most factions of the contemporary women's movement, even the most moderate of groups. The proliferation of alternative women-only institutions, the flourishing of the feminist media, and the emergence of a feminist art and literature have provided a fertile context for the elaboration of a discourse and politics of everyday resistance. Feminist writer Mary Daly (1978, 1984) is perhaps best known for embracing and politicizing language—such as the terms *hag, crone,* and *dyke*—used by dominant groups to denigrate women. In a similar vein, a lesbian organization in San Francisco dubbed itself the Damned Lesbians Coalition after conservative U.S. Senator Jesse Helms opposed the confirmation of an open lesbian, Roberta Achtenberg, to federal office on the grounds that she was a "damned lesbian" ("Dossier" 1993). The names of organizations often embody their political perspective. A militant feminist group organized against sexism, the rape culture, and the "perpetual male hard-on that crushes our [women's] spirits" on the campus of the University of California at Santa Barbara in 1991 adopted the name CUNTS, which stands for Creative Underground Network of Truthful Sisters (Sharpe unpublished). A group of men, dressed as women, call themselves Church Ladies for Choice and sing hymns such as "This Womb Is My Womb: It Is Not Your Womb" at pro-choice events; a militant lesbian group calls itself the Lesbian Avengers. Discursive strategies often promote visions of new social relations and meanings. For example, a national organization for lesbian mothers adopted the name Momazons to emphasize the previously unrecognized connection between woman loving and motherhood.

In recent work exploring the impact of media discourse on public opinion, Gamson (1988) conceptualizes discourse as the entire culture surrounding a contested issue. Issue cultures include the themes and counterthemes found in a variety of public discourses—including the discourses of specialists, the media, sponsors, and challengers. The public discourse about an issue can be thought of as a set of interpretive packages that frame or give meaning to an issue. The self-help movement that emerged to address the problem of postpartum depression illustrates the way that social movement discourse influences public discourse to create new frames that redefine experiences previously viewed in individual terms as collective and based on women's subordination as a "sex class."

The postpartum depression self-help movement crystallized in the mid-1980s out of the experiences of women who underwent major depression or psychotic illness following the birth of a child. Women who sought treatment for their conditions found established health and mental health providers unwilling to acknowledge a link between their problems and the organic and social events associated with childbirth and mothering. The dominant public discourse that activists contested framed *mother love as instinctive,* denying the existence of negative emotions, let alone serious mental illness, following childbirth. In both the popular media written to appeal to new mothers and the professional discourses of medicine and psychiatry, new mothers were depicted as fulfilled, overwhelmed with joy, and instinctively bonded with their newborn babies. The Diagnostic and Statistical Manual of the American Psychiatric Association, the official handbook of mental illness, failed to recognize postpartum conditions as a distinct syndrome, thus denying women access to medical treatment and resources.

Beginning in the mid-1980s, activists set out to call attention to what they believed to be a high incidence of depression and psychosis associated with childbirth. They drew from their experiences in the women's health movement to justify attention to the problem as a women's issue and launched a self-help movement to stake out a territory where women could define their emotional experiences for themselves, apart from male-dominated professional views, and find sources of support and treatment. The movement initially gathered steam by calling attention to the organic or hormonal basis of postpartum depression as a means of neutralizing the stigma associated with maternal mental illness. The issue of postpartum depression was packaged, that is, as *a psychiatric illness.*

Beginning with an appearance on the Phil Donahue television show in 1986, the movement sought and gained widespread media attention to the problem of postpartum depression. A critical discourse moment occurred in 1988 when a nurse from Los Angeles who had killed her nine-month-old son during a postpartum psychotic episode and was found not guilty by virtue of temporary insanity appeared with movement activists on the *Larry King Live,* *Phil Donahue,* and *Sally Jessy Raphael* shows. The issue of infanticide resonated well with the standard "newsmaking" practices of the media and resulted throughout 1988 in greater attention in the public discourse to the issue of postpartum depression and psychosis. Widespread media attention to postpartum psychosis and depression led to rapid growth in the movement and, in turn, seems to have contributed to a larger number of scholarly articles on the topic by medical professionals. But the dominant medical discourse framed in terms of psychiatric illness restated, almost more emphatically than ever, the lack of any organic basis for postpartum depression or psychosis following childbirth.

By the early 1990s, increased pressure by activists on medical providers to care for women suffering postpartum conditions combined with a growing economic crisis in health care and rising competition between hospitals for fewer patients helped to accelerate a shift from a *psychiatric illness* frame to a *women's rights* frame. From the outset, some of the movement's leaders who had a prior history of feminist and civil rights activism had traced postpartum depression to social and cultural factors, namely, the sexual division of labor in the family that gives women primary responsibility for rearing and nurturing children, the devaluation of motherhood in modern industrialized society, and the discourses and professional practices of medicine that reinforce male dominance. The movement increasingly began to promote collective as well as individual solutions to postpartum depression and psychosis. Activists promoted strategies geared toward redefining the emotional expectations of motherhood to include the negative as well as the positive emotions experienced by new mothers; pushed for changes in social policies that empower women such as increased federal funding for research on women's health, modifications in perinatal medical practices, the establishment of a postpartum psychiatric legal defense, and accessible day care and child care; and even talked openly about the redefinition of the traditional gender division of labor in the family. Ironically, medical providers, especially hospitals seeking to enlarge their domain of services by sponsoring women's health programming and community outreach, show signs of support for a women's rights frame that justifies attention to postpartum emotional problems on the basis of social rather than strictly medical criteria.

The analysis of public discourse is an important method for understanding the role of movement culture in mobilization. Further, the recent focus on movement discourse calls attention to a set of strategies and outcomes that have been overlooked by resource mobilization approaches. At the same time, it should be emphasized that discourse analysis, as practiced by scholars such as McCarthy (1994) and Gamson (1988), advocates the place of both cultural and structural factors in the analysis of mobilization. For, as Gamson (1988) contends, the relative success of a discourse can be understood only by examining factors such as the differential access to power and resources of the advocates of competing frames.

Conclusion

To call for renewed attention to the symbolic and cultural components of social movements represents, in a way, a return to questions that drove classical collective behavior theorists before resource mobilization and political process perspectives rose to dominance. But the questions we ask about culture this time around are influenced by nearly twenty years of research on social movements that has been deeply enriched by the attention to organization, political process, and rational strategic action emphasized by resource mobilization and political process approaches (Gamson 1990; McCarthy and Zald 1987; McAdam 1982; Jenkins 1983; Morris 1984).

New social movement theorists trace the renewed attention to culture to new characteristics of contemporary challenges (Cohen 1985; Touraine 1985; Melucci 1989). We think, however, that the creation of shared cultural codes and new frames of understanding that reinterpret contested issues are an element of all social movements. Empirical research on the cultural processes of social movements requires a conceptualization of culture that specifies the relationship between symbolic codes and social relations and identifies the observable components of culture. Our goal in this essay has been to draw from cultural analysis in collective behavior and social movements to lay out some possible approaches. We have framed the discussion around four key dimensions that grow out of the major theoretical approaches to culture in sociology: emergent values and norms, collective identity, ritual, and discourse.

Although cultural questions were central to classical collective behavior theorists, we come to the study of culture this time with a slightly different eye. Increasingly, the emphasis in sociology is on what Swidler (1986) terms "culture in action," or the social contexts in which culture is produced. Consistent with theorists who tie the analysis of culture to structural inequality, recent cultural analysis in the field of social movements underscores the integration of structural and cultural explanations. To understand the link between symbols, ideas, and meaning, on the one hand, and social protest, on the other, is not simply a matter of deconstructing texts and cultural codes. We must also attend to the matters of resources, power, and organization.

There are, of course, many who will insist that culture functions principally to constrain protest by symbolically reproducing social structural inequality. We argue, however, that ideas and symbols can also function as resources that supply opportunities for activists to mobilize concrete struggles for social change. If, as Swidler (1986) argues, cultural change can only be accomplished with the construction of new repertoires of action, or "tool kits," social movements surely must be considered to be among the major carpenters of change (Wuthnow 1989). Focusing on the ways that social movements are engaged in the production of culture is one of the most promising avenues of research for scholars interested in bringing the actor back into the study of social change.

Notes

This research was funded in part by the Ohio Department of Mental Health Office of Research and Evaluation, an Ohio State University Seed Grant, an Ohio State University Women's Studies Small Grant, and the Smith College Committee on Faculty and Curriculum Development. We gratefully acknowledge Rob Benford, Rick Fantasia, William Gamson, Aldon Morris, Carol Mueller, Leila Rupp, David Snow, Suzanne Staggenborg, Kate Weigand, Gilda Zwerman, and the editors of this volume, whose astute comments and criticisms helped us to revise earlier drafts of this essay.

Chapter 10

Charting Degrees of Movement Culture: Tasks of the Cultural Cartographer

John Lofland

In this chapter I will discuss topics and questions important to address in the task of charting the structure of social movement culture in terms of degree or extent. The phrase "charting the structure" is the earmark of what I will discuss—and therefore of what I will not discuss. As usefully mapped by Wuthnow and Witten, sociological studies of culture vary along the two major dimensions of (1) conceiving culture as an "implicit feature of social life" as opposed to viewing it as an "explicit social construction" and (2) focus on "social contexts in which culture is produced" (i. e., "causes" of it) as opposed to focus on "the content of these products themselves" (Wuthnow and Witten 1988: 5, 65, italics omitted).

Viewed in the Wuthnow and Witten scheme, my effort here is addressed to explicit rather than implicit culture and to the "content of the products" we call culture rather than to their causes. Historically, these combined foci provided the major approach of classic anthropological studies, which centered on mapping kinship systems but also depicted the explicit structures of many other kinds of cultural substance (Singer 1968; Kroeber and Kluckhohn 1963). Indeed, I view my treatment as very much in this classic and uncomplicatedly empirical tradition. (I am not, however, at all critical of the other three main foci formed from the conjunction of Wuthnow and Witten's two variables.)

Within this focus on charting the explicit structure of culture, I want to give central attention to the fact that human associations—social movements specifically—vary in the *amount or degree* of culture we find in them. In social movements (as in other formations) culture can usefully be thought of as a *variable,* as something that some movements have more of than do others. I will explain and apply six basic and formal dimensions of culture so conceived, showing how movements differ quite dramatically in their cultural extent or degree. I use the qualifying term *formal* to set these six dimensions of variation off from variations in substantive content. This distinction is the familiar one of form versus content, or of formal versus historically specific sociology. One might object that any discussion of culture must address content—that a purely formal discussion misses the essence of culture, which resides in such matters as the substantive goals and values involved with conduct. My answer to this objection is that the substance of culture is obviously important, and it is, indeed, something we need to take into account in complete analyses of culture and of social movements. I offer these formal matters as additions to— rather than as substitutes for—the analysis of substance.

Why Chart Degrees of Movement Culture?

Before setting out to chart degrees of movement culture, we must first answer a logically prior and key question: Why should we bother to do this? What results of this enterprise will justify the effort? I think there are at least three gains to be realized that warrant our efforts.

There is, first, the basic need for what is sometimes termed "analytic description" of movements per se, whether it is centered on culture or on some other aspect of movements. If we are to study something, one critical phase is to develop orderly (and theoretically relevant) depictions of the objects we seek to understand. Irrespective of whether we plan to treat such analytic descriptions as "dependent" or "independent" variables, in the first instance we are well advised to have solid and appropriately rich depictions of whatever the "thing" that concerns us is. This point may seem too obvious and basic to justify mentioning it, but the fact of the matter is that adequate analytic descriptions are sorely lacking in movement studies. Instead, we get all manner of anemic sketches of critical movement matters that are likely to be misleading or wrong because of their empirical thinness or their analytic over-simplification (e.g., Gamson 1990). This most basic justification, then, is generic rather than confined to culture, but no less important on that account.

Second, effectively charted degrees of movement culture should be treated as "dependent variables," as consequences of other variables that are causing variations in degrees of movement culture we are observing. Why are some movement cultures much more developed than others? What variations in social contexts lead some movements to have cultures that are differentially developed along a variety of dimensions? What about the context provided by *other* cultures in which a movement develops determines what cultural elements will or will not be adopted in a given social movement? Cast in different terms, the point is that existing cultures are resources that are differentially accessed by given movements (Swidler 1986). How does this happen and with what consequences for degrees of movement culture?

Third, formal variations in degrees of movement culture need also to be analyzed as "independent variables," as among variables that affect a wide variety of "dependent variables" of established and central interest in movement studies. One venerable proposition about social movements, for example, is that the more complex and the richer a movement culture, the higher participant morale and, therefore, commitment and tenacity in the face of adversity and retention of movement participants (e.g., Taylor 1989; Kanter 1972). While we tend to regard this proposition as a truism, we really do not know if it is true or not in the sense of having passed adequate tests of systematic inquiry. One requirement of even formulating such a test is a measure of culture, which itself presumes an analysis of degrees of movement culture of the sort I propose. Yet other propositions link degrees of culture to such dependent variables as degree of mobilization potential, degree of success in movement campaigns, and overall degree of movement success (e.g., Oberschall 1973: 144). Again, in terms of systematic empirical inquiry, we have no carefully grounded assessments of the degree to which, or ways in which, any of these variables may be linked to degrees of movement culture.

Taken overall, then, the first aim is to elevate the idea of culture to the level of a systematically conceived variable that allows us to formulate profiles of varying movement cultures. This then opens the way to the comparative analysis of movement cultures and to their scrutiny as both dependent and independent variables.

Culture and Cultural Locations

Hardly anyone agrees with anyone on a definition of the concept of "culture," but almost everyone agrees that it is among the most elusive and difficult to specify of social science concepts (Kroeber and Kluckhohn 1963; Singer 1968; Gilmore 1992). Moreover, it has been hard to get beyond regarding culture as what Gary Fine calls "an amorphous mist which swirls around society members" (1979: 733). Until recently, definitional and conceptual elusiveness has retarded efforts to analyze culture. The recent renaissance in the study of culture may have been facilitated, however, by people's deciding not to worry too much about exactly what culture "is" and how to conceive it. Instead, let us simply get on with looking at matters that we intuit to be cultural, even if we cannot provide a precise formulation of "it." I am sympathetic to this spirit of pragmatic intuition and I therefore propose not to be overly concerned here with definitions and the epistemology of conceptualization. That said, a definition in the sense of a broad orientation nonetheless remains in order, and Kroeber and Kluckhohn's synthetic effort of 1952 continues to be serviceable:

> Culture consists of patterns, explicit and implicit, of and for behavior acquired and transmitted by symbols, constituting the distinctive achievement of human groups, including their embodiments in artifacts; the essential core of culture consists of traditional (i.e. historically derived and selected) ideas and especially their attached values; culture systems may, on the one hand, be considered as products of action, on the other as conditioning elements of further action. (1963: 357)

If this is, roughly, what culture "is," one next question is how to think about it more specifically. In their elaborate review and analysis of some three hundred definitions and other discussions of the concept of culture, Kroeber and Kluckhohn conceive the task of being more specific as the question of "the components of culture," the "stuff of which culture is composed" (1963: 183-90). Surveying answers to this question, they find that anthropologists have "been reluctant to classify culture into its topical parts. They have sensed that the categories are not logically definite, but are subjectively fluid and serve no end beyond that of convenience, and thus would shift according to interest and context" (186).

Even though they are shifting and pragmatic, several schemes of compo nents of culture have been advanced. One of the most elaborate—and quaintly classic—consists of the nine categories of:

> Speech—Material traits—Art—Mythology—Knowledge—Religion—Family and Social systems—Property—Government and War. (Bose 1929: 25, quoted in Kroeber and Kluckhohn 1963: 182)

Another approach of some currency envisions a trichotomous division among (1) material culture or techniques, (2) social relationships ("social culture") or recognition, and (3) ideas, "insight," or "spiritual culture" (Kroeber and Kluckhohn 1963: 187-90).

Again, Kroeber and Kluckhohn tell us that "anthropologists have fought shy of trying to make formal classification of the components of culture. Being mostly preoccupied with dealing with cultures substantively, such classification has evidently seemed to them a matter of mainly pragmatic convenience, and they have dealt with it in an ad hoc manner" (1963: 187).

The state of efforts to classify components of culture has changed little since Kroeber and Kluckhohn's assessment, written in the early fifties. We are therefore forced to bring to the question of the components of culture the same pragmatic intuition that has also been necessary—and serves us— regarding a definition of culture. (Note, moreover, that Kroeber and Kluck- hohn tell us that a similar pragmatic spirit was very much in evidence among anthropologists historically.)

In such a spirit, let us ask, If we want to observe culture, where and at what should we look? Might there be some social locations in (or aspects of) a social movement formation where culture is more conspicuous or prominent than in other locations (or aspects)? If so, what might they be? Informed by the definitions of culture and efforts to discern components I referred to earli- er, I find it helpful to look to six kinds of matters as especially embodying this "amorphous mist" we call culture. These are:

1. Expressions of general *value*s that are distinctive enough to justify asserting that there is a "movement" in the first place.

2. Material *objects* and associated iconic personages that are held in high public esteem in a movement.

3. Everyday *stories* told and retold with strong positive or negative emo- tional expression among participants in a movement.

4. Characteristics of the movement's *occasions* (gatherings) that are regarded as positive features of the movement.

5. Social *roles* that specialize in the creation and dissemination of ideas, artifacts, and performances endowed with positive value.

6. Ways in which these specialized and other roles are expressed in the *persona* exhibited by participants.

Another way to think of these six social "locations" is as operationalizing bridges between the extremely abstract concept of culture, on the one side, and the minutiae of everyday life as it swirls around us, on the other. I must stress that in offering and using these six I do not mean to imply that there are only six, or even that these six might be the most important "locations" in all social movements or for the purposes of all analyses. Much more modest- ly and in the spirt of the historic and recent pragmatic utility I referred to ear- lier, I am only saying that it is easier—at least for me—to "see" culture in these places. Further, and this should be obvious, these six are mostly and only basic, "meat and potatoes" units of sociological analysis—such prosaic conceptual units as roles, gatherings, and the material objects found in a social scene.

Dimensions and Degrees of Movement Culture

In each of the six locations just enumerated (as well in other locations we might specify), we are likely to find that culture is developed to different degrees, that is, to different extents. Looking back at the six locations and thinking in terms of degree or extent, the notion of *enumeration* contained in the ideas of degree and extent invite us to think of each category as containing *units* of culture that we might call, simply, cultural items. In one basic form, we begin to think of the sheer number of items we might find in each of the six.

Adopting that logic, we can then go on to think about degree or extent in terms of yet other dimensions that elucidate the idea of culture as a variable. In so doing, I think at least six such dimensions are evident.

1. When we begin to compare movements we observe that they vary with respect to the degree that their participants agree on or *share* the same complex of cultural items, whether these items are distinctive to the movement or not. This is the question of cultural diversity versus consensus within a movement.

2. Holding aside (or "constant") cultural agreement or sharing, movements vary in terms of the number or proportion of their cultural items that are *distinctive* to the movement. At one extreme, a few movements elaborate a wide range of movement-distinctive cultural matters; at the other, participants are almost indistinguishable culturally from other members of society.

3. Cultures can be quite narrow or situation-specific in *scope* or quite wide, specifying, for example, appropriate beliefs and actions for every conceivable circumstance and topic.

4. Within a particular category of cultural item, we observe variation in degrees of *elaboration* or complexity.

5. Some forms of culture—particularly items of material culture—vary in terms of their sheer numbers or the *quantity* in which they are produced, a matter related to but not the same as complexity. (This is the dimension I use to typify the logic of culture as a variable.)

6. Specific items of culture and the array of cultural matters differ in the degree to which members emotionally and positively experience them as expressing or embodying their values and life circumstances, as providing occasions of transcending the mundane in *expressive symbolism* (Jaeger and Selznick 1964).

These six dimensions (and others we might use) allow us to chart degrees of movement culture, to assess the extent to which (and ways in which) one or another movement is "doing culture." Movements tending to higher values on these dimensions are—in a noninvidious and technical sense—"more cultured," "culturally rich," or "culturally developed." Movements that are "lower" in these respects are "less cultured," "culturally poor," or "culturally undeveloped." Of course, we are also likely to find that all these dimensions do not move in concert, and that, further, different classes of cultural items may have varying profiles even though there is a global movement degree of culture.

Locations and Dimensions of Degrees Conjoined and Referents Specified

The social locations or places in which to look for culture are also places in which to assess the degree of development of each of the six formal dimensions of culture. We need, that is, to inspect locations of culture vis-à-vis the dimensions of culture. This relationship is displayed graphically in Figure 10.1.

I frame my task in what follows as elaborating important questions we need to ask in assessing degrees of movement culture at the level of relatively specific cultural items. To put it another way, I seek to provide a set of guiding questions for inquiry.

My treatment is therefore programmatic in character and must be distinguished from at least two other approaches that might be taken—and that I hope that others might take. One of these is the encyclopedic task of profiling degrees of movement cultures in exhaustive detail. The other is to elaborate a detailed research protocol in terms of which movement cultures can be measured with precision. In research technology terms, this would be a code book for categorizing the minutiae of movement cultures. Viewed as a process, my effort in this chapter is temporally and conceptually prior to either of these worthy and strenuous efforts.

I have thus far been unspecific about the exact "units" or "social formations" for which we want to chart degree of movement culture. Instead, I have merely used the unspecified term *social movement*. The concept of social movement has, however, two very different referents, and we must sharply distinguish between them in order to proceed with appropriate precision.[1]

The first referent of the idea of social movement is to amorphous, sprawling, and far-flung *conglomerations* of organizations, activists, campaigns, and the like that are construed to share social or personal change goals. The concept of the "social movement industry" is an alternative label for such con-

Dimensions of degrees

Locations	Sharing	Distinctiveness	Scope	Elaboration	Quantity	Expressiveness
Values						
Objects						
Stories						
Occasions						
Roles						
Personae						

Figure 10.1. Locations and dimensions of degrees of culture

glomerations that captures the same sense of multiple movement organizations and associated persons and activities that participants believe to be
working on the same general set of problems (McCarthy and Zald 1987: 21).

The second referent of the term *social movement* is to a named formal *organization* dedicated to achieving or preventing some significant social or personal change. These entities commonly but not always have an office, phone,
publication, list of members, and other accoutrements of explicit association.
Because of such features, one can literally telephone and physically visit
movement organizations, such as, for example, the peace movement organization called Grandmothers for Peace. In contrast, as a broad bracketing of
hundreds or thousands of such movement organizations and other persons
and activities, conglomerations cannot be located in any single place or simply phoned up. You cannot, in a simple sense, telephone or visit the peace
movement in the United States. Instead, if you want to speak by phone or visit
with a conglomeration, you have to make contact with hundreds or thousands
of organizations (and individuals and activities).

In what follows I focus on conglomerations rather than on movement organizations, on sprawling mélanges of hodgepodged entities nonetheless coherent enough to justify labeling them social movements. As further background, let me also report that my discussion here is a generalization of a
case study I have published elsewhere and in which I initially generated the
outline of the present analysis. That case study is an assessment of the degree
(and form) of cultural development in the American peace movement of the
1980s (Lofland 1993: chapter 3). Indeed, after specifying questions that can
guide profiling degrees of movement culture, I will report a summary of my
assessment of that case in order to show how the guiding questions can be
applied and further to elaborate a direction in which comparative analysis of
movement cultures might move.[2]

Charting Degrees of Movement Culture: Guiding Questions

Let me now paint, in a broad-brush manner, major kinds of questions (together with some tentative answers) that can help in guiding assessment of
degrees of movement culture. As I have indicated, my discussion is organized
in terms of the "locations" of culture explained earlier.

Values

The term *values* calls attention to the positive goals that movement members want to achieve—to realize in the "real world." As highly abstract objects

that are diffuse and elusive, values can be difficult to discern. One practical way to begin catching hold of them is to give close attention to the names or labels that participants apply to their enterprises and that modify the term *movement*. In so doing, one is likely to find that participants in "a" movement use diverse labels. This diversity of adjectives modifying the word *movement* is then itself a suggestion of the multiplicity of values that may be guiding a movement that otherwise has a single and overarching name. For example, in the case of the American "peace movement" of the 1980s many people used the adjective/value *peace,* but these same people (and yet others) used a variety of other terms, including the following:

freeze movement	anti–nuclear war movement
anti-nuclear-weapons movement	disarmament movement
antiwar movement	arms control movement
citizen diplomacy movement	sister city movement
nuclear disarmament movement	arms reduction movement
anti-intervention movement	anti-imperialist movement
peace and justice movement	sanctuary movement

Such a diversity of labels suggests that while "peace" may be a shared value, this value is translated into action in a wide variety of ways. Stated in terms of the first dimension of variation in movement culture (column 1 in Figure 10.1), while peace was a shared value, values pertaining to more specific goals and foci of achieving peace were not widely shared. In fact, many people using one or another of the labels listed here were uncomfortable about also thinking of themselves as part of the "peace movement"—although yet other movement participants applied this label to them.

In order to say that there is a movement, we must be able to identify at least one such shared value, otherwise, there is, by definition, no movement (only a disparate collection of enterprises that we as analysts have ourselves fabricated in our minds as a movement). For most movements there may be, in fact, only one such value and, indeed, a value that is highly abstract. This preeminent value is commonly and publicly communicated to us in the name of the movement, as in peace, feminist, civil rights, environment, wise use, labor, pro-choice, pro-life, or whatever.

In addition to compiling names people give a movement as clues to values, it can also be helpful to compile names people give their forms of association. Elise Boulding performed such a compilation for peace groups of the 1980s, finding themes that portrayed the movement as composed of ordinary people "joining together in concern" with a sense of urgency combined with community and informality (1990: 32). Terms conveying these themes included *people, citizens, action, initiative, committee,* and *community.*

The other five dimensions of culture variation shown in Figure 10.1 encourage us to attend to these further variations and degrees concerning values.

To what degree are the movement's values different from or similar to values observed in the society at large? That is, how *distinctive* are the values? Sometimes, many if not all the movement values can also be found in the containing society. Such overlaps have been referred to as "bridges" to the host society. The degree to which there are (or are not) such bridges then enters into the degree to which the movement is defined as legitimate (Turner and Killian 1987: chapter 14). Thus, in the case of the American peace movement of the 1980s, the overwhelming proportion of Americans subscribed to the abstract ideal of "peace" (especially at Christmastime), even if they definitely did not embrace the specific actions the movement claimed would promote peace.

So, also, the more concrete and major forms of action seen within the peace movement were also valued forms of acting and believing in all or some segments of the society more generally. These major forms of conventional action were the civic and consensual boosterism of the "transcenders" cluster within the movement; the communication earnestness of the educator cluster; the scholarly disciplines of the intellectuals; the political practices of the politicians; the restrained civil disobedience of the protesters; and the radical religiosity of the prophets (Lofland 1993: chapter 1). While the substance of each of these actions was very much social movement in nature, each was *also and in form* a familiar mode of socially sanctioned—or valued—action (i.e., American boosterism, education, scholarly work, politics, nonviolent dissent, and earnest religiosity).

On the other hand, to the degree that the values are distinctive—that is, discontinuous with or in opposition to societal values—legitimacy becomes problematic. In some cases, the set of values espoused by a movement will be a complex composite of both overlapping and distinctive values. Complexity of this sort then sets the stage for contentious interactions between the movement and others over ways in which the movement is or is not legitimate.

To what degree do a movement's members espouse values that pertain to the entire range of human life? That is, how wide is the *scope* of human life for which values are enunciated? One straightforward way to conceptualize scope is in terms of major institutional realms and forms of human social organization. A fairly standard list includes these areas of human social life: economic, political, religious, social class, ethnicity, gender, age, family/intimate relations, education, criminal justice and crime, health and health care, natural environment, built environment.

At one extreme, some few movements are exceedingly ambitious and undertake to specify the values that ought to be realized with respect to each and all of these areas (and such statements are commonly accompanied by proposed schemes of action that embody the values). At least in most industrial democracies, however, many if not most movements are much more modest and confine themselves to a single institutional realm, and even to a specific area within one realm.

Movements as conglomerates, however, present a complex picture. In them, one is likely to find segments that are narrower in their value pronouncements *and* segments that move toward more all-encompassing statements of values pertaining to many or all institutional realms.

As it pertains to values, the dimension of *elaboration* refers to the degree of detail with which values are stated. At the more developed end of this dimension, a movement may feature "elaborate treatises of an abstract and highly logical character" in which the values are given "erudite and scholarly" rendition (Blumer 1969: 110). Conversely, the values may be stated in only a cryptic fashion and be quite indefinite and undefined, functioning more as vague images than as detailed renditions of ideal arrangements and positive goals.

Correlated with but separate from the dimensions of scope and elaboration is the matter of the sheer *quantity* of values in the senses of exactly how many of them we can count and the amounts of social and physical space that we find them occupying in a movement. Movements that enunciate a wide scope of values and elaborate each of them to a high degree are, of course, also likely to display larger quantities of values in these three senses.

Items of a culture are *expressive* to the degree that participants emotionally experience them as portraying their most deeply felt commitments, aspirations, and hopes and noblest sentiments. By definition, highly expressive cultural matters prompt these types of emotional experiences:

moving	poignant	touching
eloquent	rich	meaningful
alive	pregnant	spirited
lively	spiritual	

In contrast, cultural matters that lack expressiveness are experienced in these ways:

banal	drab	dull
flat	insipid	vacuous
wooden	boring	empty
vacant	dead	

These contrasting sets of adjectives address the question of the qualitative characteristics of the emotional experience of culture. The more the first set of emotional experiences is evoked, the more expressive is the culture. The more the second set is evoked, the less expressive is the culture. The theoretical framework and rationale for treating expressiveness as a variable dimension of culture has been elaborated by Jaeger and Selznick (1964). In the perspective they develop, the "symbolic value" or "expressive symbolism" of culture, arises

> in order to continue and sustain meaningful experience. The wearing of black respects and prolongs the experience of mourning, of confronted death. Festivities rich in symbolism can help consummate an experience that would otherwise be brief and incomplete. In the presence of the symbol, people respond in ways that nurture rather than attenuate the experience. Moreover, having had "an experience," [humans] . . . create a symbol of it in order that the experience may be re-evoked and relived. . . .
>
> [Expressive] symbols help to provide focus, direction, and shape to what otherwise might disintegrate into chaotic feeling or the absence of feeling. . . . By serving as vehicles of response, symbols can help transform a "mere" feeling, a vague somatic tension, into genuine emotion. Thus symbols do more than sustain emotion. They contribute to the emergence of emotion as a uniquely human attribute. (1964: 662-63)

Applying these ideas to values, we need to inquire into the degree to which the mention or other treatment of values in given situations is accompanied by what kinds of emotional experiences. For example, to what degree does the mere mention of a movement's name (its core value) send shivers up and down the necks and backs of members, move them to tears, to spasms of joy, or whatever emotional expressions?

Objects

In cultural perspective, the symbolic objects of a movement are the material items that participants view as physically expressing their enterprise, including remembrances of its successes or trials and hopes for its future. Such objects are of at least five main kinds: movement identifiers, iconic persons, key artifacts, central events, and symbolic places.

Some few social formations are strikingly lush in symbolic objects of these sorts; religious organizations are especially prone to generate ornate special buildings, garb, ceremonial objects, and even elaborate statuary.[3] Other formations generate few symbolic objects and may even explicitly oppose elaborate ones, yet the few they do generate may be distinctive (the Quakers' and the Shakers' antisymbolism, for example, itself became an elegant symbolism).

Identifiers

A great many movement *organizations* devise a distinctive symbol or logo, an eye-catching representation that serves instantly to communicate the identity of the organization. In the 1980s peace movement, for example, Beyond War used a striking green and blue representation of the planet Earth. The venerable War Resisters League continued use of its long-standing symbol of two crossed and broken rifles. In the peace movement as conglomeration, however, a large portion of movement organizations were not national in scale of operation, unlike the two just mentioned. Instead, most were local, free-standing, and all-volunteer, possessing only the most modest of financial and other resources. Consistent with such simplicity, these little entities also did not have their own identifier symbols, although some borrowed one or more that were more widely known.

Indicative of the thinness of culture at the level of movements as conglomerates, many have no instant identifiers, or there are multiple identifiers that are used by some but not all segments of the conglomerate. Continuing with the peace movement of the 1980s example, there was, of course, the "peace symbol," but it was not in fact used all that frequently and not even known to some younger participants. (It had the additional problem of not clearly symbolizing anything, and its historical origin and meaning were even disputed.) The white dove was used widely (but far from universally), rendered in a great many ways. The mushroom cloud of a nuclear explosion was seen frequently, but this was an icon of a less than positive emotional expressiveness.

Persons

The phenomenon of the charismatic leader is the most fully developed case of persons as highly expressive symbolic objects for movement organizations or conglomerates. Instances of such symbolic persons in diverse movements have included Jesus of Nazareth, Karl Marx, V. I. Lenin, Adolph Hitler, Mao Tse-tung, and Sun Myung Moon. Among movements as a general class, though, charismatic personages are rather rare. Instead, selected figures come to be venerated and endowed with symbolic expressiveness without also being thought to possess extraordinary capacities that transcend normal human limitations.

One important way to begin to gauge the cultural contours of a movement conglomerate is to conduct a census of movement persons who are mentioned publicly with some frequency and referred to as sources of authoritative or other important enunciations. This list can then be scrutinized in terms of the five dimensions of cultural development shown in Figure 10.1 regarding the degree to which they:

- are known to and revered by participants in the movement conglomerate (sharing);
- overlap with revered figures in the larger society (distinctiveness);
- represent diverse institutional realms (scope);
- are subjects of a great deal of or very little symbolic representation, as in hanging their pictures or placing their statues in conspicuous places, distributing writings by and about them (elaboration);
- are many or few in number when viewed in comparative movement perspective (quantity);
- stimulate expressive emotional experiences in movement members (expressiveness).

Artifacts

Perhaps the most physically cultural way to look at a movement is simply to inventory the transportable and literal objects that are "part" of it. Such inventories vary across movements in terms of their number, size and weight, market value, distinctiveness, and the like. Presumptively, the higher a movement's rank on these dimensions (comparatively speaking), the more materialistic it is, as well as the more cultured.

Like values and other aspects of culture, artifacts divide into those endowed by participants with symbolic value or expressive symbolism and those regarded as mere neutral instruments. One further way, then, to scrutinize the artifacts observed on the bodies of participants, brought to their gatherings, and found at places of movement habitation is in terms of which, if any, of those artifacts are fondly regarded (i.e., have symbolic significance) as distinct from merely used. Prime candidates for such expressive symbolism in movements include certain prized posters from past campaigns, particular copies of certain books and other publications, unusual souvenirs from past striking events, and photographs of movement people.

Events

The histories of human striving are punctuated by space- and time-bracketed actions in which long-term and diffuse fears or aspirations are rendered momentarily visible in decisive victories or defeats. The crucifixion and "resurrection" of Jesus and the signing of the Declaration of Independence are examples of such events in their respective movements. Each is commemorated and celebrated as an occasion of value clarification and rejuvenation. Such iconic events are, of course, as much constructed as objectively perceived. Therefore, many more episodes are candidates for use than actually get constructed as such, and the degree to which a movement "has" them tells us more about the level of its cultural enterprise and development than about its iconic history (though not all events are equally suitable for iconic construction).

One way cultural entrepreneurs in some movements seek to develop iconic events is to piggyback on established (mainstream) symbolic days by overlaying the mainstream symbolism with movement symbolism. Mother's Day and Good Friday have been the particular objects of such overlaying by, especially, the feminist and peace movements. For example, peace movement acts of civil disobedience have sometimes been scheduled on Good Friday and accompanied by appropriate religious ceremonials as a way of encouraging people to think of civil resistance as a religious activity. An effort is made, that is, to elevate an otherwise simply political or illegal action to the level of the expressively spiritual and cosmic. The piggybacking aspect resides in using traditional religious cultural significance expressively to define movement purposes and acts. (Relative to the distinctiveness dimension, such piggybacking also serves as a bridge to the encompassing culture.)

Places

Movements vary in the degree to which given spaces or places come to be defined as recalling and expressing "the movement." For a few movements, a single, particular place gets defined as *the* revered place—the either literal or metaphorical Mecca of the movement. Movement places can be analyzed in the same way as the cast of venerated persons in order to reveal degrees and forms of cultural development. To what degree are culturally endowed movement places:

- known to movement members (shared in the sheer sense of knowledge)?

- the same as or different from revered places in the culture at large (distinctiveness)?

- addressed to a diverse or narrow range of matters of concern in human life (scope)?

- simple or complex (or expensive or inexpensive) in their construction and furnishing (elaboration)?

- abundant versus few in number (quantity)?

- evocative of intense emotional experiences and scenes of public and dramatic emotional display (as in gyrations of joy or torrents of tears) (expressiveness)?

Stories

We commonly observe a movement's people espousing distinctive values, propounding various kinds of substantive beliefs about desired social changes, and expressing and acting on diverse theories of the actions required to achieve those changes. These three activities do not, however, exhaust the ideological work that we observe in the everyday life of movements. To read the writings of movement members and to listen to them talk among themselves is to encounter a stream of what we might think of as "movement stories," or, when they're compressed, as "movement slogans" (Wuthnow and Witten 1988: 67). These are homely folktales, pithy sayings, and special labels that contribute to a movement's distinctive cultural ambience. In his classic depiction of social movements, Herbert Blumer calls attention to such storytelling as the "popular character" of ideology in "the form of emotional symbols, shibboleths, stereotypes, smooth and graphic phrases, and folk arguments" (1969: 111). In chapter 7 of this volume, Gary Fine treats this aspect of culture as "bundles of narratives," focusing on the three major types of such narratives: horror stories, war stories, and stories with happy endings.

Movements vary in the degree to which such "stories" circulate among the members. In some few movement organizations, ordinary language is so laced with argot that day-to-day talk and common movement writing is virtually unintelligible to outsiders—or if it is intelligible, it seems strikingly novel or alien. At the level of movement conglomerates, though, there are likely to be relatively few of these forms of special understanding. In whatever event, the cartographer of movement culture seeks to enumerate stories and to assess them as a set in terms of the six dimensions of degree of cultural development.

Occasions

The occasions on which movement participants assemble face to face provide many opportunities for richer or poorer cultural enactment. Even gatherings that are for instruction or work—as opposed to celebrations—can vary in the distinctiveness and extent of cultural display.

On a virtually global scale, the quintessential form of movement occasion has become the march/rally. Irrespective of society, culture, or movement, march/rallies exhibit a remarkably similar form that features marchers carrying banners and placards and a parade of speakers from organizations in coalition that is punctuated by folksy musical entertainment. One cultural challenge to social movements is, indeed, to avoid the deadly sameness of this kind of key event. In recent times, cultural innovation with respect to the march/rally has, in fact, been seen with increasing frequency, and these innovations are reasonably viewed as responding to a need for increased degrees of cultural expressiveness (see, for example, B. Epstein 1990a).

The music sung (or not sung) at movement occasions is always, of course, of particular cultural interest. Similar to the prevalence of the standard march/rally, the song "We Shall Overcome" has become the virtually global and all-purpose movement anthem, sung even in conservative movements despite its leftish origin.

Roles

While culture pertains to everyone, everyone does not have an equal relation to it or an equal role in its creation, elaboration, preservation, chronicling, performance, or dissemination. Instead, some people are likely to "do" culture much more than others and to do so in specialized roles. And movements differ in the degree, *variety,* and *number* engaged in such specialized roles. These specialized roles themselves divide into those that create (or elaborate) culture and those that are particularly occupied with disseminating it.

Creators

One key category of culture is the ensemble of concepts, assertions, precepts, presumed facts, and other cognitions labeled "knowledge." This body of knowledge is mostly created by people who work at that task with continuity and diligence. They are therefore "knowledge workers," otherwise called intellectuals, artists, and scholars. So, too, the products of knowledge workers divide roughly into items that are more scientific, or analytic, versus more artistic, or humanistic. The former are said to produce analysis or science, while the latter provide art and literature.

Institutions of higher education and journalism, along with the wealth of foundations and individuals, have created an infrastructure on which has risen a social class of intellectuals. Portions of this social class function as the continuing culture creators (and elaborators) of many social movements. In inspecting social movements as conglomerates, in particular, one basic task is to identify their strata of analytic and and humanistic intellectuals and to profile each in terms of the six dimensions of cultural development. In particular, there are these kinds of questions:

- How many people can we say function as analytic or humanistic intellectuals for a given movement?

- Among the analytic intellectuals, how many journals and other publications claim to be doing serious scholarship and seek to engage mainstream intellectuals working on the same topics?

- How productive are the analytic and humanistic intellectuals along such lines as the number of books, journal articles, novels, poems, plays, musical compositions, literary criticisms, and the like that they create in given units of time?

- Using conventional categories of scholarship, what sort of intellectuals (historians, physicists, economists, or whatever) do these tend to be?

- What is the general size of the corpus of movement intellectual materials that these intellectuals have produced over one or more decades?

Disseminators

While creators of a movement's culture obviously also disseminate it to some degree, culture is probably most effectively spread when people set about doing it in social roles geared to that objective. There are at least three major sorts of specialized disseminator roles, not all of which appear with much force in all movements.

Culture retailers.   The creators may produce materials that can be assigned monetary value and offered to a market. Given such a supply, we can then ask: How many retailers of the movement's culture are there? What is the scale of their operation? What is the range of their offerings?

Social movements are centered on ideals and ideas and, consequently, publications expressing such ideals and ideas are key items of retail. Concerning these publications, there is the question of whether or not there is *a* preeminent and regular one that deals with movement matters. The least developed movement conglomerates do not have such a publication, or even a small number of them. Instead, there are diverse magazines and newsletters that are read by only a small portion of movement participants. A movement that is more (or most?) developed, in contrast, is one with a regular publication that everyone "has" to read to claim to be abreast of movement concerns. In fullest form, this is a daily newspaper—or, at the very least, a weekly newspaper or magazine.

Although I have not surveyed all social movements in the current world, it is my impression that daily movement publications are exceedingly rare and that weekly movement publications are not much more common. In the United States, for example, no recent social movement, to my knowledge, produces a daily newspaper (in contrast to hundreds of occupations and industries that produce them) (see, for example, Georgakas 1990; Buhle 1990). There are, though, a few (and struggling) weeklies, mostly representing the American left (e. g., the *Nation, In These Times*). Most commonly, movement ideas and ideals are expressed in monthly magazines.

The qualitative characteristics of movement publications obviously require inspection. Most conspicuously in the case of newspapers and magazines, there are questions of the degree of their "slickness," which refers first to the literal slickness of the paper on which they are printed. As enterprises that seem almost always on the edge of financial collapse, most movement publications are definitely not "slick"—in the paper used, the number of ink colors employed, the complexity or professionalism of the graphics and photographs, and the like. They do vary among themselves, though, and a few recent movement periodicals have had "slick" features (*Mother Jones* and *Ms*, for example, both also widely accused of "selling out" their respective movements).

Artistic performers.   Movement-based or movement-oriented dance, drama, comedy, music, and kindred performers in troupe or solo form differ in the degree to which they can make a living from a movement or must depend on broader audiences. Only a very few recent movements have sustained artistic performers, and these only for brief periods. That is, most of the time, most movements tend to be so small that a "movement" performer must reach out beyond a movement in order to make a living. Generally movement-based but broader-reaching performers of the American left have included Pete Seeger, Joan Baez, Holly Near, Jackson Browne, Bruce Cockburn, and Tom Paxton.

Formal educators. Formal educators are people who make a living teaching in educational institutions from kindergarten through the most advanced graduate training. The way they earn their livelihood encourages them to be more than normally sensitive to ideas and ideals, to conceptions of the way the world is, what is wrong with it, and how it might and should be changed. We ought therefore not be surprised to discover that the ranks of formal educators are disproportionately populated with activists, participants, fellow travelers, and sympathizers for virtually every movement—left, right, or whatever.

Social movements differ, though, in the degree of their respective strengths among formal educators, including the extent to which educators overtly promote movement ideas and culture in educational activities. For some few movements, movement ideas and culture have achieved formal curricular recognition and a measure of legitimacy, especially in postsecondary educational organizations. This is particularly true of the women's movement, several ethnic movements, the peace movement, and movements of the left. Yet others are in the process of striving with some success for formal incorporation. Among basic ways to measure degrees of cultural development within institutions of formal education is to count numbers of programs, departments, professorships, and courses that bear the movement's name (or entailed concepts), and students enrolled in such entities.

In contrast to the culture retailers and the performers, formal educators have greater access to people who can be influenced by their views, and they work at their task over a great many years. In this sense, movement formal educators are likely to be among the most salient and potent of movement cultural disseminators. Therefore, profiles of movement cultures can usefully give sustained attention to their sheer number in a movement, their curricular endeavors, and their broader activities. Further, when they're placed in the context of all social roles in a movement, formal educators in many movements may be the most dominant disseminators. Indeed, although this is not widely known, some social movements consist significantly if not largely of current, former, and retired formal educators of various sorts. Formal educators are the unsung or "secret," sleeper class of the social movement industry.

Persona

The term *persona* is intended to direct our attention to cultural styles of interaction—to motifs of emotional expression and physical gestures commonly enacted and culturally approved by participants in a social organization. Personae are enormously complex composites of myriad features that are nonetheless identifiable "packages" of ways of speaking and interacting. Major matters of variation we are often pointing to in attending to an actor's persona include the degree to which it is cool, contained, and analytic versus fiery and emotional, or friendly, warm, amiable, or loving versus angry, distant, or hostile. Sometimes, we can think of persona as involving a dominant emotional content, forms of which include anger, fear, joy, shame, and cool civility, among many others.

Personae are real as social facts, but it must also be appreciated that they are subjective and subject to contentious perception among varying observers. For example, a movement spokesperson might be commonly perceived in a movement as an infectious personality who buoys up other participants and delivers humorous, learned, and inspiring speeches. Looking at exactly the same behavior, others might regard this person as a loudmouthed buffoon who masks an inability to lead with glib, artfully delivered rhetoric. If a person is perceived as the former much more commonly than the latter, the person's persona, is, as a *cultural fact*, the former rather than the latter. Therefore, in treating personae as cultural items, we need not adjudicate the "real reality."

The topic of persona is especially relevant to the study of social movements because these enterprises are so integrally about objection and protest or conflict. Authorities and others are being targeted with "demands" that they—the authorities—would rather not hear, much less grant. Such a mismatch of desires is fertile ground for frustration on both sides and, therefore, for angry and aggressive interpersonal personae. For these reasons, people in social movements are in more stressful situations than are persons in ordinary life, and as a consequence are more likely to call out and culturally sanction personae that are hostile and snarling. Indeed, the upstretched arm with a clenched fist is among the classic all-purpose symbols of social movements, and this gesture is only one element in a larger persona of anger that is often associated with movements. The task of the student of movement personae is therefore to be alert to both main and variant interaction styles as they are seen in various kinds of situations, especially in situations of public address.

The distinction between main and variant personae calls attention to the possibility that while movement personae might be quite different in some ways, they can also simply be variations on an overarching manner in which they are the same. Thus, in the American peace movement of the 1980s, conspicuous differences were abundantly evident, but the range of these differences was limited. Taken as a set and at a higher level of abstraction, they were quite similar and remarkable in their cordial civility and lack of the menacing edge more frequently observed as a prominent element of other movements. Even the most ideologically radical of leaders struck postures of religious contemplation and serenity. Many other leaders were trained as ministers or other church functionaries and had the platform and interpersonal styles of mainstream preachers. More secular leaders were not unlike corporate press spokespersons reading press releases or were otherwise text-dependent when they were speaking in public. Moreover, peace movement leaders with the flamboyant or dramatic public persona of people such as Adolf Hitler, Winston Churchill, John L. Lewis, Martin Luther King Jr., Jimmy Swaggart, Molly Yard, Eleanor Smeal, and Desmond Tutu were decidedly rare. The single prominent spokesperson who tended *not* to exhibit cordial civility was the subject of rather sharp criticism from other prominent movement people. I speak of Dr. Helen Caldicott—called Helen Holocaust by her critics—who was characterized as "direct and blunt, eschewing the need to be moderate and respectable" (Neal 1990: 177). Other terms applied to her included "hysterical," and "shrieking." But even though she exhibited a certain unusual toughness, it was, comparatively, a rather mild toughness.

This or some other similarity in movement persona does not necessarily mean that its participants are "persona clones," a characterization ventured with justification about members of some movement organizations. (For example, in their respective soaring periods, the Black Panthers appear to have sponsored a cloned persona of anger and the "Moonies" promoted one of "gung-ho bliss" [Lofland 1985: chapter 9].) Instead, in the context of limited variation, there is a great deal of variety. In the case of the American peace movement of the 1980s, despite virtual unity on cordial civility, there was an enchanting multiplicity of other patterns. Here are the captions I assigned to the descriptions of the more publicly prominent of those that I treat in my profile of peace movement culture: restrained alarmist, cool intellectual, gee-whiz enthusiast, spirited grandmother, assured elite, solemn believer (Lofland 1993: chapter 3).

One task of the cultural cartographer, then, is profiling personae with respect to these considerations and to the six dimensions of sharing, distinctiveness, scope, elaboration, quantity, and expressiveness.

Conclusions

In the foregoing I have set forth the task of charting degrees of movement culture, specified dimensions of such degrees, indicated a number of locations in which to observe culture, and outlined a series of questions that can guide the cultural cartographer. I want to conclude with an example of how this approach has been applied to a movement conglomerate, with a restatement of the purposes of this effort, and with a hypothesis I caption "the dilemma of culture."

Example of a Charted Culture: The Sparse, Uneven, Two-Tiered Culture of the 1980s Peace Movement

As I mentioned earlier, I developed the scheme presented in this chapter as a way to chart the culture of the American peace movement of the 1980s (Lofland 1993: chapter 3). As a step in the larger and long-term process of working toward the comparative analysis of movement cultures, I want to summarize the charting or "profile" I constructed for that case.

Our perception of the case (and of cultural charting itself) is sharpened, I think, by beginning with a statement of features of an ideal, typical, maximally developed movement culture. In an ideal, typically "rich" or "developed" movement culture:

1. Participants *share* knowledge and veneration of a set of cultural items—values, iconic persons, key artifacts, historic events, places, features of occasions, roles, persona, and the like.

2. These shared cultural matters are *distinctive* and not largely imported from the host culture.

3. The values and practices are wide in *scope*. The culture applies not merely to politics and public policy but also to the entire array of human activities and, most especially, to the conduct of economic institutions and to the organization of domestic or family life.

4. Cultural matters in all the areas just mentioned are quite complex and *elaborate,* including diverse and artful *dramatizations* of cultural themes, as in artistic performances and varied *roles* dedicated to cultural elaboration.

5. There is a great *quantity* of culture in the sense that we observe it prominently "everywhere." It is expressed via diverse media of *dissemination* (publications, motion pictures, and the like).

6. Matters of cultural import are experienced by participants as the positive *emotional and symbolic expressions* of their highest aspirations, hopes, and longings.

Viewed against this ideal type of cultural development, the American peace movement of the 1980s was, *at the movementwide level,* quite sparse.

However, movementwide sparsity stood in contrast to culture at a lower *cluster level,* where it varied widely in substance and was developed to a much greater degree, although unevenly. The movement was, in this sense, *culturally two-tiered.*

1. At the movementwide level participants shared some basic and abstract values and the practices of a polite persona, but little else. Much more sharing of iconic persons, artifacts, and so on was found at the cluster level, although the clusters varied among themselves in the degrees of their cultural development. By clusters I mean that the movement was internally differentiated in terms of the main ways in which participants went about seeking social change. There were six main forms of seeking, each expressing a theory, as it were, of how one acts effectively to accomplish social change. Briefly, these clusters and their change theories were: transcenders, who promote rapid shifts of consciousness; educators, who communicate facts and reasoning; intellectuals, who produce new facts and reasoning; politicians, who undertake political electioneering and lobbying; protesters, who force issues by noncooperation and disruption; and prophets, who affect deep moral regeneration (Lofland 1993: chapter 1).

2. The small number of shared values and civil personae at the movementwide level were to a significant degree distinctive in the sense that in critical policy circumstances most members of the larger American society did not adhere to them. Fortunately for the movement, however, in less policy-relevant contexts—and especially at Christmastime—most Americans also professed a desire for "peace" and what it implies about how to act and interact. At the cluster level, some of the culture was distinctive, but much, if not most, was clearly imported; that is, it partook of cultural patterns found in the larger society. One found the boosterism of the transcenders, the communication earnestness of the educators, the scholarly disciplines of the intellectuals, the political practices of the politicians, the civil disobedience of the protesters, and the fervent religiosity of the prophets.

3. The scope of institutional matters to which the core values were applied was quite narrow at the movementwide level. This was also true at the cluster level except among the neocounterculture elements of the protesters and among the prophets, who led distinctive lives of dissent. That is, these two groupings seriously modified their economic and family lives in terms of peace movement values to a degree and in ways not seen in other clusters.

4. Movementwide culture was quite simple and lacking in dramatization and culturally enacting roles. This, again, was in contrast to the cluster level, where intellectuals, especially, had produced enormously elaborate, erudite,

and scholarly forms of culture. The intellectuals seemed to me, indeed, to be far and away the strongest or richest cluster in the sense of sheer elaboration—which of course implies a relatively large quantity of cultural objects.

5. Perhaps befitting a movement in which a significant portion of the participants questioned materialism, the movement was not overrun with "objects" at the movementwide or cluster level, nor were those that did exist especially wide in scope. In contrast, I think of movements that develop distinctive attire either as accoutrements of daily life or for draping the body during ceremonial occasions.

6. Objects and occasions of symbolic expressiveness were quite evident although not abundant at the second-tier level of clusters. This was especially the case among the prophets and other clusters of explicitly religious peace movement people (who, however, were using symbols that were imported from other traditions rather than generated by the movement).

Three aspects of this summary profile require underscoring. First, at the movementwide level, culture was relatively weak, sparse, and impoverished in the senses elucidated here. This is not to say, however, that what we found at this level was insignificant. A commitment to peace and the relative absence of abrasive personae may not have been much culture, but was surely of importance for the contrast with other movements and social life that it presented. Second, there was quite a clear contrast between the modesty of movementwide culture and its much greater development at the cluster level; that is, the movement was two-tiered. Third, in the second tier, peace movement culture was uneven in the sense that sharing, distinctiveness, scope, elaboration, quantity, and symbolic expression were not equally developed across clusters. Overall, the neocounterculture protesters and prophets had proceeded furthest on these dimensions, while clusters further to the "right" had proceeded least. As a summary caption, then, we can think of the peace movement as exhibiting a *civil, uneven, two-tiered culture.*

The Objectives Restated

The case I have just summarized is but one of a much larger number of studies that are required in order to depict comprehensively the range of formal shapes that are observed among social movement conglomerates. Profiles can then be arrayed in terms of their degree and forms of cultural development. That is, the array becomes a "dependent" or "independent" variable depending on whether one is asking a question of causes or of consequences.

With regard to *causes* of various profiles, we need to examine such variables as the age and rate of growth of movement conglomerates. Thus, in the case of the 1980s peace movement, the sparsity of culture at the movement-wide level was in part a consequence of the movement's extremely rapid growth and the short period of time over which the movement, in the form I have described, had existed. That is, it went through a soaring rate of growth in 1981-83, springing rapidly from a variety of social groupings, occupations, and other enclaves (Lofland 1993). Focused on whatever was the peace task at hand in one's cluster, there was no time or inclination to promote the culture of one's cluster to other clusters. Sparsity is, in this sense, simply another way of speaking of newness. Newness also meant that not enough time had yet passed for simple processes of diffusion to have occurred on any scale.

Examined in terms of *consequences,* the 1980s peace movement suggests the hypothesis that sparse culture of the type it exhibited is indicative of a profound fragility in the face of resistance and deflating countermoves by, in particular, ruling elites. Because the movement was culturally fragile, when it encountered resistance, reversal, and setback, the consequence was a rapid and steep slump in levels of mobilization. Because it was so new, sparse, and fragile, the movement flowered only briefly and wilted quickly in the face of elite heat (Lofland 1993: 281-87).

Of course, sparsity of culture was not the only variable that accounted for the peace movement's rapid slump when it encountered adversity. Additional variables such as the predominance of a volunteer workforce and one-shot funding from dissident elites must also be factored in as important elements in explaining fragility and slump (Lofland 1993: chapter 7). Even so, the thinness of the culture uniting the movement's clusters seems also clearly to have played a key role.

In addition to effects that different degrees of culture have on mass mobilization levels, other areas in which to look for consequences of variations in culture include the individual level of recruitment, maintenance of individual participation, flexibility of strategic action, degrees of coercion or subordination of members, and demeaning treatment of outsiders. Coercion, subordination, and demeaning others are of particular interest, and I therefore want to conclude with a hypothesis about their relation to degrees of culture. I caption this hypothesis "the dilemma of culture."

The Dilemma of Culture

Most of us tend to think that culture is "a good thing." Therefore, the more of it we have, presumably the better off we are. Yet for movements this does not appear to be the case. Cultures that are shared, distinctive, wide in scope, elaborated, large in quantity, and intensely expressive tend often—and perhaps always—to be stifling and oppressive. To discuss culture in terms of its degrees of development, of "richness" or "poverty," as I have done, is not to say that a culture is preferable simply because it is "rich" or that it is less than desirable only because it is, technically speaking, "poor."

More specifically, movement cultures that are especially rich tend also to be religious in the conventional sense and, along with this, intolerant of other perspectives. Outsiders apply such terms as *dogmatic, hard-eyed, sectarian,* and *true believer* to them—and these labels are often descriptively accurate, as well as pejoratively appropriate. Consider, also, a second kind of example, the highly developed culture of the American military. It begins at the skins of its participants in the form of attire that is *uniform* in critical respects within organizational categories, but quite dramatically *differentiated* from those who are not members. It continues through an enormously complicated panoply of equipment and lifestyle. Aside from the intriguing and challenging complexity of military gear, there are prolific forms of colorful insignia, flags, and regalia. To this is added a vast body of celebratory traditions (ceremonies, books, historical reenactments, and so forth). Whatever else may be said of the military, its designers are experts in creating a culture that is highly developed and "rich" in the sense in which I use this term. Compared to the military, virtually all movements are culturally anemic.

I am not advocating that movement people imitate religions or the military by devising elaborate countercultures with such things as movement uniforms. There seems, in fact, to be a dilemma of culture: truly strong movement cultures tend to stimulate commitment and participation but to be authoritarian, while weak cultures, even though they are democratic and participatory, understimulate commitment and participation (Lofland 1985: chapter 9). That is to say, culture is a double-edged sword. On the one side, more culture probably means greater capacity for collective action, greater tenacity in the face of target resistance and campaign reversals, and a membership that derives greater satisfaction from movement participation. With this comes, however, higher degrees of membership coercion, narrowing of the number and range of people who will participate, and reduction in the civility of the participants' personae and relations among themselves and with outsiders. The trick is to elaborate culture that sustains participation without stifling democratic participation and sponsoring demeaning treatment of nonmembers. The likelihood that a given movement is stronger if it has "more culture" is therefore qualified by the realization that one can have too much of a good thing—that one can socially overdose with consequent social illness, so to speak. Further and finally, relations among degrees of movement culture and other movement features are, of course, not necessarily linear. There might also be threshold effects in which culture can develop in certain ways and up to certain points without becoming stifling or oppressive.

Notes

I am very grateful to Hank Johnston, Bert Klandermans, Lyn H. Lofland, Sam Marullo, David Meyer, and Carol Mueller for their constructive suggestions on drafts of this chapter.

1. There are, arguably, more than two main referents, but the two I distinguish here are sufficient to the task at hand. For a glimmer of how three or four main referents might usefully be employed, see Herbert Blumer's classic distinctions among cultural drifts, general social movements, and specific social movements (1969: 99-103).

2. Readers interested in assessing degrees of movement culture in movement organizations might want to inspect my effort at this focused on an especially "cultured" organization, the Unification Church (the "Moonies") (Lofland 1985: chapter 9, 1987). Although complex, a movement organization is still reasonably compact and circumscribed, a fact that makes analysis rather more manageable.

3. In such terms, it is especially interesting to peruse the catalogs of wholesale houses merchandising objects for furnishing churches and clothing people who conduct religious services. See, for example, the 1992-93 wholesale catalog of the Wheaton Religious Gift Shoppe and Church Supply.

Chapter 11

A Methodology for Frame Analysis: From Discourse to Cognitive Schemata

Hank Johnston

In social movement analysis, the framing perspective has been at the forefront of renewed interest in cultural and ideational processes. But several persistent problems in frame analysis remain: how to do it systematically, for example, and how to verify the content and relationships between the concepts within frames that have been identified. This chapter is a methodological essay—both practical and conceptual—that introduces one way by which frames can be studied. It specifies certain procedures that allow the analyst to demonstrate the relations between concepts, knowledge, and experience that constitutute social movement frames, and to speak more convincingly about the effects of frames on mobilization.

Frame analysis began to attract attention over a decade ago with Gamson, Fireman, and Rytina's concept of an injustice frame (1982). Drawing on Erving Goffman's *Frame Analysis* (1974), frames were defined as mental orientations that organize perception and interpretation.[1] From a cognitive perspective, frames are problem-solving schemata, stored in memory, for the interpretative task of making sense of presenting situations. They are based on past experiences of what worked in given situations, and on cultural templates of appropriate behavior. Early forays into frame analysis emphasized the social and cultural processes by which frames were generated, but they also preserved the essential definition of a frame as a mental structure that organized perception and interpretation.

Subsequent elaboration of the framing perspective by Snow et al. (1986) and Snow and Benford (1988, 1992) tended to shift the focus away from cognition and toward collective and organizational processes appropriate to mobilization. Gamson (1988) has looked at framing processes as the intentional assembly of frame packages, both for media consumption and as a stage in consensus mobilization. Johnston (1991) looked at frames as the result both of strategic planning and of cultural currents of international scope. In these studies, the notion of frame is similar to a Weberian ideal type. It assumes the aggregation of numerous individual interpretative schemata around a norm and holds in abeyance idiosyncratic differences in order to approximate the essence of the phenomenon.

But for purposes of verification and proof, the "true location" of a frame is in the mind of the social movement participant, and ultimately frame analysis is about how cognitive processing of events, objects, and situations gets done in order to arrive at an interpretation. As framing concepts have become more general, the tendency has been to move away from empirical references to individual cognitive organization and to blur the distinctions between frames and other ideational factors such as values, norms, identity, solidarity, and grievances. Penetrating the "black box" of mental life has always been a challenge to social science, but with the use of questionnaires and focus groups, or by inferring from observed behavior, it has been possible to see the influence of collective behavior frames. In this essay, however, I will show how the structure of mental frames can be reconstructed through the close analysis of the discourse of social movements. The goal is to present a method by which frame analysis might strengthen its case through reference to the spoken and written texts of social movement participants.

If frame analysis has been at the forefront of the cultural trend in social movement research, "discourse analysis" has dominated cultural perspective in general—in sociology, history, literature, and political science. Discourse is typically defined as the summation of symbolic interchange, of what is being talked and written about, of the interrelations of symbols and their systematic occurrence. For the historian, it refers to the sum total of the "manifestos, records of debates at meetings, actions of political demonstrators, newspaper articles, slogans, speeches, posters, satirical prints, statutes of associations, pamphlets, and so on" of a time, a place, and a people (Sewell 1980: 8-9). For the scholar of contemporary social movements, it can refer to, in addition to documents, spoken words that can be overheard and annotated, and to interaction that can be observed, audiorecorded, and videotaped.

But in focusing on the general patterns and tendencies of what is being talked about, by whom, and in what ways, this brand of discourse analysis rarely makes concrete reference to the documents, speeches, or minutes of meetings. When it does, reasons justifying why a particular text is taken as representative, or how we can be sure interpretations are correct, are usually left implicit. These different varieties of "texts" are all vessels in which cultural influences can be demonstrated and analyzed. The concepts of public discourse, media discourse, and movement discourse all imply the aggregation of specific speech or documents or both. Ultimately, to make a convincing case for the influence of a particular style of discourse, reference to these empirical building blocks is necessary.

This chapter is about the relationship between the concrete and the aggregate expressions of discourse and frames, between the microscopic concerns of cognitive organization and how textual materials are actually produced, and the macrosociological concerns of explaining mobilization. I will argue that with a microfocus on discourse, namely on the spoken and written texts of social movement participants, and with a microanalysis of frames, namely of the mental schemata by which experience is interpreted, the cultural analysis of social movements can become more conceptually specific and systematic. The discussion that follows is predicated on the view that there is an inextricable link between discourse and frames: it is through intensive discursive analysis that the mental structures of social movement participants are best reconstructed—from the bottom up, from the text to the frame. It is a relationship that is often obscured by analyses that work at a more general level, but keeping it in mind requires an ongoing empirical dialogue between linguistic behavior and the mental processes they are said to manifest.

Gaining Access to Frames: Micro–Discourse Analysis

The poststructuralist definition of discourse is generally macroscopic. It refers to broad patterns of what is talked and written about, by whom, their social location, when—in terms of broad historical currents—and why. In the terminology of poststructuralism, specifying all this adds up to the "decomposition" of a text. In the pages that follow, I will call this brand of analysis *macro–discourse analysis.* I will contrast it with *micro–discourse analysis,* a more intensive approach that takes a specific example of written text or bounded speech and seeks to explain why the words, sentences, and concepts are put together the way they are.

Micro–discourse analysis is based on an established body of knowledge that traces its roots to linguistics. For a long time, linguistic researchers were concerned primarily with questions of grammar, namely, how people composed well-formed sentences. Gradually, linguists realized that sentences were but the building blocks of larger textual units—stories, speeches, essays, letters, diaries, and interactional episodes—and that grammatical rules do not explain how sentences are put together into these larger units.

The boundaries of larger texts are set by the introduction and resolution of themes and by their own internal structures. Cultural knowledge of appropriate forms of speech and writing is a crucial factor. Also, interactional considerations—with whom one is communicating, and in what circumstances—affect the shape of what gets said and written. It is also necessary to account for the fact that communication does not always occur by the most direct means. Especially in speech, other channels of information such as intonation or facial expression often indicate when different or shaded interpretations of texts are required.

This approach shares several analytical tools with Michael Billig's rhetorical psychology, presented in chapter 4. There is a key difference, however: in contrast to Billig's "anticognitivism," the present goal is to integrate a recognition of the importance of language with the concept of a mental schema borrowed from cognitive science. The rationale is that, through close attention to language, the analyst can reconstruct a schema that systematically shows the relationships between concepts and experience represented in speech. As imperfect as such a schema might be, it is a gain over more tacit approaches to the content and structure of frames because it systematizes presentation—facilitating comparison—and justifies their organization by close empirical reference to the speech. It has been shown that there is a fundamental relationship between the structures of mental life and the production of written or verbal discourse (Bartlett 1932; Kintsch and van Dijk 1978; Thorndyke 1977; Rumelhart 1975; Buschke and Schaier 1979), and because social movement frames are cognitive structures, a window of access exists through the spoken words of participants and written texts of social movement organizations. It is no easy task to reconstruct the mental processes behind a text, but there are tools by which the task can be undertaken, if only in a partial way. A brief foray into the methods of textual analysis is therefore necessary, but, as I will argue, the theoretical payoffs are substantial.

The fundamental task in the microanalysis of discourse and text is the specification of all sources of meaning—all that is left implicit in a text, and all that is taken for granted in its interpretation. In some respects the task is easier with documents because the written word is the only channel used to convey information, whereas in spoken texts, natural speaker-hearers process numerous incoming channels of information. On the other hand, contextual and biographical information pertinent to the production of documents is often lost with the passage of time.[2] The microanalysis of discourse employs a wide variety of interactional, biographical, and behavioral data to verify and broaden interpretations of text. While the method is not perfect, it represents an empirically grounded approach to the "black box" of mental life, to the structures of social experience that are resident therein, and therefore to the frames by which social experience is organized. This approach has a strong empirical and positivist focus that contrasts with textual analysis in the hermeneutic tradition (Ricoeur 1976, 1981; see also Gadamer 1976). While it is strongly influenced by linguistics, Ricoeur's approach recasts all social action as meaningful text, including the action of social research itself, thereby challenging the possibility of social science traditionally conceived. Micro–discourse analysis as presented here works on the assumption that, while not perfect, a more rigorous exegesis of meaning can advance the scientific enterprise of building social movement theory.

There have been several different approaches to the microanalysis of discourse, all of which share the goal of explaining the shape and content of speech. Labov and Fanshel (1977) devised procedures to analyze a psychoanalytic interview. Grimshaw (1982) adapted their methods to analyze a doctoral dissertation defense. Stubbs (1983) subsequently offered a general codification of analytic procedures. Van Dijk (1987) has applied discourse analysis in conjunction with other methodologies to questions of racial antagonism. From this work, and from that of others, I have distilled five key principles for the interpretation of texts that are fundamental to micro–discourse analysis.

Text as a Holistic Construct

Information needed for micro–discourse analysis is frequently found in other parts of the text, and sometimes quite distant from the segment under consideration. There are two fundamental reasons why this information must be included in the analysis. First, because the overall structure of the text is often isomorphic with the structure of the frame, textual integrity must be kept intact if the ultimate goal of reproducing the shape of interpretative frames is to be achieved. Second, because written and spoken texts are often full of unclear and vague references, information from distant sections is often necessary for clarification. The referents of pronouns, for example, may not be immediately clear. Vague or cryptic semantic choices (such as "these things," "that stuff," or "those guys") may require a distant search for what they refer to. Also, factual material from outside the immediate text can shed light on knowledge that is tacitly understood between the interlocutors, yet necessary for full interpretation by a third party. Private understandings about what the interaction is about and how it is progressing are typically left unvoiced. These can be illuminated by reference to other parts of the text.

The text is the central empirical referent in micro–discourse analysis, and its integrity should be maintained. On a practical level, this carries with it some constraints on the types of data gathered and how this is accomplished. Written texts in their entirety become the units of analysis, and often information about the organizational and personal contexts of their composition is necessary. Speeches, recorded episodes of interaction, and loosely structured interviews are the best sources of verbal texts for micro–discourse analysis. In my own experience, I have found that interview protocols that are informal and open-ended encourage the respondent's narrative accounting of initial adherence, participation, and events (see Johnston 1991). Studies of recall and traditional storytelling have demonstrated that the way events are stored in memory relates directly to the narrative form of recitation. Limiting the interactional constraints on the speech situation to manageable and known quantities more clearly reveals the participant's cognitive structuring of accounts. As I will discuss, this is important as we seek to reconstruct the shape of social movement frames.

Finally, a sample of even fifty narrative texts produces an overwhelming profusion of words. While transcription of all interviews is the ideal, a more parsimonious strategy is to first summarize and code them (using audiotape counter markers for oral texts, lines for written documents) and choose the more informative and representative narratives for verbatim transcription and close analysis. For documents, key texts can be selected and closely analyzed after a general review. In both cases, texts and interviews not subjected to close scrutiny at first can be returned to, transcribed, and closely analyzed if warranted. There is clearly a qualitative element to the selection of texts, but the point is that while this strategy—like other methods—invariably limits the universe of what gets analyzed, it also preserves data that can be returned to at a later point.

The Speech Situation

A speech situation is a bounded episode of interaction in which there are specific social rules for what should and should not be said. For the most part these rules are well understood by speaker-hearers for common interactive situations, and they constitute part of the unspoken context. Rules for the hows and whys of speech come from the general culture, from subcultural and interactional relations, and from formal organizations. Part of what constitutes a social movement culture is the understandings of what constitutes appropriate speech in the appropriate situations. They serve as baseline determinants for how interactants define the course of interaction. It should also be noted that these the rules can change in the course of interaction and are often marked by changes in other aspects of speech or composition such as formality of address, tone, or writing style.

The concept of a speech situation was derived from the observation of verbal exchange, but similar cultural, interactional, and organizational constraints are operative when written documents are produced.[3] For example, there are understood rules for what goes into an interdepartmental academic memo, how it is phrased, and the physical form it should take. For the most part, the rules and understandings that constitute the context of textual production are not problematic in the interpretation of text, and social science reporting almost always disregards them. But in doing so, one runs the risk of confusing the culturally or organizationally prescribed forms of the text with the intended meaning. This would occur, to take two obvious examples, if terms of deference and respect in eighteenth-century French correspondence were mistaken as genuine sentiments or, conversely, if the sterile form of contemporary office memos was taken as evidence of the absence of personal relationships.

In a plural, urban, postindustrial society, there are numerous speech situations known and shared within small groups that may not be widely understood by outsiders. Regarding social movement research, there are several culturally or socially defined situations that may demand different forms of speech. Rallies and protest gatherings carry with them certain understandings about what is said and how. Informal conversations between participants would typically follow culturally accepted rules, but there will also be some idiosyncratic and tacitly shared understandings about what can and cannot be said. For social movement analysis, cases of misinterpretation arise when the researcher enters movement subcultures—religious, youth, ethnic, or lifestyle—where expectations of appropriate speech may not be fully understood. Briggs (1986) discusses several instances of cross-cultural interaction in which different definitions of the speech situation lead to outright misunderstanding between the interviewer and respondent.

Other speech situations that are pertinent to social movements are media announcements, announcements to potential participants, and speech appropriate to organizational settings such as meetings, strategy planning sessions, and recruitment activities. These examples suggest a public-private continuum in which the audience and the scope of diffusion are important determinants of what gets said (see Figure 11.1). Public situations mean wider diffusion and suggest constraints that derive from persuasion, recruitment, and countermovement strategy. Public speech situations also are influenced by culturally appropriate forms of argumentation. What are generally referred to as "public discourse" and "media discourse" are concrete texts produced in public speech situations where certain constraints in form and content are operative. Less public situations may limit diffusion of the message to movement participants, as in organizational meetings, or to prospective recruits, as in canvassing situations. At this level, two key variables are the relations of power and solidarity between interlocutors. They influence the assessment of appropriate degrees of formality or informality and goal-directedness versus spontaneity in speech. Finally, there are highly personal speech situations, which may also be infused with strategic and ideological considerations. These are also important loci for the production of social movement culture. These relationships are schematically represented by Figure 11.1.

Role Analysis

What gets said or written is also influenced by social role. One speaks differently as a sociologist, a father, or a teacher. One writes differently in a diary, a letter, or an official document, partly because of changing speech situations, but also partly because changing role perspective changes assessments of what is important to say and what is not. Although social roles are usually correlated with specific speech situations, it is common that role perspectives from which people speak can change in the course of a narrative—often constituting a story within a larger story. Thus, the complete analysis of text requires knowledge of the speaker/writer's role repertoire, and of the contents of those roles.

The concept of role is in part institutionally or organizationally based, and in part idiosyncratic insofar as it must be played out situationally. The social actor typically assumes a role with incomplete information about other interactants and often incomplete information about the institutional requirements of the role itself. The actor also brings a unique assemblage of skill and experience to the role that imparts an additional indeterminacy. As imprecise as the concept of role may be, there nevertheless are continuities and a certain boundedness to the various roles that each social actor plays, and in lieu of an alternative, it remains a useful concept.

Regarding the interpretation of speech and documents, there are two key points: first, that speech or writing is produced from within a role perspective; and, second, role perspectives frequently change in the course of textual production, with commensurate changes in what gets said, and often subtle changes in what is meant. Clearly, understanding textual production from the perspective of role requires that the analyst know something about the

Public (widest audience)	Less public		Increasingly private (smaller audiences)			Intimate
Announcements directly to public	**Declarations** to kindred social movement organizations	**Addresses** to social movement organizations	**Statements** to meetings, committees, etc.	**Discussions** among leaders, activists	**Conversations** among rank and file	**Chats** between members and with their primary relations
For indirect consumption by government, elite groups, countermovements	*For indirect consumption by government, elites, countermovements*	*For indirect consumption by other leaders, factions, and activists*	*For indirect consumption by kindred social movement organizations, other leaders, factions, and activists*	*For indirect consumption by factions and activists*	*For indirect consumption by factions and leaders; interactional goals become salient*	*Indirect consumption is limited; interactional goals become salient*
For consumption by movement members, potential members, countermovements, or government						

Figure 11.1. Social movement speech situations

speaker/writer. Biographical data about the respondent is sometimes available elsewhere in the text (see "Text as a Holistic Construct" earlier in this chapter). Otherwise it can be gathered from organizational sources, and from other participants. In long interviews, this information may be widely distributed; bits and pieces may come early on, but, more likely than not, there is a good deal to be found later in the interview when the situation relaxes.

It is well known that speech and interaction are influenced by prevailing patterns of class, gender, and ethnic stratification. In face-to-face interchange, initial attributions constitute the foundation of role-based constraints on speech, and subsequent markers of group membership perceived in the course of interaction further modify role attributions. Blom and Gumperz (1972) have shown how, if group affiliation is not known at the outset of interchange, cues picked up in the course of interaction impart role identities to interlocutors and affect how things are said. In the analysis of political and social movements, organizational struggles over policy, strategy, or leadership can color what is said or written publicly, or stated in interviews.

Social roles are not always as clearly defined for the analyst. In one interview with a socialist militant, I observed alternation between no less than three role postures in the course of a long narrative (see Johnston 1991: 179-94). At first, the respondent spoke from the role of a socialist functionary, and his speech was peppered with the programmatic rhetoric of socialist politics. Later, speaking as an immigrant, he described ethnic discrimination and blended class and ethnic politics. Finally, he spoke as a husband and father, and he made some very unproletarian claims about the social mobility that he hoped for his children. When they were compared, different speech segments seemed contradictory and confusing, but by identifying the role transformations, I was able to see how the speech logically progressed. When interviews do not evince internal consistency the tendency is to disregard them as lacking validity. Role analysis puts fluctuations and inconsistencies in a different light. It gives the analyst access to additional data—data that may have been lost without taking into consideration the multiple social roles that each person plays every day and that, in some speech situations, evince a leakage and overlap that determines what is said.

Role analysis is perhaps the most overlooked aspect of taking organizational texts as data. When textual materials from archives are used as measures of organizational strategy, rarely is information about who composed the text provided. Rather, written texts are taken as self-apparent reflections of the organization. Partly this is because record of the actual writer of the text has been lost with the passage of time, or by the vagaries of organizational record keeping. In other instances, the identity of the writer is intentionally obscured because the text is intended as a collective statement rather than a personal one. On this latter point, the analyst must determine if the personal has permeated the political, and if indeed it is worth the time and effort to attempt bringing personal data into the textual analysis. Close attention to the content and structure of text can suggest the best strategy.

Pragmatic Intent

A propos of roles within the movement, and the organizational and political strategies pursued by occupants of those roles, movement texts must be analyzed with an eye to what the speaker/writer is trying to accomplish, or the *pragmatic intent* behind the words. That people do things with words, to use John Austin's (1962) phrase, is a commonsense and everyday input to interpretation. A salesman's speech is often understood in terms of his overarching goal of selling a product, and depending on the sensitivity of the hearer (one's cynicism) or lack thereof (one's naïveté), his words can be interpreted with that pragmatic intent in mind. Wilson (1990) has shown how the vagueness of political speech can be analyzed from a pragmatic perspective. Similarly, in interview situations or archival research, misapprehension of pragmatic intent raises the possibility of invalid interpretations. If pronouncements do not correlate with other documents or with information in other parts of the interview, inconsistencies (and outright lies) can nevertheless be taken as data if one can reconstruct the reasoning behind them.

Pragmatic intent is often closely linked to speech situations. Proselytizing, for example, is a goal behind many social movement texts. Like sales pitches, relatively fixed (sometimes memorized) "scripts" can occur within more general ones, representing stages in the proselytizing effort—a kind of seduction by which the hearer's defenses are lowered through speech that has the goal of concealing any broader goal-directedness. On a practical level, the pragmatic intent of a script is often revealed by looking at the overall structure of the text, especially toward the end when the goals of interaction become more transparent. The same is true of narratives that superficially seem less goal-directed. All speech and writing embody interactional goals that can often be ascertained by looking at the overall structure of the text in terms of "where it is moving."

The concepts of frame alignment, frame bridging, and frame extension can be found as pragmatic goals in some speech situations. These concepts were originally introduced to describe organizational strategy and are often reflected in movement documents, but it makes sense that, depending on how deeply embedded participants are in the social movement organization, these goals can be reflected in social movement speech at the interactional level. For others, perhaps more distant from the social movement organization and less "strategically cynical" about their speech, what is said might reflect alignment actions based on established styles of organizational speech. Here, in substantive terms, what gets said, and how, are part of the social movement culture, and pragmatic intent behind the utterances is not so much a case of frame alignment as it is a reflection of group cohesiveness. Pragmatic intent in this case may be to assert membership status and cohesiveness with the group. What exactly is confronting the researcher—an intentional act or a learned reflection of social movement organization culture—is often difficult to determine. Reference to other parts of the discourse again can offer clues, but it is a question of weighing the costs and benefits of making the determination.

Discursive Cues

In face-to-face interaction, it is common that nonverbal channels of information also convey meaning. These aids to interpretation include inflection, tone, pitch, cadence, melodic contours of speech. In written documents, the use of alternate channels is limited (although perfumed letter paper or a document hastily scribbled on a scrap of paper are examples of meaning conveyed outside the text itself). Yet for the researcher who is analyzing recorded speeches, group interaction, or interviews, it is widely recognized that nonverbal channels can bend and change meanings significantly. Also, Gumperz (1982) has shown that nonverbal information often marks changes in role status, speech situation, and discursive style. He refers to these markers as *contextualization conventions*. They represent a shared "language" about when changes in the context of interaction are appropriate—such as when there is a joint recognition that the interaction is becoming more informal or intimate. Questions regarding participation, motivation, and beliefs, especially regarding recollection of past events, often create highly complex speech situations in which this kind of information may be crucial for complete and valid interpretations.

Nonverbal channels are typically lost in most data-gathering methods but can be retrieved on audio- or videotape, especially if the tape is reviewed shortly after the interview with the intention of noting nonverbal elements. They are surprisingly retrievable from short-term memory because they are almost always cognitively processed as factors in meaning, but typically via channels that are not consciously recognized the way semantic and syntactic channels are. The same is true of extralinguistic information such as facial expressions, posture, and gestures.

Specifying these data is labor intensive, and an initial rule of thumb is that this level of analysis is indicated if there is difficulty in making sense of a section, or if the analyst—employing his or her own cultural sensitivity to these cues—suspects something is being communicated beyond the words alone. It is much more difficult to recognize these cues in foreign cultural settings.

Microanalysis of a Participation Text

The way that these five principles are applied to micro–discourse analysis will vary according to the larger goals of research. Also, the role and significance that each one will have will be different according to the texts under consideration. Microanalysis is so labor intensive that it is not practical to apply it to all documents or narratives. Rather, the insights it provides can be particularly useful for important documents or interview segments—perhaps from critical junctures in the movement, or when the text is articulated particularly well, or when the text is highly representative. These are the circumstances in which the kind of microscopic scrutiny that these methods allow can increase validity of interpretation, capture data that would otherwise be lost, and reveal connections in different parts of the text that give insight into the thought processes of the producer.

In Table 11.1 I analyze a segment of interview text from my own field research in Spain in order to illustrate the principles I have described. On the left is a verbatim transcription of the interview; running parallel on the right is a "textual expansion" that is matched line for line with text on the left. This approach to microanalysis is similar to the method employed by Jefferson (1985). It stands halfway between the highly formalistic analysis of Labov and Fanshel (1977), which stresses the linguistic processes over substantive goals, and one in which the microanalysis is less formalized and is presented in a narrative fashion as part of the broader theoretical discussion (see, for example, Johnston 1991). In the textual analysis on the right, several procedures highlight the five principles. Items relating to definitions of the speech situation are underlined. Points related to role analysis are placed in italics, nonverbal cues in bold type. Pragmatic aspects of the interaction are in capital letters, and sections in which a holistic view of the text is indicated are marked by references to other sections of the interview and placed in parentheses.

The segment comes from an interview with a nationalist activist who participated in two key social movement organizations in Barcelona in the mid-

Table 11.1. Microanalysis of a "participation text"

Verbatim transcription	Textual expansion
1 R: [There were] two impressive demonstrations	Topic of demonstrations introduced independently by the
2 in February '76. On the first and the	respondent immediately after a discussion of a social
3 eighth, when Franco had just recently	movement organization, underline{suggesting that this is the kind of}
4 died, there was on Sunday, it was one day	underline{information he thinks the interviewer wants.} (This group
5 for amnesty and the other Sunday was for	organized the demonstrations. He participated with friends
6 autonomy. And for the first time in	who were members.)
7 Barcelona, seventy, eighty thousand people	**Here a change in tone,** suggesting the drama of the
8 went into the streets, hounded by the	encounter.
9 police, still, still, struck by the police,	Repetition with **forceful tone,** suggesting dramatic effect.
10 and some detained. But it was, all	
11 of Barcelona was a battle during the	
12 entire morning for two consecutive	
13 Sundays. The police couldn't do anything!	**Forceful tone** again. This topic is a common theme in
14 They ran around a lot and at times they'd	other interviews—police inefficiency.
15 arrive at a spot in a police jeep and get	
16 down and find some isolated people.	
17 I: Did you go out?	
18 R: Eh? Yes, yes, of course, evidently. In	**Pause, almost disbelief.** Laugh. underline{It was taken for granted}
19 these cases you have to go. H:hhh. You	underline{that his attendance was understood—likely by his defini-}
20 can't stop.	underline{tion of why he was being interviewed.}
21 I: Why?	
22 R: Because we thought it was a necessary	
23 thing at that time. Come on! These	underline{Understanding of participation assumed.} "You must be
24 mobilizations, uh, come on! I couldn't	able to understand." **Lower pitch,** disbelief.
25 have stayed in the house, H:hhhh,	Laugh. A break in narrative flow when interactive expecta-
26 evidently, nor could have any of my family	tions are broken. ATTEMPT TO FILL IN BACKGROUND
27 either.	INFORMATION.
28 I: But, let's say five years earlier, would	
29 you have gone out into the streets?	
30 R: Well, it's that in the period of Franco,	**Slower, considered speech contour.** SPEAKING AS AN AU-
31 the things were much more serious. You had	THORITATIVE OBSERVER. Contrasts with informality above.
32 to think twice. Then too, we went but with	"We" is unclear, but can refer to family (as indicated in 26
33 much fear, and the demonstrations were	above, or "we Catalans," 38 and 49 below).
34 small. There was one on May 1, it was a	(This demonstration occurred May 1, 1974.)
35 small thing but, well, with a lot of fear	
36 and much caution. But these two	The impressive demonstrations of 1976. HE WANTS TO
37 demonstrations were the first in which the	SPEAK ABOUT THESE EVENTS.
38 people massively risked to go out into the	
39 streets, because they thought . . . I think	
40 it was decisive for the politics that	**Slower speech** here marks a change in discursive focus—
41 developed later in Catalonia, because the	a less informal and more didactic "political analysis" for
42 Spanish state, well, the gentlemen in	interviewer, *in response to a more detached question.* Shift to
43 Madrid, saw that we were serious, that it	formality accompanied by use of the generalized "we"
44 wasn't a minority, because to send police	referring to all Catalans.

45	to repress seventy, eighty thousand	
46	people, you pay a high price, because	
47	there's many more who think the same way.	
48	And it was—come on!—it was marvelous for	Pause, and shift to informal mode. Utterance "Come on!"
49	us, to be in the street, in Calle Aragon,	**spoken in lower pitch, quickly.** SEEKS TO ELICIT
50	you know it, filled from one end to the	UNDERSTANDING OF WHAT IT WAS LIKE. Again a
51	other, and people came from Grand Via. In	sense of collective effervescence from participation.
52	each neighborhood, there was a small	
53	gathering, which, when they arrived in the	
54	center of Barcelona, was a mess of people.	

Key: PRAGMATIC ASPECTS OF SPEECH—capital letters
Changing definition of speech situation—underline   **Non-verbal cues in speech**—bold
(Information from other sections of text)—parentheses   *Changing role postures in speech*—italics

1970s. This was a time when the regime of General Francisco Franco was weakening, and nationalist and oppositional mobilizations were increasing. This segment originally was selected for intensive analysis because the respondent was representative of a large and significant group of "latecomer" activists whose participation in mass demonstrations after the death of Franco in 1975 was crucial in the transition to democracy. On a practical level, the segment eloquently describes what it was like to participate in mass demonstrations and provides abundant and complex text for microanalysis. It may be argued that the latter criterion mitigates the representativeness of the text, and especially that eloquence is related to embellishment and selective recitation of facts. While this is no doubt true in some respects, it is important to recognize that all narrative accounts are selective and embellished to varying degrees, and it is through microanalysis that the researcher can deal with issues of selective recall and the social presentation of the narrative in a systematic way. The text in Table 11.1 was chosen for this chapter because, as an example of a method of analysis, its topic transcends the political context of Francoist Spain. This segment is part of a larger text upon which, later in this chapter, the reconstruction of a collective behavior frame for participation is based.

Regarding theoretical interests in mobilization, the skeptic asks what is gained by the time-consuming analysis on the right over the clear and seemingly self-apparent verbatim text on the left. Yet the point of the earlier discussion was that as everyday speaker-hearer-readers of text we take the complexity and skillful execution of everyday communicative processes largely for granted. Ethnomethodological and sociolinguistic studies have demonstrated that there is considerable complexity to interpretative processes that usually goes unnoticed, that there is a great deal of background information that mostly goes unvoiced, and that there is more misunderstanding than we would normally think that is allowed to pass. The vagueness and imprecision of everyday language are not only requisite to smooth the ongoing flow of interaction, but are made possible by the unrecognized linguistic and extralinguistic skills participants have as native speakers of a language.[4] When analysis of mobilization directs analytical attention to important documents or to key interviews, then these methods ensure the validity of interpretation by bringing new data to bear.

One way this is achieved is by preventing the tentative imputation of meaning that naturally occurs as part of everyday speech. In lines 30-36 the respondent briefly answers a question about whether he would have participated in demonstrations five years earlier. His response, "Then too, we went but with much fear" (lines 32-33), seems to indicate that his participation dates to 1971. On closer examination, the referent of the "we" in line 32 is not really clear. It can refer to him and his family as in lines 22-27, but just a few lines further (line 38) he speaks in terms of "the [Catalan] people," and this too could be the "we" who went "with much fear" in lines 32-33. A further point of information is that his narrative returns to the more recent demonstrations quickly (line 36), suggesting that these are the ones he wants to talk about—*perhaps because these are the ones in which he has, in fact, participated.* Although there is not enough information here to decide either way, a superficial reading would have attributed activism several years earlier, while a closer reading reveals evidence to the contrary.

In this case microanalysis cautions the interpretation, but elsewhere it can fortify it. This is seen in lines 13 and 48-54, where the tonal quality functions to affirm the intensity of the experience. It is common, however, that tonal change parallels textual change, and that correct interpretations can usually be made by a reading of the text alone. Working one's way through a document, there is no way of telling which items will prove significant and which will not. Many of the other changes in pitch and tone are noted in the analysis (lines 9, 13, 30), but do not seem important. This may be because they accompany clear textual assertions, but is also because their significance becomes apparent only when the text is considered as a whole.

Viewed in this light, several tonal changes function as markers to reorient the focus of the narrative. In line 39, the respondent assumes a more considered and deliberate way of talking compared to earlier sections (lines 22-27, for example). Here we find a more formal "political analysis" of events, rather than a personal account. A change from informal to formal discursive style represents a variation in the definition of the interview situation and in what the respondent is trying to accomplish with his words. Apparently insignificant tonal changes can accompany more significant discursive shifts and can function as markers for key concepts in the organization of frame structure (Gumperz 1982). As we will see later in the discussion of social movement frame structures, "sending a message to the government" is a key concept in the organization of information about protest participation. We have here a rule of thumb for micro–discourse analysis: that the convergence of several textual characteristics, such as changes in style of speech, definitions of speech situation, or role perspective can both indicate and serve as evidence of key orienting principles in the frame.

Elsewhere, there are other indications of how the respondent defines the interview situation and of what kind of shared background knowledge he thinks he can assume. We see this in his responses to several of the interviewer's questions. In line 17, following a description of the two demonstrations, the interviewer, apparently not having understood that a firsthand account was just provided, asks of the respondent, "Did you go out [and attend]?" This is followed by the interrogative "Eh?" (uttered with a tonal contour suggesting disbelief) and then a pause and stutter. This reaction suggests that the question did not fit the respondent's expectations, and in a vague and unsure attempt to provide background, he continues, "In these cases you have to go," meaning, of course, he participated. In line 21, the interviewer probes with a simple "Why?" but in lines 23-25 the respondent is taken again by the apparent lack of shared knowledge on the part of the interviewer. He answers with "Come on" twice—both calls for the interviewer to try to empathize. When the interviewer asks a more detached, analytical question (lines 28-29), the respondent speaks in a more detached and analytical way, but it does not last long. He returns to a more informal mode of speech in order to describe the two demonstrations that he attended—and about which he apparently wants to talk.

When I first reviewed this section, the key analytical codes were "family ties," "police inefficiency," a sense of compulsion about participation that reflects an "emergent norm," and the "exuberance" in his participation. I had coded for these concepts in other interviews and documents, and their analytical importance increased as they occurred more often—according to the standard canons of research. Yet microanalysis yields another genre of data that derives from seeing the text in a broader context as a negotiated document. By taking the document as a whole, we see how important these two demonstrations were to the respondent. In the structure of this discourse, he initially chose the topic, and returned to it; he assumed a great deal of back-ground knowledge on the part of the interviewer, and was frustrated when his expectations were not met. What we have here is a datum that derives not from what a participant says but from how he says it. It enables the recon-struction of a mental state from the structure of speech rather than from the expression of speech itself. Moreover, by identifying the importance of these demonstrations, we now know something about the cognitive organization of this respondent's participation. Because of their importance, it is likely that a great deal of other experience is organized—"framed" in memory—under them, ready to be invoked in situations appropriate to social movement ac-tivism.

All this has particular importance for questions of framing. By analyzing the spoken texts of respondents, one is able to approximate the underlying cognitive organization that structures experience and influences behavior. Bartlett's early studies (1932) demonstrated that the way people remember is related to how they initially experienced events and stored them in memory. Because speech production and memory are isomorphic processes, the spo-ken accounts of social movement participants give access to the individual cognitive schemata that define situations as warranting action (or inaction). If we are to research interpretative frames more rigorously, as I think we can, the most compelling data are to be found in how speech and text are struc-tured. This kind of data provide a new way of analyzing the structure of men-tal life and a more rigorous method of verifying the cultural content contained therein.

The Structure of Frames

At the epistemological rock bottom of any framing activity is the individual interpretative schema. Whether framing activities are done by the media or by a social movement organization, they count only insofar as they penetrate the "black box" of mental life to serve as determinants of how a situation is defined, and therefore acted upon. Collective action frames are "bundles of beliefs and meanings" that are related in a systematic way. They are system-atic because they are related in the cognitive organization of social movement participants. Frame analysis, implicitly or explicitly, is about cognitive pro-cesses; and while we cannot see the brain synapses firing, we can approxi-mate an organization of concepts and experience that indicates how a situa-tion is to be interpreted.

I will be arguing in this section that the goal of visually representing the structure of a mental schema, even of the roughest sort (which is all that I will offer at this time) is worthwhile. I have in mind a structure that portrays the various factors and their relationships to each other that go into making sense of a situation for a typical kind of behavior in social movement participation. Such a structure would approximate an aggregation of individual cognitive schemata by stating the probable experiential elements for a particular group and how they are related.

A good deal of frame analysis to date interprets whether a frame is being applied by movement members or by the media, and traces its ideological sources and effects. The problem is that there are no shared criteria about how to do this, nor are there rules to ascertain whether a frame has been correctly interpreted. To make a convincing case, it would be useful if the analyst could trace how beliefs, meanings, and experiences are related in the frame; and, just as importantly, this must be done in a way that can be verified. Demonstrating how one arrives at a frame structure through microanalysis of a social movement text makes the shape of the frame openly available to discussion and debate. The final test of whether a social movement frame has been correctly described is if these reconstructions help the analyst understand why individual participants and social movement organizations act the way they do. Otherwise, there is a tendency toward the kind of conceptual and terminological elaboration discussed in chapter 1 rather than refining and testing.

This notion of a collective behavior frame parallels the definition of *frame* as it is used in the cognitive science literature. The analogy that best captures the essence of the field is the brain *qua* computer. Experience is organized, encoded, stored, and retrieved by "mental programs" (Miller and Johnson-Laird 1975). According to Ableson, frames are "structures that when activated reorganize comprehension of event-based situations . . . [and invoke] . . . expectations about the order as well as the occurrence of events" (1981: 717). What we know about the organization of interpretative frames also comes from cognitive science. While we are far from consensus on the shape and content of these mental programs, there is overlap in two fundamental areas that are important for frame analysis of social movements.

First, all models of cognitive processes share some form of hierarchical organization. Higher levels, or nodes as they are sometimes called, subsume a multiplicity of detail and can serve as points of access for retrieval from memory. One approach to the hierarchical organization of text falls under the rubric of story grammars (Thorndyke 1977; Rumelhart 1975). Story grammars are normative schematic forms by which stories, tales, accounts, and histories are organized and remembered. According to Thorndyke (1977), simple stories are organized by deep structures. General descriptions of settings, themes, plots, and characters all subsume substructures in which appropriate details are organized. Rumelhart (1975) suggests a somewhat different structure whereby the story line is organized according to different schemata for episodes, action, and events that subsume the details of the story. This approach suggests that the deep structure of a narrative telling or writing of social movement participation gives a good idea of how experiences were stored in memory. Another approach also focuses on the cognitive processes of producing well-formed texts. Kintsch and van Dijk (1978) have specified two levels at which spoken and written texts are organized: a microstructure that orders the specific ideas contained in the text and a macrostructure "where a list of macropropositions represents a kind of abstract of the text" (Hormann 1986: 181). In the analysis of social movement frames, it is these macrostructures that are widely shared between participants, and that organize a multiplicity of idiosyncratic personal detail in a common (and often solidifying) way.

Second, the shape of frames or schemata will vary according to their content. In cognitive science, the relation between the content of memory and the structure in which it is stored is a basic theme, exemplified by the treatment of cognitive processes by Schank and Abelson: "It does not take one very far to say that schemas are important: one must account for the content of schemas.... In other words, a knowledge structure theory must make commitment to a particular content schema" (1977: 10). Schemata for collective behavior and social movement activities will have their own unique form, and will vary according to roles in the movement and presenting situations.

A key interpretative process is to recognize similarities with past experiences. When a framework that organizes past experience is present in memory, it is assessed for "goodness of fit" with the presenting situation and drawn upon for knowledge that has been useful in the past. Schank and Abelson term these standardized general episodes "scripts." They are economy measures in storing episodes in that they require access only to the abstract categories rather than numerous details, allowing people to deal with a great deal of material in little time.

Accessing certain scripts brings up a wide array of subevents with which experience can be compared.[5] For example, a typical script or file may be RESTAURANT. The "scripted" events include entering, taking a table, ordering, consuming the food, paying, tipping, and exiting—all indexing a variety of more detailed events representing different ways each of these actions could be accomplished. For our purposes, another script might be DEMONSTRATION for social movement activists, which provides access to subscripts such as placard making, gathering, singing, chanting, marching, responding to police, asserting of solidarity, and even appropriate modes of socializing. Another script would be STRATEGIZING (for movement leaders), which includes templates for thinking about movement goals and interaction with other leaders.

Representations of Frames

At this stage, there are three key points to keep in mind. The first is that frames are hierarchical cognitive structures that pattern the definition of a situation for individual social action. Second, individual frames can be aggregated for subgroups within social movements that share general cognitive orientations toward events. Idiosyncratic experiences will occur at lower levels of cognitive organization, but higher-level nodes will be shared so that they coordinate and interpret experiences for participants in a common way. In terms of what frame analysis can contribute to the study of social movements, these higher-level concepts are the basis of sharing and coordination for many social movement actions, and it is through their systematic reconstruction and verification that the real contribution of micro–frame analysis lies. Third, the structure of a frame is contingent on the situation that it represents.

The kind of micro-frame analysis that I am suggesting involves approximating the hierarchical relationships that constitute frames and scripts appropriate to typical or crucial situations in a movement career. The kinds of situations and role perspectives within the movement are narrowed by the definition of the research problem, and by identification of the critical junctures and important groups in movement development. For example, depending on the aspect of mobilization in question, an interpretative frame relevant to any number of confronting situations could be reconstructed for each of the groups represented in Figure 11.2. Government personnel, although not specified here, are important players in many movement environments as well.

Because it is impossible to microanalyze all texts or interviews, a sampling of texts to assure some degree of representativeness is necessary. Figure 11.3 represents a sample schema for participation in an antigovernment demonstration in Barcelona, Spain. It is based on a broader section of the interview analyzed earlier in Table 11.1. The respondent was a nationalist acti-

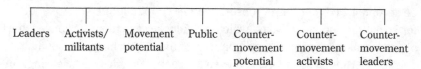

Figure 11.2. Groups for micro–frame analysis

vist who attended two mass demonstrations in the mid-1970s and participated in some dissident organizations but, according to the scale in Figure 11.2,
fell somewhere between the active militant role and the latent potential of a
movement. In the mid-1970s, participation of the urban middle classes in
demonstrations against the regime was crucial in spurring democratic transition, and the text was chosen as representative of this level and type of
activism. Thus, while the schema in Figure 11.3 is for just one individual, it is
offered as a representative statement of a kind of participation judged to be
crucial in the overall analysis. In the present case, the respondent was selected by nonprobability sampling of theoretically important groups. In other
cases, random sampling procedures can be used to assure representativeness.

At the very top of the schema is listed the location on the audiotape of the
speech segment, defined by development and resolution of the participation
theme. Numbers in parentheses at the lower levels or nodes indicate lines in
the verbatim transcription. Note that some information pertinent to participation through friendship networks (the branches on the far left) is located
much further on in the interview. The mechanics of presentation are important checks for the reliability of the schema through reference to the original
text. While a full line-by-line transcription of text is the ideal, pertinent information is often located so far from the central text that more parsimonious
presentations are necessary. In the present case, only the central text has
been reproduced (see Table 11.1) in order to convey the kind of detail that
allows verification of the structure of the frame. An alternative strategy is to
construct an ideal-typical schema by melding together several representative
interview transcripts, although the mechanics of referencing several tran-
scriptions is cumbersome.

Figure 11.3 is a visual reconstruction of the collective action frame for a
representative social actor at a particular juncture in a movement career. The
goal is to present a schema that accounts for the actions of other members
sharing similar role perspectives for the same situation. If the analysis had
been of a key movement document, the analysis would yield the structure of

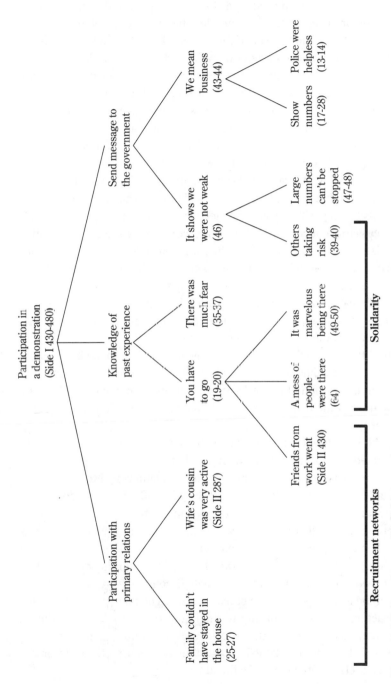

Figure 11.3. Schema for attending a demonstration

key concepts for those who produced the document and, depending on its ideological importance, for the rank and file. The upper levels of the structure are where the generalizing power of the method lies. The support of friends and family, past experience of demonstrations, and the conscious intent to send a message to the government are general concepts under which a variety of experience and knowledge are organized. Another way of putting it is that, for Figure 11.3, these three upper nodes are points of access to memory wherein information pertinent to a decision to participate in a demonstration is stored. These upper levels are the "key framing concepts" that orient and shape participants' interpretations of the world.

The lower levels of the frame will vary according to the source of text, but the expectation is that, through the shared experiences and social location of the participants, they will vary in patterned ways. In Figure 11.3, these levels are not necessarily couched in the analytical concepts of the social scientist, although there is often overlap. At the third and fourth levels, there are nodes in the form of the utterances "You have to go!" and "It was marvelous being there." These carry the sense of emergent normative expectations—an important analytical point—but the information is organized not according to the concepts of the researcher, but in the center tree under "past episodes." Herein lies the key difference between the analysis of the social scientist and the practical thinking of the social actor: movement participation is not *cognitively organized* according to the concepts of the analyst. These concepts are, however, often to be found in the frame structures, as demonstrated by the horizontal lines at the bottom of Figure 11.3 labeled "recruitment networks" and "solidarity."

Figure 11.3 represents one form in which an interpretative schema might be represented. For example, Gamson notes that a key aspect of a frame is its ability to encompass a variety of different interpretations and to incorporate new and unforeseen events (1988: 222-23). Figure 11.3 might include alternative scripts or courses of action for variations in the presenting situations. If friends brought news that the police were out in force the day of the demonstration, alternative actions based on past experience could be plotted as part of the schematic representation at lower levels. Although this question was not asked, we cannot assume that alternative courses were not stored in memory, to be invoked should the situation arise. The point is that the shape of the structure will vary according to the idiosyncrasies of the situation in which the text was produced, but, if a social movement frame is operative, the upper-level nodes will be relatively consistent between participants or are likely to occur elsewhere in organizational texts.

While this kind of analysis is far from perfect, it does permit a systematic and fine-tuned discussion about frames and framing processes.[6] In schematic form with accompanying text an "individual rights frame" (Gamson 1992a) or a "no gain without cost frame" (Donati 1992: 234) could be represented in ways that show (1) what concepts make up the frame, (2) the relations between concepts, (3) the basis for arriving at the connections, (4) the degree of carryover to other levels and types of participation, and (5) how interpretations might vary with changing situations. If the analysis focuses on media frames (Gamson 1988, 1992a), then one would expect to find parallels between the structure of media texts at these upper levels and the structures of movement documents and the speech of participants. Similarly, if a social movement organization promotes frame extension and frame bridging, then one would expect similarities between organizational texts and participants' spoken texts. Lower-level experiences and knowledge that are "bridged" or "extended" will be subsumed by the more encompassing frames at the upper levels, the "bridges." Thus, micro–frame analysis provides a way of verifying the presence and influence of several framing processes.

A Theoretical Conclusion

Using micro–discourse analysis to graphically reconstruct frames for representative social movement participants creates a different idiom for talking about ideational factors and their influence on behavior. This kind of *micro–frame analysis* (in contrast to traditional frame analysis) enables the researcher to speak about frames with a great deal more empirical grounding. It answers the criticism, often directed at the analysis of mentalities and macrodiscourse in history and literary criticism, that there is too much loose interpretation taking place too far from the data (see Gray 1986; Palmer 1987).

Micro–frame analysis has two methodological goals. First, regarding the reliability of the analysis, it seeks a more systematic approach to the content of social movement frames through an intensive dialogue between the general concepts represented in frame structures and the textual materials on which they are based. Second, regarding validity, it confronts head-on the fundamental problem in analyzing textural materials: namely, their infusion with cultural, organizational, and interactional considerations that always—in varying degrees—bend and shape what gets said. Less rigorous discourse analysis tends to make two inappropriate assumptions in this regard: first, that what the text means is self-evident; and second, that what the text *apparently* means is all that is important. The first implies that the cultural and interactional constraints that hold for the researcher and audience are shared by those producing the text; the second that other factors in textual production, such as prosodic, pragmatic, situational, and biographical elements, do not carry information pertinent to the analysis. Without them, however, not only is important information often missed, but outright misinterpretation can occur.

Micro–frame analysis is more than just another way of presenting concepts that could be discussed by more traditional narrative exposition. I say this because its application carries with it a clear theoretical focus. Visually representing knowledge in the form of frames and scripts anchors the analysis in a Weberian *verstehenze soziologie.* In the past, sociology and anthropology have dichotomized the locus of culture, of opportunity structures and historical influences, in terms of either "out there," in social structure, or "in here," in the mental life of the social actor. Micro–frame analysis follows Weberian nominalism in that abstracted cultural, historical, and social influences are always viewed through the lens of individual cognition. Structural factors find their way into the analysis insofar as they are *perceived and interpreted* by social actors. That is not to say that they do not have effects beyond their perception, only that, *in this brand of analysis,* objective (as opposed to subjectively perceived) structural factors must be considered separately.

Out of this brand of nominalism, therefore, there are several other theoretical spin-offs. First, social role as an analytical category is reintroduced into social movement analysis. This occurs via the observation that textual materials are produced from within discursive role perspectives, and that interpretation of presenting situations is for the most part organized according to social roles. In fact, social roles are almost always implied at the highest level of frame organization, such as in Figure 11.3, where the entire frame is organized ("stored in memory") under the respondent's role of an activist—as we saw in Table 11.1 with his repeated attempts to move the discussion to two demonstrations. Moreover, this particular segment of text was chosen because of the critical importance of this movement role—the recently incorporated activist—in the course of mobilization. Also, Figure 11.3 shows that information and experience that are more extensively organized under *other* role perspectives may be invoked from within the current discursive role, such as when the respondent speaks of his family's attending demonstrations, secondarily invoking his roles of father and husband. Thus, there is interpenetration and overlap in roles even though the social role remains a fundamental category of mental life.

If one takes seriously the notion that social movement frames are, at their base, cognitive structures, then social role must have a place in the analysis.

But apart from this, role analysis has a place in the study of social movements beyond methodological perspective. Substantively, there has been renewed interest in what might loosely be called identity movements, especially work focusing on new social movements. Role analysis should be central to understanding identity movements, and the concept of collective identity, so central to the new social movement perspective, can be fruitfully reconceptualized as a social-role-based group membership. What is rarely brought into the analysis is the relation of other social roles the participant may play to the emergent role as member in a movement. It makes sense that these relations could be fruitfully studied via micro–frame analysis.

Second, micro–frame analysis has the effect of bringing grievances back into the analysis. The emphasis on resources over the past twenty years, and a growing emphasis on identity during the past ten, has had the effect of relegating grievances to secondary status. My experience in talking to participants about their activities in movements, or perusing key organizational documents, has been that justifications for action invariably include reference to what is unjust and what needs to be changed. To put it in the language of micro–frame analysis, grievances—regardless of whether they are key elements in movement success or movement strategy—often occur as higher-level organizing concepts of participation frames. We saw this in Figure 11.3 with the need to "send a message to the government," a concept that at its base characterizes the perceived injustices of the Franco regime. Collective grievances represent the most widely shared and most facile explanations for collective action, and that is because, to the extent that there is a group, the articulation of grievances—of what is wrong and what must be done—constitutes a process fundamental to group formation. The voicing of grievances establishes the boundaries of the group and serves as a primary source of legitimacy for coordination and action. Hearing about shared grievances from movement participants reintroduces practical reasoning into social movement analysis. The extent to which they play a role in social movement formation will vary between movements, and, via the framing perspective, grievances and interpretation of them should be a key empirical focus in future research.

Third, one of the recent insights of social movement research has been the extent to which the personal is political. In many contemporary movements there is a close relation between the organization of everyday life and the movement. A propos of the discussion here, everyday experience is often where injustice is experienced, and where the need for change is first articulated. Also, there may be a large overlap between movement activities and the course of daily events for participants. To the extent that these experiences are organized under social movement frames, or necessary for the analysis of social movement texts, a microanalysis of cognitive frames takes the researcher into the private corners of social life. Recall how easily the respondent in Table 11.1 lapsed into discussion of his family, and in other sections of the interview of his cousins and friends. This is what people know best, and it is crucially important in their daily actions. To the detriment of theory, this kind of data has not typically found a place in thinking about political and social change, but primary interaction is a central arena from which public behaviors in the form of protest and revolt often rise up: family, friends, the dinner table, and the coffee shop.

Finally, micro–frame analysis helps explain the content of social movements. I began this essay by moving away from the broader definitions of discourse and frame, but with this final point I come full circle: to what I had called "macrodiscourse," the broad definitions of culturally appropriate speech and text. In recognizing that some groups articulate fears and grievances better than others, and that some seize upon symbols and vocabularies more appropriate to cultural patterns, macro–discourse analysis helps explain the success of some social movements. There exist no contradictions between this and the kind of micro-frame analysis I have discussed, only differences in focus and in the kind of evidence needed for a convincing argument. But I also think that an important test of the insights of macro–discourse analysis, especially the organizational insights of Gamson (1992a), Snow and Benford (1992), and others, is the presence of the concepts at higher-level nodes in the cognitive organization of participants. This can be empirically demonstrated with microanalysis. Furthermore, why certain frames resonate and others do not can be tested at the level of the individual participant in terms of the connections, continuities, overlaps, and parallels in cognitive organization. For these two reasons I think that the *microanalysis* of member speech is an important test for several *macroscopic* perspectives on social and political movements.

Notes

1. Goffman's frame analysis has been criticized as being too general, relying too much on impressionistic data, and failing to provide concrete empirical examples of frames themselves (Swanson 1976: 218).

2. In this essay there is a clear emphasis on naturally occurring speech, but if documents are being analyzed, the general principles still apply. This stands in contrast to Ricoeur's (1971) assertion that there is a distinct "spiritual" quality to written texts because they are not addressed to a concrete other. I would argue that the complex of interactional, organiza-

tional, and cultural constraints that typically constrain speech between specific interlocutors also are determinants of all but the most unusual kinds of written texts. Social movement records and manifestos are just as much contextually produced and directed at audiences as any conversational utterance. To bring these factors to bear in the analysis, however, the researcher must have ethnographic knowledge of the situations in which these texts are produced—sometimes a very tall order.

3. Anthropologists have extended the contextual parameters of speech to include the cultural knowledge that enables a member to speak and act appropriately. Knowing what should be said, how, and at what time requires knowledge of the norms governing specific speech situations in addition to considerations of interactional influences and tacit assumptions that are part of the more general culture. Thus, the social encounter rather than the speech itself becomes the analytical focus. For example, Susan Phillips (1974) analyzed the structure of a Warm Springs Indian meeting and the contextual structure that enabled a participant to know how "to fit into the meeting," and for how long. Collections in the ethnography of speaking include Pier Paolo Giglioli 1972, J. Gumperz and Dell Hymes 1972, and Dell Hymes 1974a, 1974b.

4. Perhaps first pointed out in Harold Garfinkel's well-known article "The Routine Grounds of Everyday Activities" (1967). In discussing types of social knowledge other than purely linguistic or conversational, he was one of the first sociologists to recognize the degree to which everyday social activities are based on assumed background knowledge and skills. His initial insights were developed further by Harvey Sacks (1972) and his colleagues Sacks, Schegloff, and Jefferson (1974). Out of this work grew the subfield of conversation analysis, which systematically examined examples of naturally occurring talk to specify the rules and mechanisms fundamental to its occurrence. Cicourel (1974, 1982, 1986) has subsequently developed an awareness of the taken-for-grantedness of language insofar as it relates to the research process.

5. For the purposes of this essay, it is not necessary to explain these processes in detail. For Schank and Abelson, the concept of script was an extension of their earlier work called conceptual dependency theory. They sought to represent meaning of words through combining a limited number of primitive (or basic) actions and states. While this seemed to account for the fundamental semantic content of some speech, it became apparent that some often repeated and often used words are not broken down into primitives but rather are directly accessed by higher-level schemata (Schank and Abelson 1977: 12-15).

6. It should be mentioned that in focusing just on frames and scripts, we have only the tip of the cognitive iceberg, so to speak. Mental life requires several other kinds of interpretative structures to accommodate situations that have never previously been encountered. Schank and Abelson introduce several other theoretical structures that are complementary repositories of knowledge: plans (and "planboxes"), goals, and themes. All three represent places where information connecting events that cannot be connected by scripts is stored (Schank and Abelson 1977: 70). Plans are composed of general information on how actors achieve goals. By finding a plan, the subject can make guesses about the intentions of an action in an unfolding situation (or story) and use these guesses to make sense of the story. Understanding an actor's plans—by access to what the authors call planboxes—involves examining experience with reference to defined sets of possible action that can be called up to achieve a goal. Goals are also organized in a hierarchy. Proposing a main goal automatically invokes specific subgoals to be pursued in interaction. Finally, themes are packages of goals that tend to occur together because of some property of one or more actors. Themes contain the background knowledge upon which we base information that an individual will have certain goals. Themes can be organized around the social roles, around interpersonal

relationships (such as probable goals of a person who is in love), and general life themes that describe a general position or aim that a person wants in life. As goal bundles, the various types of themes generate predictions about other people's actions and, in stories, about the protagonists (ibid.: 123-24). It is important to note the highly social nature, the cultural specificity, and the situational predication of scripts, plans, goals, and themes.

Bibliography

Abelson, Robert P. 1981. "The Psychological Status of the Script Concept." *American Psychologist* 36:715-29.

Abu-Lughod, Lila. 1990. "The Romance of Resistance: Tracing Transformations of Power through Bedouin Women." *American Ethnologist* 17:41-55.

———.1985. "A Community of Secrets." 10:637-57.

Adam, Barry D. 1987. *The Rise of a Gay and Lesbian Movement.* Boston: Twayne.

Agger, Ben. 1991. "Critical Theory, Poststructuralism, Postmodernism: Their Sociological Relevance." *Annual Review of Sociology* 17:105-31.

Aguirre, B. E., E. L. Quarantelli, and J. L. Mendoza. 1988. "Collective Behavior of Fads: The Characteristics, Effects, and Career of Streaking." *American Sociological Review* 53:569-84.

Alexander, Jeffrey C. 1990. "Analytic Debates: Understanding the Relative Autonomy of Culture." In *Culture and Society,* edited by Jeffrey C. Alexander and Steven Seidman. Cambridge: Cambridge University Press.

Alexander, Jeffrey C., ed. 1988. *Durkheimian Sociology: Cultural Studies.* New York: Cambridge University Press.

Alexander, Jeffrey C., and Steven Seidman, eds. 1990. *Culture and Society.* Cambridge: Cambridge University Press.

Almond, Gabriel, and Sidney Verba. 1964. *The Civic Culture.* Boston: Little, Brown.

Alperovitz, Gar, and Jeff Faux. 1982. "The Youngstown Project." In *Workplace Democracy and Social Change,* edited by Frank Lindenfeld and Joyce Rothschild-Whitt. Boston: Porter Sargent.

Amrane, Djamila. 1982. "Algeria: Anti-Colonial War." In *Female Soldiers: Combatants or Non Combatants?* edited by Nancy Loring Goldman. Westport, Conn.: Greenwood.

Anderson, Benedict. 1991. *Imagined Communities: Reflections on the Origins and Spread of Nationalism.* London: Verso.

Andrews, Florence. 1987. "An Analysis of an Organization through Its Means of Social Control: The Case of the La Leche League." Unpublished paper.

Aristotle. 1909. *Rhetoric.* Cambridge: Cambridge University Press.

Austin, John L. 1962. *How to Do Things with Words.* London: Oxford University Press.

Bacon, F. 1858. *Of Dignity and Advancement of Learning.* London: Longman.

Bakhtin, M. M. 1986. *Speech Genres and Other Late Essays.* Austin: University of Texas Press.

———. 1981. *The Dialogic Imagination.* Austin: University of Texas Press.

Bales, Robert Freed. 1970. *Personality and Interpersonal Relations.* New York: Holt, Rinehart, & Winston.

Balthazar, Louis. 1986. *Bilan du nationalisme au Québec.* Montreal: L'Hexagone.

Barlow, Maude, and Bruce Campbell. 1991. *Take Back the Nation.* Toronto: Key Porter.

Barsh, Russel Lawrence, and James Youngblood Henderson. 1982. "Aboriginal Rights, Treaty Rights, and Human Rights: Indian Tribes and 'Constitutional Renewal.'" *Journal of Canadian Studies* 17, no. 2.

Barthes, Roland. 1982. "Inaugural Lecture, College de France." In *Barthes: Selected Writings,* edited by S. Sontag. London: Fontana/Collins.

————. 1975. *The Pleasure of the Text.* New York: Hill and Wang.

————. 1970. *Writing Degree Zero.* Boston: Beacon.

Bartholomew, Anne, and Margit Mayer. 1992. "Nomads of the Present: Melucci's Contribution to 'New Social Movement' Theory." *Theory, Culture and Society* 9, no. 3.

Bartlett, F. C. 1932. *Remembering.* Cambridge: Cambridge University Press.

Bashevkin, Sylvia B. 1991. *True Patriot Love: The Politics of Canadian Nationalism.* Toronto: Oxford University Press.

Bateson, Gregory. 1979. *Mind and Nature.* New York: Dutton.

————. 1972. *Steps to an Ecology of Mind.* New York: Ballantine.

Baudrillard, Jean. 1975. *The Mirror of Production.* St. Louis: Telos.

Bellah, Robert N. 1973. Introduction to *Emile Durkheim on Morality and Society,* edited by Robert Bellah. Chicago: University of Chicago Press.

Benedict, Ruth. 1961. *Patterns of Culture.* London: Routledge.

Benford, Robert D. Unpublished. "Social Movement Organizations and Collective Identities: A Constructionist Approach to Collective Identity Claims-Making."

Benford, Robert D., and Scott A. Hunt. 1992. "Dramaturgy and Social Movements: The Social Construction and Communication of Power." *Sociology Inquiry* 62:35-55.

Bennett, W. Lance. 1988. *News: The Politics of Illusion.* New York: Longman.

Bergeron, Gérard. 1991. "Le devenir de l'etat du Québec." In *Le Québec et la restructuration du Canada,* edited by L. Balthazar et al. Sillery, Quebec: Septention.

Bertaux, Daniel. 1981. *Biography and Society.* London and Beverly Hills: Sage.

Best, Joel. 1990. *Threatened Children: Rhetoric and Concern about Child-Victims.* Chicago: University of Chicago Press.

————. 1989. "Extending the Constructionist Perspective." In *Images of Issues,* edited by Joel Best, New York: Aldine de Gruyter.

Billig, M. 1993. "Nationalism and Richard Rorty: The Text as a Flag for *Pax Americana.*" *New Left Review,* no. 202, 69-83.

————. 1992. *Talking of the Royal Family.* London: Routledge.

————. 1991. *Ideology and Opinions: Studies in Rhetorical Psychology.* London: Sage.

————. 1990a. "Collective Memory, Ideology and the British Royal Family." In *Collective Remembering,* edited by D. Middleton and D. Edwards. London: Sage.

————. 1990b. "Stacking the Cards of Ideology: The History of the Sun's 'Royal Souvenir Album.'" *Discourse and Society* 1:17-37.

————. 1989. "The Extreme right: Continuities In Anti-Semitic Conspiracy Theory in Post-War Europe." In *The Nature of the Right,* edited by R. Eatwell and N. O'Sullivan. London: Frances Pinter.

————. 1987. *Arguing and Thinking: A Rhetorical Approach to Social Psychology.* Cambridge: Cambridge University Press.

————. 1985. "Prejudice, Categorization and Particularization: From a Perceptual to a Rhetorical Approach." *European Journal of Social Psychology* 15:79-103.

————. 1978. *Fascists: A Social Psychological View of the National Front.* London: Academic Press.

————. Forthcoming. "Celebrating Argument in Psychology: Dialogue, Negation and Feminist Critique." *Argumentation*.

Billig, Michael, S. Condor, D. Edwards, M. Gane, D. Middleton, and A.R. Radley. 1988. *Ideological Dilemmas: A Social Psychology of Everyday Thinking*. London: Sage.

Blee, Kathleen. 1991. *Women of the Klan*. Berkeley: University of California Press.

Bleyer, Peter. 1992. "Coalitions of Social Movements as Agencies for Social Change: The Action Canada Network." In *Organising Dissent: Contemporary Social Movements in Theory and Practice,* edited by W.E. Carroll. Toronto: Garamond.

Blom, Jan-Peter, and John J. Gumperz. 1972. "Social Meaning in Linguistic Structures: Code-Switching in Norway." In *Directions in Sociolinguistics,* edited by John J. Gumperz and Dell Hymes. New York: Holt, Rinehart & Winston.

Blumer, Herbert. 1969. "Collective Behavior." In *Principles of Sociology,* edited by A. M. Lee. New York: Barnes & Noble.

————. 1955. "Social Movements." In *Principles of Sociology,* edited by A. M. Lee. New York: Barnes & Noble.

Boggs, Carl. 1986. *Social Movements and Political Power*. Philadelphia: Temple University Press.

Bose, N. K. 1929. *Cultural Anthropology*. Calcutta: NPG.

Boulding, Elise. 1990. "The Early Eighties Peak of the Peace Movement." In *Peace Action in the Eighties,* edited by S. Marullo and J. Lofland. New Brunswick, N. J.: Rutgers University Press.

Bourdieu, Pierre. 1990. *The Logic of Practice*. Stanford, Calif.: Stanford University Press.

————. 1984. *Distinction: A Social Critique of the Judgement of Taste,* translated by R. Nice. Cambridge, Mass.: Harvard University Press.

————. 1977. *Outline of a Theory of Practice*. Cambridge: Cambridge University Press.

————. 1972. *Algeria 1960*. New York: Cambridge University Press.

Breines, Wini. 1982. *Community and Organization in the New Left, 1962-68*. New York: Praeger.

Breton, Gilles, and Jane Jenson. 1991a. "After Free Trade and Meech Lake: *Quoi de neuf?*" *Studies in Political Economy,* no. 34.

————. 1991b. "La nouvelle dualité canadienne: L'entente de libre-échange et l'après-Meech." In *Le Québec et la restructuration du Canada,* edited by L. Balthazar et al. Sillery, Quebec: Septention.

Breton, Raymond. 1985. "Multiculturalism and Canadian Nation-Building," In *The Politics of Gender, Ethnicity and Language in Canada,* edited by A. Cairns and C. Williams. Toronto: University of Toronto Press.

Briggs, Charles L. 1986. *Learning How to Ask*. New York: Cambridge University Press.

Brown, Michael, and Amy Goldin. 1973. *Collective Behavior*. Pacific Palisades, Calif.: Goodyear.

Buechler, Steven M. 1990. *Women's Movements in the United States*. New Brunswick, N.J.: Rutgers University Press.

Buhle, Paul. 1990. "Daily Worker (and Successors)." In *Encyclopedia of the American Left,* edited by M. J. Buhle, P. Buhle, and D. Georgakas. New York: Garland.

Burke, Kenneth. 1969. *A Rhetoric of Motives*. Berkeley: University of California Press.

Burke, Peter. 1992. "We, the People: Popular Culture and Identity in Modern Europe." In *Modernity and Identity,* edited by S. Lash and J. Friedman. Oxford: Blackwell.

Buschke, H., and A. H. Schaier. 1979. "Memory Units, Ideas, and Propositioning in Semantic Remembering." *Journal of Verbal Learning and Verbal Behavior* 18:549-63.

Calhoun, Craig. 1983. "The Radicalism of Tradition: Community Strength or Venerable Disguise and Borrowed Language?" *American Journal of Sociology* 88:886-914.

Cameron, Duncan. 1992. Introduction to *Constitutional Politics,* edited by D. Cameron and M. Smith. Toronto: Lorimer.

Capek, Stella. 1993. "The 'Environmental Justice' Frame: A Conceptual Discussion and an Application." *Social Problems* 40, no.1: 5-24.

Caplow, Theodore. 1984. "Rule Enforcement without Visible Means: Christmas Gift Giving in Middletown." *American Journal of Sociology* 89:1306-23.

——. 1982. "Christmas Gifts and Kin Networks." *American Sociological Review* 47:383-92.

Carlson, Allan. 1986. "Family Abuse." *Reason,* May, 34-41.

Cassell, Joan. 1977. *A Group Called Women: Sisterhood and Symbolism in the Feminist Movement.* New York: David McKay.

Castells, Manuel. 1983. *The City and the Grassroots: A Cross-Cultural Theory of Urban Social Movements.* Berkeley: University of California Press.

Chartrand, Paul L. A. H. 1993. "Aboriginal Self-Government: The Two Sides of Legitimacy." In *How Ottawa Spends 1993-94: A More Democratic Canada?,* edited by Susan D. Phillips. Ottawa: Carleton University Press.

——. 1992. "The Claims of Aboriginal Peoples in Canada: A Challenge to the Ideas of Confederation in 1867." Presented to a conference on Federalism and the Nation State, University of Toronto.

——. 1991. "'Terms of Division': Problems of 'Outside-Naming' for Aboriginal People in Canada." *Journal of Indigenous Studies* 2, no.2.

Chodorow, Nancy. 1978. *The Reproduction of Mothering: Psychoanalysis and the Sociology of Gender.* Berkeley: University of California Press.

Cicourel, Aaron V. 1986. "Elicitation as a Problem of Discourse." In *Sociolinguistics: An International Handbook of the Science of Language and Society.* Berlin: Walter de Gruyter.

——. 1982. "Interviews, Surveys, and the Problem of Ecological Validity." *American Sociologist* 17:11-20.

——. 1975. "Discourse and Text: Cognitive and Linguistic Processes in Studies of Social Structure." *Versus: Quaderni de Studi Semiotici,* September-December, 33-84.

——. 1974. *Cognitive Sociology.* New York: Free Press.

Clarke, H., J. Jenson, L. LeDuc, and J. Pammett. 1991. *Absent Mandate: Interpreting Change in Canadian Politics.* Toronto: Gage.

Clifford, James. 1988. *The Predicament of Culture.* Cambridge, Mass.: Harvard University Press.

Coakley, John. 1992. *The Social Origins of Nationalist Movements.* London: Sage.

Cohen, Jean L. 1985. "Strategy or Identity: New Theoretical Paradigms and Contemporary Social Movements." *Social Research* 52, no.4: 663-716.

Coleman, William. 1984. *The Independence Movement in Quebec, 1945-1980.* Toronto: University of Toronto Press.

Collins, Randall. 1990. "Stratification, Emotional Energy and the Transient Emotions." In *Research Agendas,* edited by Theodore O. Kemper. Albany: State University of New York Press.

——. 1989. "Toward a Neo-Meadian Sociology of Mind." *Symbolic Interaction* 12:1-32.

——. 1988. "The Micro Contribution to Macro Sociology." *Sociological Theory* 6 (Fall): 242-53.

——. 1981. "On the Microfoundations of Macrosociology." *American Journal of Sociology* 86:984-1014.

——. 1975. *Conflict Sociology.* New York: Academic Press.

Colvin, Lucy. 1993. "Thousands of Women Are Throwing Up Their Food Today." *Off Our Backs,* July, 7.

Cornell, Stephen. 1988. *The Return of the Native.* New York: Oxford University Press.

Daly, Mary. 1984. *Pure Lust: Elemental Feminist Philosophy*. Boston: Beacon.

———. 1978. *Gyn/Ecology: The Metaethics of Radical Feminism*. Boston: Beacon.

Daly, Mary, and Jane Caputi. 1987. *Webster's First New Intergalactic Wickedary of the English Language*. Boston: Beacon.

D'Anjou, Leon J. M. 1990. "Social Movements and Collective Definitions of the Situation." Paper presented at the 13th World Congress of Sociology, Madrid.

Darnton, Robert. 1984. *The Great Cat Massacre and Other Episodes in French Cultural History*. New York: Basic Books.

Davies, James C. 1969. "The J-curve of Rising and Declining Satisfaction as a Cause of Some Great Revolutions and a Contained Rebellion." In *Violence in America: Historical and Comparative Perspectives*. Washington, D.C.: Government Printing Office.

Davis, Natalie Zemon. 1975. *Society and Culture in Early-Modern France*. Stanford, Calif.: Stanford University Press.

Della Porta, Donatella. 1992. "Life Histories in the Analysis of Social Movements Activists." In *Studying Collective Action*. London: Sage.

D'Emilio, John. 1983. *Sexual Politics, Sexual Communities*. Chicago: University of Chicago Press.

Denzin, Norman K. 1991. "Empiricist Cultural Studies in America: A Deconstructive Reading." *Current Perspectives in Social Theory* 11:17-39.

———. 1987. *The Recovering Alcoholic*. Newbury Park, Calif.: Sage.

Diamond, Edwin. 1975. *The Tin Kazoo: Television, Politics, and the News*. Cambridge, Mass.: MIT Press.

Diani, Mario, and Ron Eyerman, eds. 1992. *Studying Collective Action*. London: Sage.

Dobrowolsky, Alexandra, and Jane Jenson. 1993. "Reforming the Parties: Prescriptions for Democracy." In *How Ottawa Spends 1993-94: A More Democratic Canada?* edited by Susan D. Phillips. Ottawa: Carleton University Press.

Donati, Paolo. 1992. "Political Discourse Analysis." In *Studying Collective Action*, edited by Mario Diani and Ron Eyerman. London: Sage.

"Dossier." 1993. *The Advocate*, July 13, 7.

Douglas, Mary. 1986. *How Institutions Think*. Syracuse, N.Y.: Syracuse University Press.

Dundes, Alan. 1977. "Who Are the Folk?" In *Frontiers of Folklore*, edited by William R. Bascom. Boulder, Colo.: Westview.

Durkheim, Emile. 1973. "Individualism and the Intellectuals." In *Emile Durkheim on Morality and Society*, edited by R. N. Bellah. Chicago: University of Chicago Press.

———. 1965, 1961 [1915]. *The Elementary Forms of the Religious Life*. Translated by Joseph Ward Swain. New York: Free Press.

———. 1964 [1895]. *Rules of the Sociological Method*. New York: Free Press.

———. 1933. *The Division of Labor in Society*. New York: Free Press.

Edelman, Murray J. 1988. *Constructing the Political Spectacle*. Chicago: University of Chicago Press.

Eder, Donna, Suzanne Staggenborg, and Lori Sudderth. Unpublished. "The National Women's Music Festival: A Community That Works?"

Eder, Klaus. 1982. "A New Social Movement?" *Telos* 52:5-20.

Edwards, D. 1991. "*Categories Are for Talking*." *Theory and Psychology* 1:515-42.

Edwards, D., and J. Potter. 1993a. *Discursive Psychology*. London: Sage.

———. 1993b. "Language and Causation: A Discursive Action Model of Description and Attribution. *Psychological Review* 100: 23-41.

Edwards, D., D. Middleton, and J. Potter. 1992. "Toward a Discursive Psychology of Remembering. *Psychologist* 15:441-46.

Eiser, J. R. 1980. *Cognitive Social Psychology*. London: McGraw-Hill.

Elshtain, Jean Bethke. 1985. "Invasion of the Child Savers: How We Succumb to Hype and Hysteria." *Progressive,* September, 23-26.

Epstein, Barbara. 1990a. *Political Protest and Cultural Revolution: Nonviolent Direct Action in the 1970s and 1980s.* Berkeley: University of California Press.

———. 1990b. "Rethinking Social Movement Theory." *Socialist Review* 20:35-66.

Epstein, Edward J. 1973. *News from Nowhere.* New York: Random House.

Epstein, Steven. 1987. "Gay Politics, Ethnic Identity: The Limits of Social Constructionism." *Socialist Review* 17:9-54.

Essed, P. 1988. "Understanding Verbal Accounts of Racism: Politics and the Heuristics of Reality Constructions." *Text* 8:5-40.

Evans, Sara. 1980. *Personal Politics: The Roots of Women's Liberation in the Civil Rights Movement and the New Left.* New York: Vintage.

Evans, Sara, and Harry Boyte. 1986. *Free Spaces.* New York: Harper & Row.

Fanon, Frantz. 1967. *A Dying Colonialism.* New York: Grove.

Fantasia, Rick. 1988. *Cultures of Solidarity.* Berkeley and Los Angeles: University of California Press.

Feldman, Steven P. 1990. "Stories as Cultural Creativity: On the Relation between Symbolism and Politics in Organizational Change." *Human Relations* 43:809-28.

Fernea, Elizabeth, and Basima Qattan Berzirgan, eds. 1977. *Middle Eastern Muslim Women Speak.* Austin: University of Texas Press.

Ferree, Myra Marx. 1992. "The Political Context of Rationality: Rational Choice Theory and Resource Mobilization." In *Frontiers of Social Movement Theory,* edited by Aldon Morris and Carol Mueller. New Haven, Conn.: Yale University Press.

Ferree, Myra Marx, and Frederick D. Miller. 1985. "Mobilization and Meaning: Toward an Integration of Social Psychological and Resource Perspectives on Social Movements." *Sociological Inquiry* 55:38-51.

Feuer, Lewis S. 1975. *Ideology and the Ideologists.* Oxford: Blackwell.

Fine, Gary Alan. 1989. "The Process of Tradition: Cultural Models of Change and Content." In *Studies in Comparative Historical Sociology,* edited by Craig Calhoun. Greenwich, Conn.: JAI Press.

———. 1987. *With the Boys: Little League Baseball and Preadolescent Culture.* Chicago: University of Chicago Press.

———. 1985. "Can the Circle Be Unbroken?: Small Groups and Social Movements." In *Advances in Group Processes.* Vol. 2. Edited by Edward Lawler. Greenwich, Conn.: JAI Press.

———. 1982. "The Manson Family as a Folk Group: Small Groups and Folklore." *Journal of the Folklore Institute* 19:47-60.

———. 1981. "Friends, Impression Management, and Preadolescent Behavior." In *The Development of Children's Friendships,* edited by Steven R. Asher and John M. Gottman. New York: Cambridge University Press.

———. 1979. "Small Groups and Cultural Creation: The Idioculture of Little League Baseball Teams." *American Sociological Review* 44:733-45.

Fireman, Bruce, and William H. Gamson. 1979. "Utilitarian Logic in the Resource Mobilization Perspective." In *The Dynamics of Social Movements,* edited by Mayer N. Zald and John D. McCarthy. Cambridge, Mass.: Winthrop.

Fisher, Berenice, and Joan Tronto. 1990. "Toward a Feminist Theory of Caring." In *Circles of Care: Work and Identity in Women's Lives,* edited by Emily K. Abel and Margaret K. Nelson. Albany, N.Y.: SUNY Press.

Flacks, Richard. 1988. *Making History.* New York: Columbia University Press.

Foucault, Michel. 1983. "Afterword: The Subject and Power." In *Michel Foucault: Beyond*

Structuralism and Hermeneutics. Edited by Hubert Dreyfus and Paul Rabinow. Chicago: University of Chicago Press.

———. 1980. *Power/Knowledge: Selected Interviews and Other Writings, 1972-1977,* edited by Colin Gordon. New York: Pantheon.

———. 1978. *The History of Sexuality.* Vol. 1. London: Penguin.

———. 1977. *Discipline and Punish.* New York: Vintage.

———. 1965. *Madness and Civilization: A History of Insanity in the Age of Reason.* New York: Random House.

Fraser, Nancy. 1989. *Unruly Practices: Power, Discourse, and Gender in Contemporary Social Theory.* Minneapolis: University of Minnesota Press.

Freeman, Jo. 1975. *The Politics of Women's Liberation.* New York: David McKay.

———. 1972-73. "The Tyranny of Structurelessness." *Berkeley Journal of Sociology* 17:151-64.

Friedman, Debra, and Doug McAdam. 1992. "Collective Identity and Activism: Networks, Choices, and the Life of a Social Movement." In *Frontiers in Social Movement Theory,* edited by Aldon Morris and Carol Mueller. New Haven, Conn.: Yale University Press.

Gadamer, Hans Georg. 1976. *Philosophical Hermeneutics.* Translated and edited by David E. Linge. Berkeley: University of California Press.

Gagne, Patricia L. 1993. "The Battered Women's Movement in the 'Post-Feminist' Era." Unpublished doctoral dissertation, Ohio State University.

Gagnon, Alain-G., and Mary Beth Montcalm. 1990. *Quebec: Beyond Quiet Revolution.* Toronto: Nelson.

Gamson, Josh. 1989. "Silence, Death, and the Invisible Enemy: AIDS Activism and Social Movement 'Newness.'" *Social Problems* 36:351-67.

Gamson, William A. 1992a. "The Social Psychology of Collective Action." In *Frontiers in Social Movement Theory,* edited by Aldon Morris and Carol McClurg Mueller. New Haven, Conn.: Yale University Press.

———. 1992b. *Talking Politics.* Cambridge: Cambridge University Press.

———. 1990. *The Strategy of Social Protest.* Belmont, Calif.: Wadsworth.

———. 1988. "Political Discourse and Collective Action." In *International Social Movement Research: From Structure to Action,* edited by Bert Klandermans, Hanspeter Kriesi, and Sidney Tarrow. Greenwich, Conn.: JAI Press.

Gamson, William A., Bruce Fireman, and Steven Rytina. 1982. *Encounters with Unjust Authority.* Homewood, Ill.: Dorsey.

Gamson, William, and Andre Modigliani. 1989. "Media Discourse and Public Opinion on Nuclear Power." *American Journal of Sociology* 95:1-37.

Gans, Herbert. 1988. *Middle American Individualism.* New York: Free Press.

Garfinkel, Harold. 1967. "The Routine Grounds of Everyday Activities." *Studies in Ethnomethodology.* Englewood Cliffs, N.J.: Prentice-Hall.

Gartman, David. 1991. "Culture as Class Symbolization or Mass Reification? A Critique of Bourdieu's Distinction." *American Journal of Sociology* 97:421-47.

Gazzaniga, Michael. 1987. *The Social Brain.* New York: Basic Books.

Geertz, Clifford. 1976. "Art as a Cultural System." *Modern Language Notes* 91:1473-99.

———. 1973. *The Interpretation of Cultures.* New York: Basic Books.

———. 1968. *Islam Observed: Religious Development in Morocco and Indonesia.* New Haven, Conn.: Yale University Press.

———. 1966. "Religion as a Cultural System." In *Anthropological Approaches to the Study of Religion,* edited by Michael Banton. London: Tavistock.

———. 1960. *The Religion of Java.* New York: Free Press of Glencoe.

Gellner, Ernst. 1987. *Culture, Identity and Politics.* Cambridge: Cambridge University Press.

———. 1983. *Nations and Nationalism.* Oxford: Blackwell.

Georgakas, Dan. 1990. "National Guardian and Guardian." In *Encyclopedia of the American Left,* edited by M. J. Buhle, P. Buhle, and D. Georgakas. New York: Garland.

Gergen, K. J. 1989. "Social Psychology and the Wrong Revolution." *European Journal of Social Psychology* 19:463-84.

———. 1985. "The Social Constructionist Movement in Modern Psychology." *American Psychologist* 40:266-75.

———. 1982. *Towards Transformation in Social Knowledge.* New York: Springer.

Gerhards, Jurgen, and Dieter Rucht. 1992. "Mesomobilization: Organizing and Framing in Two Protest Campaigns in West Germany." *American Journal of Sociology* 98:555-95.

Giddens, Anthony. 1991. *Modernity and Self-Identity: Self and Society in the Late Modern Age.* Stanford, Calif.: Stanford University Press.

———. 1987. *Social Theory and Modern Sociology.* Cambridge, Mass. Polity.

———. 1985. *The Nation-State and Violence.* Cambridge, Mass. Polity.

———. 1984. *The Constitution of Society.* Berkeley: University of California Press.

Gieryn, Thomas F. 1983. "Boundary-Work and the Demarcation of Science from Non-Science: Strains and Interests in Professional Ideologies of Scientists." *American Sociological Review,* 48:781-95.

Giglioli, Pier Paolo, ed. 1972. *Language and Social Context.* London: Penguin Education.

Gilbert, G. N., and M. Mulkay. 1984. *Opening Pandora's Box.* Cambridge: Cambridge University Press.

Gilligan, Carol. 1982. *In a Different Voice.* Cambridge, Mass.: Harvard University Press.

Gilmore, Samuel. 1992. "Culture." In *Encyclopedia of Sociology.* Vol. 1. Edited by E. Borgatta and M. Borgatta. New York: Macmillian.

Gitlin, Todd, 1980. *The Whole World Is Watching.* Berkeley and Los Angeles: University of California Press.

Glendon, Mary Ann. 1991. *Rights Talk: The Impoverishment of Political Discourse.* New York: Free Press.

Goffman, Erving. 1974. *Frame Analysis.* Cambridge, Mass.: Harvard University Press.

———. 1967. *Interaction Ritual.* Chicago: Aldine.

———. 1959. *The Presentation of Self in Everyday Life.* Garden City, N.Y.: Doubleday Anchor.

Goldstein, Marilyn. 1987. "Presumed Guilty." *Newsday,* July 16.

Goodenough, Ward. 1964. "Cultural Anthropology and Linguistics." In *Language in Culture and Society,* edited by Dell Hymes. New York: Harper & Row.

———. 1956. "Componential Analysis and the Study of Meaning." *Language* 32:195-216.

Gordon, David C. 1968. *Women of Algeria: An Essay on Change.* Cambridge, Mass.: Harvard University Press.

Gordon, Steven. 1981. "The Sociology of Sentiments and Emotion." In *Social Psychology, Social Perspectives,* edited by Morris Rosenberg and Ralph Turner. New York: Basic Books.

Gramsci, Antonio. 1971. *Prison Notebooks.* London: Lawrence and Wishart.

Granatstein, J. L., and Kenneth McNaught, eds. 1991. *"English Canada" Speaks Out.* Toronto: Doubleday.

Graumann, C. F., and S. Moscovici, eds. 1987. *Changing Conceptions of Conspiracy.* New York: Springer.

Gray, Robert. 1986. "The Deconstruction of the English Working Class." *Social History* 11:363-73.

Greenblatt, Stephen. 1980. *Renaissance Self-Fashioning: From More to Shakespeare.* Chicago: University of Chicago Press.

Grimshaw, Allen D. 1982. "Comprehensive Discourse Analysis: An Instance of Professional Peer Interaction." *Language in Society* 11:15-47.

Guindon, Hubert. 1988. *Quebec Society: Tradition, Modernity and Nationhood.* Toronto: University of Toronto Press.

Gumperz, John J. 1982. *Discourse Strategies.* Cambridge: Cambridge University Press.

Gumperz, John, and Dell Hymes. 1972. *Directions in Sociolinguistics.* New York: Holt, Rinehart, & Winston.

Gurr, Ted. 1970. *Why Men Rebel.* Princeton, N.J.: Princeton University Press.

Gusfield, Joseph R. 1989. "Constructing the Ownership of Social Problems: Fun and Profit in the Welfare State." *Social Problems* 36:431-41.

———. 1981. "Social Movements and Social Change: Perspectives of Linearity and Fluidity." In *Research in Social Movements, Conflict, and Change,* vol. 4, edited by Louis Kriesberg. Greenwich, Conn.: JAI Press.

Haaken, Janice. 1993. "From Al-Anon to ACOA: Codependence and the Reconstruction of Caregiving." *Signs* 18:321-45.

Habermas, Jürgen. 1987. *The Theory of Communicative Action.* Vol. 2, *Lifeworld and System: A Critique of Functionalist Reason.* Boston: Beacon.

———. 1984. *The Theory of Communicative Action.* Vol. 1, *Reason and the Rationalization of Society.* Boston: Beacon.

Hall, Tony. 1991. "Aboriginal Issues and the New Political Map of Canada." In *"English Canada" Speaks Out,* edited by J. L. Granatstein and Kenneth McNaught. Toronto: Doubleday.

Hardesty, Monica, and Patricia Geist. 1987. "Stories of Choice and Constraint in the Pursuit of Quality Medical Care." Paper presented to the Society for the Study of Symbolic Interaction, Urbana, Illinois.

Harding, Sandra. 1991. *Whose Science? Whose Knowledge?* Ithaca, N.Y.: Cornell University Press.

Hebdige, Dick. 1979. *Subculture: The Meaning of Style.* London: Methuen.

Hewitt, J. P., and R. Stokes. 1975. "Disclaimers." *American Sociological Review* 40:1-11.

Hilgartner, Steven, and Charles Bosk. 1988. "The Rise and Fall of Social Problems: A Public Arenas Model." *American Journal of Sociology* 94:53-78.

Hill Collins, Patricia. 1990. *Black Feminist Thought.* New York: Routledge.

Hiltermann, J. R. 1991. "The Women's Movement During the Uprising." *Journal of Palestine Studies* 20:48-57.

Hirsch, Eric L. 1990a. *Urban Revolt: Ethnic Politics in the Nineteenth Century Chicago Labor Movement.* Berkeley: University of California Press.

———. 1990b. "Sacrifice for the Cause: Group Processes, Recruitment and Commitment in a Student Movement." *American Sociological Review* 55: 243-54.

———. 1986. "The Creation of Political Solidarity in Social Movement Organizations." *Sociological Quarterly* 27:373-87.

Hobsbawm, E. J. 1959. *Primitive Rebels.* New York: Norton.

Hobsbawm, E. J., and Terrence Ranger, eds. 1983. *The Invention of Tradition.* Cambridge: Cambridge University Press.

Hochschild, Arlie. 1990. "Ideology and Emotion Management: A Perspective and Path for Future Research." In *Research Agendas in the Sociology of Emotions,* edited by Theodore D. Kemper. Albany, N.Y.: SUNY Press.

———. 1983. *The Managed Heart.* Berkeley: University of California Press.

———. 1979. "Emotion Work, Feeling Rules, and Social Structure." *American Journal of Sociology* 35:551-73.

Hollander, Edwin. 1958. "Conformity, Status, and Idiosyncracy Credit." *Psychological Review* 65:117-27.

hooks, bell. 1993. *Sisters of the Yam: Black Women and Self-Recovery.* Boston: South End Press.

256   BIBLIOGRAPHY

Hormann, Hans. 1986. *Meaning and Context.* New York: Plenum.
Horowitz, Donald L. 1977. "Cultural Movements and Ethnic Change." *Annals of the American Academy of Political and Social Sciences* 433:6-18.
Hunt, Lynn. 1984. *Politics, Culture and Class in the French Revolution.* Berkeley and Los Angeles: University of California Press.
Hunt, Scott A., and Robert D. Benford. Unpublished. "Constructing Personal and Collective Identities."
Hymes, Dell. 1974a. "Social Anthropology, Sociolinguistics, and the Ethnography of Speaking." In *Foundations in Sociolinguistics,* edited by Dell Hymes. Philadelphia: University of Pennsylvania Press.
――――. 1974b. *Directions in Sociolinguistics.* Philadelphia: University of Pennsylvania Press.
Inglehart, Ronald. 1990. *Culture Shift in Advanced Industrial Society.* Princeton, N.J.: Princeton University Press.
――――. 1977. *The Silent Revolution: Changing Values and Political Styles among Western Publics.* Princeton, N.J.: Princeton University Press.
Iyengar, Shanto. 1991. *Is Anyone Responsible?: How Television News Frames Political Issues.* Chicago: University of Chicago Press.
Iyengar, Shanto, and Donald R. Kinder. 1987. *News That Matters.* Chicago: University of Chicago Press.
Jacobs, Mark D. 1987. "Probation Officers' Tragic Narratives." Presented at the annual meetings of the American Sociological Association, Chicago.
Jaeger, Gertrude, and Phillip Selznick. 1964. "A Normative Theory of Culture." *American Sociological Review* 29: 653-69.
Jaggar, Alison. 1983. *Feminist Politics and Human Nature.* Totowa, N.J.: Rowman and Allanheld.
Jaspars, J. M. F., and C. Fraser. 1983. "Attitudes and Social Representations." In *Social Representations,* edited by Serge Moscovici. Cambridge: Cambridge University Press.
Jefferson, Gail. 1985. "On the Interactional Unpacking of a 'Gloss.'" *Language in Society* 14:435-66.
Jenkins, J. Craig. 1983. "Resource Mobilization Theory and the Study of Social Movements." *Annual Review of Sociology* 9:527-53.
Jenson, Jane. 1992. "Beyond Brokerage Politics: Towards the Democracy Round." In *Constitutional Politics,* edited by D. Cameron and M. Smith. Toronto: Lorimer.
――――. 1991. "All the World's a Stage: Ideas, Spaces and Time in Canadian Political Economy." *Studies in Political Economy,* no. 36.
――――. 1990. "Representations in Crisis: The Roots of Canada's Permeable Fordism." *Canadian Journal of Political Science* 23:4.
――――. 1989. "Paradigms and Political Discourse: Protective Legislation in France and the United States before 1914." *Canadian Journal of Political Science* 22:2.
――――. 1987. "Changing Discourse, Changing Agendas: Political Rights and Reproductive Policies in France." In *The Women's Movements of the United States and Western Europe,* edited by Mary F. Katzenstein and Carol McClurg Mueller. Philadelphia: Temple University Press.
Jepperson, Ronald L. 1991. "Institutions, Institutional Effects, and Institutionalism." In *The New Institutionalism in Organizational Analysis,* edited by Walter W. Powell and Paul DiMaggio. Chicago: University of Chicago Press.
Jhappan, Radha. 1993. "Inherency, Three Nations and Collective Rights: The Evolution of Aboriginal Constitutional Discourse from 1982 to the Charlottetown Accord." *International Journal of Canadian Studies,* no.7-8 (Spring-Fall).
――――. 1992. "Aboriginal Peoples' Right to Self-Government" In *Constitutional Politics,* edited by D. Cameron and M. Smith. Toronto: Lorimer.

Johnson, John. 1989. "Horror Stories and the Construction of Child Abuse." In *Images of Issues,* edited by Joel Best. New York: Aldine de Gruyter.

Johnson-Laird, Phillip N. 1983. *Mental Models.* Cambridge, Mass.: Harvard University Press.

Johnston, Hank, 1993. "Religio-Nationalist Subcultures under the Communists: Comparisons from the Baltics, Transcaucasia and the Ukraine." *Sociology of Religion* 54, no.3: 237-55.

———. 1992. "Religion and Nationalist Subcultures in the Baltics." *Journal of Baltic Studies* 23, no.2: 133-48.

———. 1991. *Tales of Nationalism: Catalonia, 1939-1979.* New Brunswick, N.J.: Rutgers University Press.

———. 1989. "Toward an Explanation of Church Opposition to Authoritarian Regimes: Religio-Oppositional Subcultures in Poland and Catalonia." *Journal for the Scientific Study of Religion* 28:493-508.

———. 1987. "Textual Analysis of Archival Documents: Microsociological Critique of Historical-Comparative Data Bases." Paper presented at the American Sociological Association annual meeting, Section on Sociolinguistics "Talk as Social Structuration: Implications for Theory and Methods," Chicago.

———. 1985. "Catalan Ethnic Mobilization: Some 'Primordial' Modifications of the Ethnic Competition Model." In *Current Perspectives in Social Theory.* Edited by Scott McNall. Greenwich, Conn.: JAI Press.

Johnston, Hank, Enrique Laraña, and Joseph R. Gusfield. 1994. "New Social Movements: Identities, Grievances and Ideologies of Everyday Life." In *New Social Movements: From Ideology to Identity,* edited by Enrique Laraña, Hank Johnston, and Joseph R. Gusfield. Philadelphia: Temple University Press.

Kalcik, Susan. 1975. ". . . Like Ann's Gynecologist or the Time I Was Almost Raped: Personal Narratives in Women's Rap Groups." *Journal of American Folklore* 88:3-11.

Kanter, Rosabeth. 1972. *Commitment and Community.* Cambridge, Mass.: Harvard University Press.

Katzenstein, Mary. Unpublished. "Discursive Politics and Feminist Activism in the Catholic Church." Presented at a conference entitled Feminist Organizations: Harvest of the Women's Movement held in Washington, D.C., in February 1992.

Kauffman, L. A. 1990. "The Anti-Politics of Identity." *Socialist Review* 20:67-80.

Keane, John. 1988. *Civil Society and the State.* London: Verso.

Keesing, Roger M. 1974. "Theories of Culture." In *Annual Review of Anthropology 3.* Palo Alto: Annual Reviews.

Kemper, Theodore D. 1981. "Social Constructionist and Positivist Approaches to the Sociology of Emotions." *American Journal of Sociology* 87:336-62.

———. 1978. *A Social Interactional Theory of Emotions.* New York: Wiley.

Kintsch, W., and Teun A. van Dijk. 1978. "Toward a Model of Text Comprehension and Production." *Psychological Review* 85:363-94.

Klandermans, Bert. 1994. "Transient Identities?: Membership Patterns in the Dutch Peace Movement." In *New Social Movements: From Ideology to Identity,* edited by Enrique Laraña, Hank Johnston, and Joseph R. Gusfield. Philadelphia: Temple University Press.

———. 1992. "The Social Construction of Protest and Multiorganizational Fields." In *Frontiers in Social Movement Theory,* edited by Aldon Morris and Carol McClurg Mueller. New Haven, Conn.: Yale University Press.

———. 1989. "Grievance Interpretation and Success Expectations: The Social Construction of Protest." *Social Behaviour* 4:113-25.

———. 1988. "The Formation and Mobilization of Consensus." In *International Social Movement Research.* Vol. 1, *From Structure to Action: Comparing Movement Participa-*

tion across Cultures, edited by Bert Klandermans, Hanspeter Kriesi, and Sidney Tarrow. Greenwich, Conn.: JAI Press.

———. 1984. "Mobilization and Participation: Social-Psychological Expansions of Resource Mobilization Theory." *American Sociological Review* 49:583-600.

Klandermans, Bert, and Sidney Tarrow. 1988. "Mobilization into Social Movements: Synthesizing European and American Approaches." In *International Social Movement Research.* Vol. 1, *From Structure to Action: Comparing Movement Participation across Cultures,* edited by Bert Klandermans, Hanspeter Kriesi, and Sidney Tarrow. Greenwich, Conn.: JAI Press.

Klandermans, Bert, Hanspeter Kriesi, and Sidney Tarrow. 1988. *International Social Movement Research.* Vol. 1, *From Structure to Action: Comparing Movement Participation across Cultures.* Greenwich, Conn.: JAI Press.

Klapp, Orrin. 1991. *Inflation of Symbols.* New Brunswick, N.J.: Transaction.

———. 1969. *Collective Search for Identity.* New York: Holt, Rinehart & Winston.

Klein, Ethel. 1984. *Gender Politics.* Cambridge, Mass.: Harvard University Press.

Kluckhohn, Florence R., and Fred Strodtbeck. 1961. *Variations in Value Orientations.* New York: Row, Peterson.

Knauss, Peter R. 1987. *The Persistence of Patriarchy: Class, Gender, and Ideology in Twentieth Century Algeria.* New York: Praeger.

Kriesi, Hanspeter. 1991. "The Political Opportunity Structure of New Social Movements: Its Impact on Their Mobilization." Berlin: WZB Working Paper.

Kristeva, J. 1986. "Word, Dialogue and Novel." In *The Kristeva Reader,* edited by T. Moi. Oxford: Blackwell.

Kroeber, A. L. 1963. *Anthropology: Culture, Patterns, and Processes.* New York: Harcourt Brace.

Kroeber, A. L., and Clyde Kluckhohn. 1963. *Culture: A Critical Review of Concepts and Definitions.* New York: Vintage. Originally published in 1952 as vol. 47, no. 1 of the Papers of the Peabody Museum of American Archaeology and Ethnology, Harvard University.

Krosenbrink-Gelissen, Lilianne. 1993. "The Canadian Constitution, the Charter, and Aboriginal Women's Rights: Conflicts and Dilemmas." *International Journal of Canadian Studies,* no.7-8, (Spring-Fall).

Kymlicka, Will. 1991. "Liberalism and the Politicization of Ethnicity." *Canadian Journal of Law and Jurisprudence* 4, no.2 (July).

Labov, William, and David Fanshel. 1977. *Therapeutic Discourse.* New York: Academic Press.

Lalljee, M., L. B. Brown, and G. P. Ginsberg. 1984. "Attitudes: Disposition, Behaviour or Evaluation?" *British Journal of Social Psychology* 23:233-44.

Lamont, Michele, and Robert Wuthnow. 1990. "Betwixt and Between: Recent Cultural Sociology in Europe and the United States." In *Frontiers of Social Theory: The New Synthesis,* edited by George Ritzer. New York: Columbia University Press.

Lang, Kurt, and Gladys Lang. 1961. *Collective Dynamics.* New York: Crowell.

Lapassade, Georges. 1981. *L'analyse et l'analyste.* Paris: Gauthier Villars.

Laraña, E., H. Johnston, and J.R. Gusfield, eds. 1994. *New Social Movements.* Philadelphia: Temple University Press.

LeBon, Gustave. 1960. *The Crowd: A Study of the Popular Mind.* New York: Viking.

Lichterman, Paul. 1992. "When Is the Personal Political? Class, Culture and Political Style in U.S. Grassroots Environmentalism." Paper presented at the annual meeting of the American Sociological Association, Pittsburgh.

Lofland, John. 1993. *Polite Protesters: The American Peace Movement of the 1980s.* Syracuse, N.Y.: Syracuse University Press.

———. 1992. "Movement Culture: Sparse, Uneven, Two-Tiered." Unpublished manuscript.

———. 1989. "Consensus Movements: City Twinning and Derailed Dissent in the American Eighties." In *Research on Social Movements*. Vol. 11. Greenwich, Conn.: JAI Press.

———. 1987. "Social Movement Culture and the Unification Church." In *The Future of the New Religious Movements*, edited by D.G. Bromley and P. E. Hammond. Macon, Ga.: Mercer University Press.

———. 1985. *Protest: Studies of Collective Behavior and Social Movements*. New Brunswick, N.J.: Transaction.

Long, David. 1992. "Culture, Ideology, and Militancy: The Movement of Native Indians in Canada, 1969-91." In *Organising Dissent: Contemporary Social Movements in Theory and Practice*, edited by W. E. Carroll. Toronto: Garamond.

Lopes, L. L. 1991. "The Rhetoric of Irrationality." *Theory and Psychology* 1:65-82.

Loureau, René. 1977. *Le gai savoir des sociologues*. Paris: Editions 10/18.

Lyotard, Jean-François. 1984. *The Postmodern Condition: A Report on Knowledge*. Minneapolis: University of Minnesota Press.

MacLeod, Arlene Elowe. 1991. *Accommodating Protest: Working Women, the New Veiling, and Change in Cairo*. New York: Columbia University Press.

Malinowski, Bronislaw A. 1944. *A Scientific Theory of Culture*. Chapel Hill: University of North Carolina Press.

Mannheim, K. 1960. *Ideology and Utopia*. London: Routledge and Kegan Paul.

Manning, David J. 1980. "The Place of Ideology in Political Life." In *The Form of Ideology*, edited by David J. Manning. London: Allen & Unwin.

———. 1976. *Liberalism*. New York: St. Martin's.

Martin, J., and M. E. Powers. 1983. "Organizational Stories: More Vivid and Persuasive Than Quantitative Data." In *Psychological Foundations of Organizational Behavior*, edited by B. Staw. Glenview, Ill: Scott, Foresman.

Martin, J., M. S. Feldman, M. S. Hatch, and S. B. Sitkin. 1983. "The Uniqueness Paradox in Organizational Stories." *Administrative Science Quarterly* 28:438-53.

Martin, Joanne. 1992. *Cultures in Organizations*. New York: Oxford University Press.

Martin, Patricia Yancey. 1990. "Rethinking Feminist Organizations." *Gender and Society* 4, no.2: 182-206.

Marx, John H., and Burkart Holzner. 1975. "Ideological Primary Groups in Contemporary Cultural Movements." *Sociological Focus* 8:311-29.

Marx, Karl, and Friedrich Engels. 1970. *The German Ideology*. London: Lawrence and Wishart.

Matthews, Nancy. 1992. "Managing Rape: The Feminist Anti-rape Movement and the State." Paper presented at the Working Conference on Feminist Organizations: Harvest of the New Women's Movement, Washington D.C.

Maxwell, Madeline M., and Pam Kraemer. 1990. "Speech and Identity in the Deaf Narrative." *Text* 10:339-63.

Mayer, Adrian C. 1966. "The Significance of Quasi-Groups in the Study of Complex Societies." In *The Social Anthropology of Complex Societies*, edited by Michael Banton. London: Tavistock.

McAdam, Doug. 1988. *Freedom Summer*. New York: Oxford University Press.

———. 1982. *Political Process and the Development of Black Insurgency 1930-1970*. Chicago: University of Chicago Press.

McAdam, Doug, and Dieter Rucht. 1993. "The Cross-National Diffusion of Movement Ideas." *Annals of the American Academy of Political and Social Sciences* 528:56-74.

McCall, Christina, et al. 1992. "Three Nations: Eleven of Canada's Leading Intellectuals Declare Their Support for a Canada Equitable from Sea to Sea to Sea." *Canadian Forum*, March.

McCarthy, John D. 1994. "Activists, Authorities and the Media Framing of Drunk Driving."

In *New Social Movements: From Ideology to Identity,* edited by Enrique Laraña, Hank Johnston, and Joseph R. Gusfield. Philadelphia: Temple University Press.

McCarthy, John D., and Mark Wolfson. 1992. "Consensus Movements, Conflict Movements, and the Cooptation of Civic and State Infrastructures." In *Frontiers of Social Movement Theory,* edited by Aldon Morris and Carol McClurg Mueller. New Haven, Conn.: Yale University Press.

McCarthy, John D., and Mayer N. Zald. 1987. "Resource Mobilization and Social Movements: A Partial Theory." In *Social Movements in an Organizational Society: Collected Essays,* edited by M. Zald and J. McCarthy. New Brunswick, N.J.: Transaction.

———. 1973. *The Trend of Social Movements in America.* Morristown, N.J.: General Learning Press.

McCracken, Samuel. 1979. "The Harrisburg Syndrome." *Commentary* 67:27-39.

———. 1977. "The War against the Atom." *Commentary* 64:33-47.

McFeat, Tom. 1974. *Small Group Cultures.* New York: Pergamon.

Melucci, Alberto. 1992. "Frontier Land: Collective Action between Actors and Systems." In *Studying Collective Action,* edited by Mario Diani and Ron Eyerman. London: Sage.

———. 1989. *Nomads of the Present: Social Movements and Individual Needs in Contemporary Society.* Philadelphia: Temple University Press.

———. 1988 "Getting Involved: Identity and Mobilization in Social Movements." In *International Social Movement Research.* Vol. 1. Edited by Bert Klandermans, Hanspeter Kriesi, and Sidney Tarrow. Greenwich, Conn.: JAI Press.

———. 1985. "The Symbolic Challenge of Contemporary Movements." *Social Research* 52:781-816.

———. 1984. *Altri codici. Aree di movimento nella metropoli.* Bologna: Il Mulino.

Merelman, Richard M. 1984. *Making Something of Ourselves: On Culture and Politics in the United States.* Berkeley: University of California Press.

Meyer, David S., and Nancy Whittier. 1994. "Social Movement Spillover." *Social Problems* 41:277-98.

Middleton, D., and D. Edwards, eds. 1990. *Collective Remembering.* London: Sage.

Miller, George A., and Phillip N. Johnson-Laird. 1975. *Language and Perception.* Cambridge, Mass.: Belknap and Harvard University Press.

Miller, Mark Crispin. 1988. *Boxed-In: The Culture of TV.* Evanston, Ill.: Northwestern University Press.

Mills, C. Wright. 1959. *The Sociological Imagination.* New York: Oxford University Press.

Mirowsky, John, and Catherine E. Ross. 1989. *Social Causes of Distress.* New York: Aldine de Gruyter.

Moaddel, Mansoor. 1992. "Ideology as Episodic Discourse: The Case of the Iranian Revolution." *American Sociological Review* 57:353-79.

Morantz, Toby. 1992. "Aboriginal Land Claims in Quebec." In *Aboriginal Land Claims in Canada: A Regional Perspective,* edited by Ken Coates. Toronto: Copp Clark.

Morgen, Sandra. 1983. "Towards a Politics of Feelings: Beyond the Dialectic of Thought and Action." *Women's Studies* 10, no. 2: 203-23.

———. Unpublished. "'It Was the Best of Times, It Was the Worst Of Times': Work Culture in Feminist Health Clinics."

Morris, Aldon D. 1992. "Social Movement and Oppositional Culture." Paper presented at the Workshop on Culture and Social Movements, University of California, San Diego.

———. 1984. *The Origins of the Civil Rights Movement: Black Communities Organizing for Change.* New York: Free Press.

Morris, Aldon D., and Carol McClurg Mueller, eds. 1992. *Frontiers in Social Movement Theory.* New Haven, Conn.: Yale University Press.

Moscovici, Serge. 1993. *The Invention of Society.* London: Polity.

———. 1988. "Notes Towards a Description of Social Representations." *European Journal of Social Psychology* 18:211-50.

———. 1987. "Answers and Questions." *Journal for the Theory of Social Behaviour* 17:513-29.

———. 1985. "Comment on Potter and Litton." *British Journal of Social Psychology* 24:91-93.

———. 1983. "The Phenomenon of Social Representations." In *Social Representations*, edited by R. Farr and S. Moscovici. Cambridge: Cambridge University Press.

———. 1982. "The Coming Era of Representations." In *Cognitive Approaches to Social Behaviour*, edited by J. P. Codol and J. J. Leyens. The Hague: Nijhoff.

———. 1981. *L'age des foules*. Paris: Fayard.

Moscovici, Serge, G. Mugny, and E. Van Avermaet. 1985. *Perspectives on Minority Influence*. Cambridge: Cambridge University Press.

M'Rabet, Fadela. 1964. *La femme algérienne*. Paris: François Maspero.

Mueller, Carol McClurg. 1994. "Collective Identities and the Mobilization of the U.S. Women's Movement, 1960-1970." In *New Social Movements: From Ideology to Identity*, edited by Enrique Laraña, Hank Johnston, and Joseph R. Gusfield. Philadelphia: Temple University Press.

———. 1992. "Building Social Movement Theory." In *Frontiers in Social Movement Theory*, edited by Aldon D. Morris and Carol McClurg Mueller. New Haven, Conn.: Yale University Press.

———. 1987. "Collective Consciousness, Identity Transformation, and the Rise of Women in Public Office in the United States." In *The Women's Movement of the United States and Western Europe*, edited by Mary F. Katzenstein and Carol M. Mueller. Philadelphia: Temple University Press.

Mugny, G., and J. A. Perez, 1991. *The Social Psychology of Minority Influence*. Cambridge: Cambridge University Press.

Nairn, Tom. 1988. *The Enchanted Glass: Britain and Its Monarchy*. London: Hutchinson Radius.

Nakagawa, Gordon. 1990. "'No Japs Allowed': Negation and Naming as Subject-Constituting Strategies Reflected in Contemporary Stories of Japanese American Internment." *Communication Reports* 3:22-27.

Neal, Mary. 1990. "Rhetorical Styles of the Physicians for Social Responsibility." In *Peace Action in the Eighties*, edited by S. Marullo and J. Lofland. New Brunswick, N.J.: Rutgers University Press.

Neisser, Ulrich. 1976. *Cognition and Reality*. San Francisco: Freeman.

Nemni, Max. 1991. "Le dés'accord du Lac Meech et la construction de l'imaginaire symbolique des Québécois." In *Le Québec et la restructuration du Canada*, edited by L. Balthazar et al. Sillery, Quebec: Septention.

Newman, Katherine S. 1987. "PATCO Lives! Stigma, Heroism, and Symbolic Transformations." *Cultural Anthropology* 2:319-46.

Nicholson, Linda, ed. 1990. *Feminism/Postmodernism*. London: Routledge.

Oberschall, Anthony. 1973. *Social Conflict and Social Movements*. Englewood Cliffs, N.J.: Prentice-Hall.

Oliver, Michael. 1991. *The Passionate Debate: The Social and Political Ideas of Quebec Nationalism 1920-1945*. Montreal: Véhicule.

Oliver, Pamela E., and Gerald Marwell. 1993. "Mobilizing Technologies for Collective Action." In *Frontiers in Social Movement Theory*, edited by Aldon D. Morris and Carol McClurg Mueller. New Haven, Conn.: Yale University Press.

Omstein, R., and D. Sobel. 1987. *The Healing Brain*. New York: Simon & Schuster.

Ong, W. J. 1989. *Fighting for Life*. Amherst: University of Massachusetts Press.

Oring, Elliot. 1992. *Jokes and Their Relations*. Lexington: University Press of Kentucky.

Ortner, Sherry. 1984. "Theory in Anthropology since the Sixties." *Comparative Studies in Society and History* 26:126-66.

Pal, Leslie and F. Leslie Seidle. 1993. "Constitutional Politics 1990-92: The Paradox of Consultation." In *How Ottawa Spends 1993-94: A More Democratic Canada?* edited by Susan D. Phillips. Ottawa: Carleton University Press.

Palmer, Bryan D. 1990. *Descent into Discourse.* Philadelphia: Temple University Press.

———. 1987. "Response to Scott." *International Labor and Working Class History* 31:14-23.

Parker, I. 1992. *Discourse Dynamics.* London: Routledge.

Parker, I., and J. Shotter, eds. 1990. *Deconstructing Social Psychology.* London: Routledge.

Parsons, Talcott. 1961. "An Outline of the Social System." In *Theories of Society,* edited by T. Parsons et al. New York: Free Press.

———. 1951. *The Social System.* Glencoe, Ill.: Free Press.

———. 1937. *The Structure of Social Action.* New York: Free Press.

Perelman, C., and L. Olbrechts-Tyteca. 1971. *The New Rhetoric.* Notre Dame, Ind.: University of Notre Dame Press.

Phillips, Marilynn. 1990. "Damaged Goods: Oral Narratives of the Experience of Disability in American Culture." *Social Science Medicine* 30:849-57.

Phillips, Susan. 1974. "Warm Springs 'Indian Time.'" In *Ethnography of Speaking,* edited by Richard Bauman and Joel Sherzer. New York: Cambridge University Press.

Pizzorno, Alessandro. 1986. "Some Other Kind of Otherness: A Critique of Rational Choice Theories." In *Development, Democracy and the Art of Trespassing,* edited by A. Foxley, M. McPherson, and G. O'Donnell. Notre Dame, Ind.: University of Notre Dame Press.

———. 1978. "Political Exchange and Collective Identity in Industrial Conflict." In *The Resurgence of Class Conflict in Western Europe since 1968,* edited by C. Crouch and A. Pizzorno. New York: Holmes and Meier.

Plummer, Ken, and Arlene Stein. Forthcoming. "I Can't Even Think Straight: Queer Theory and the Missing Sexual Revolution in Sociology." *Sociological Theory.*

Potter, J., and M. Billig, 1992. "Re-representing Representations: Discussion of Raty and Snellman." *Ongoing Production on Social Representations* 1:15-20.

Potter, J., and I. Litton, 1985. "Some Problems Underlying the Theory of Social Representations." *British Journal of Social Psychology* 24:81-90.

Potter, J., and M. Wetherell, 1988. "Accomplishing Attitudes: Fact and Evaluation in Racist Discourse." *Text* 8:51-68.

———. 1987. *Discourse and Social Psychology.* London: Sage.

Potter, J., D. Edwards, and M. Wetherell, 1993. "A Model of Discourse in Action." *American Behavioral Scientist* 36:383-401.

Quandt, William B. 1969. *Revolution and Political Leadership: Algeria, 1954-1968.* Cambridge, Mass.: MIT Press.

Ransdell, Lisa. Forthcoming. "Lesbian Feminism and the Feminist Movement." In *Women: A Feminist Perspective.* 5th Ed. Edited by Jo Freeman.

Reddy, William Jr. 1984. *The Rise of Market Culture: The Textile Trade and French Society, 1750-1900.* Cambridge: Cambridge University Press.

Resnick, Philip. 1989. *Letters to a Québécois Friend.* Montreal: McGill-Queen's University Press.

———. 1977. *The Land of Cain: Class and Nationalism in English Canada 1945-75.* Vancouver: New Star.

Rice, John S. 1992. Discursive Formation, Life Stories, and the Emergence of Codependency: 'Power/Knowledge' and the Search for Identity." *Sociological Quarterly* 33:337-64.

Richardson, Laurel. 1991. "Speakers Whose Voices Matter: Toward a Feminist Postmodernist Sociological Praxis." *Studies in Symbolic Interactionism* 12:29-38.

Ricoeur, Paul. 1981. *Hermeneutics and Human Sciences: Essays on Language, Action, and Interpretation.* Edited and translated by John B. Thompson. Cambridge: Cambridge University Press.

———. 1976. *Interpretation Theory: Discourse and the Surplus of Meaning.* Fort Worth: Texas Christian University.

———. 1971. "The Model of the Text: Meaningful Action Considered as a Text." *Social Research* 38:3.

Robinson, John A. 1981. "Personal Narrative Reconsidered." *Journal of American Folklore* 94:58-85.

Rocher, François. 1992. "Quebec's Historical Agenda." In *Constitutional Politics,* edited by D. Cameron and M. Smith. Toronto: Lorimer.

Rokeach, Milton. 1973. *The Nature of Human Values.* New York: Free Press.

Rowbotham, Sheila. 1972. *Women, Resistance & Revolution.* New York: Vintage.

Rumelhart, D. E. 1975. "Notes on a Schema for Stories." In *Representation and Understanding,* edited by S. A. Bobrow and S. M. Collins. New York: Academic Press.

Rupp, Leila J., and Verta Taylor. 1987. *Survival in the Doldrums: The American Woman's Rights Movement, 1945 to the 1960s.* New York: Oxford University Press.

Ryan, Barbara. 1992. *Feminism and the Women's Movement.* New York: Routledge.

Ryan, Charlotte. 1991. *Prime Time Activism.* Boston: South End Press.

Sacks, Harvey. 1972. "An Initial Investigation of the Usability of Conversational Materials for Doing Sociology." In *Studies in Social Interaction,* edited by D. Sudnow. New York: Free Press.

Sacks, Harvey, Emmanuel Schegloff, and Gail Jefferson. 1974. "A Simplest Systematic for the Organization of Turn-Taking for Conversation." *Language* 50:696-735.

Sampson, E. E. 1993. *Celebrating the Other.* Hemel Hempstead: Harvester/Wheatsheaf.

———. 1981. "Cognitive Psychology as Ideology." *American Psychologist* 36:730-43.

Sawchuk, Joe, ed. 1992. *Readings in Aboriginal Studies.* Vol. 2, *Identities and State Structures.* Brandon, Manitoba: Bear Paw Press.

Schank, Roger C., and Robert P. Abelson. 1977. *Scripts, Plans, Goals and Understanding.* Hillsdale, N.J.: Lawrence Erlbaum Associates.

Scheff, Thomas J. 1990. *Microsociology: Discourse, Emotion, and Social Structure.* Chicago: University of Chicago Press.

Schneider, Joseph W. 1985. "Social Problems Theory: The Constructionist View." *Annual Review of Sociology* 11:209-29.

Scott, James. 1990. *Domination and the Arts of Resistance.* New Haven, Conn.: Yale University Press.

Scott, Joan W. 1988. "Deconstructing Equality Versus Difference; The Uses of Poststructuralist Theory for Feminism, *Feminist Studies* 14:33-50.

———. 1987. "Re-writing History." In *Behind the Lines: Gender and the Two World Wars,* edited by M. R. Higonnet et al. New Haven, Conn.: Yale University Press.

Scott, W. Richard. 1992. "Institutions and Organizations: Toward a Theoretical Synthesis." Unpublished paper, Department of Sociology, Stanford University.

Sewell, William H. Jr. 1992. "A Theory of Structure: Duality, Agency, and Transformation." *American Journal of Sociology* 98:1-29.

———. 1990. "Collective Violence and Collective Loyalties in France: Why the French Revolution Made a Difference." *Politics and Society* 18, no.4:527-52.

———. 1985. "Ideologies and Social Revolutions: Reflections on the French Case." *Journal of Modern History* 57:57-85.

———. 1980. *Work and Revolution in France.* Cambridge: Cambridge University Press.

Sharpe, Valerie. Unpublished. "A Cunt until My Dying Day."

Shils, Edward. 1981. *Tradition.* Chicago: University of Chicago Press.

————. 1968. "The Concept and Function of Ideology." *International Encyclopedia of the Social Sciences* 7:66-76. New York: Macmillan.

Shotter, J. 1993a. *Cultural Politics of Everyday Life*. Buckingham: Open University Press.

————. 1993b. *Conversational Realities: Studies in Social Constructionism*. London: Sage.

————. 1992. "Social Constructionism and Realism: Adequacy or Accuracy?" *Theory and Psychology* 2:175-82.

————. 1991. "Rhetoric and the Social Construction of Cognitivism." *Theory and Psychology* 1:495-513.

Shotter, J., and K. J. Gergen. Forthcoming. "Conversation in Practice: Issues Regarding the Social Construction of the Person." In *The Communication Yearbook*. Vol. 17. Edited by S. A. Deetz.

Simeon, Richard, and Ian Robinson. 1990. *State, Society and the Development of Canadian Federalism*. Toronto: University of Toronto Press.

Simonds, Wendy. 1992. *Women and Self-Help Culture*. New Brunswick, N.J.: Rutgers University Press.

Simons, H. W. 1990. "Rhetoric of Inquiry as an Intellectual Movement." In *The Rhetorical Turn*, edited by H. W. Simons. Chicago: University of Chicago Press.

Singer, Milton. 1968. "Culture: The Concept of Culture." In *International Encyclopedia of the Social Sciences*. Vol. 3. Edited by D. Sills. New York: Macmillan and Free Press.

Skevington, Suzanne. 1989. "A Place for Emotion in Social Identity Theory." In *The Social Identity of Women,* edited by Suzanne Skevington and Deborah Baker. London: Sage.

Skocpol, Theda. 1985. "Cultural Idioms and Political Ideologies in the Revolutionary Reconstruction of State Power: A Rejoinder to Sewell." *Journal of Modern History* 57:86-96.

Smelser, Neil. 1962. *Theory of Collective Behavior*. New York: Free Press.

Smith, Anthony D. 1991. *National Identity*. Reno: University of Nevada Press.

Smith, Dorothy. 1990. *The Conceptual Practices of Power*. Boston: Northeastern University Press.

————. 1987. *The Everyday World as Problematic: A Feminist Sociology*. Boston: Northeastern University Press.

Snow, David A., and Robert D. Benford. 1992. "Master Frames and Cycles of Protest." In *Frontiers in Social Movement Theory,* edited by Aldon Morris and Carol McClurg Mueller. New Haven, Conn.: Yale University Press.

————. 1988. "Ideology, Frame Resonance, and Participant Mobilization." In *International Social Movement Research: From Structure to Action,* edited by Bert Klandermans, Hanspeter Kriesi, and Sidney Tarrow. Greenwich, Conn.: JAI Press.

Snow, David A., E. Burke Rochford Jr., Steven K. Worden, and Robert D. Benford. 1986. "Frame Alignment Processes, Micromobilization and Movement Participation." *American Sociological Review* 51: 456-81.

Snow, David A., Louis A. Zurcher, and Robert Peters. 1981. "Victory Celebrations as Theater: A Dramaturgical Approach to Crowd Behavior." *Symbolic Interaction* 4:21-41.

Spector, Malcolm, and John Kitsuse. 1977. *Constructing Social Problems*. Menlo Park, Calif.: Cummings.

————. 1973. "Social Problems: A Re-formulation." *Social Problems* 21:145-59.

Stahl, Sandra Dolby. 1989. *Literary Folkloristics and the Personal Narrative*. Bloomington: Indiana University Press.

Steinem, Gloria. 1992. *Revolution from Within*. Boston: Little, Brown.

Stubbs, Michael. 1983. *Discourse Analysis*. Chicago: University of Chicago Press.

Swanson, Guy E. 1976. "Review of Erving Goffman's Frame Analysis." *Annals of the American Academy of Political and Social Science* 420:218-20.

Swidler, Ann. 1987. "The Uses of Culture in Historical Explanation." Paper presented at the annual meeting of the American Sociological Association, Chicago.

————. 1986. "Culture in Action: Symbols and Strategies." *American Sociological Review* 51:273-86.

————. Forthcoming. *Talk of Love: How Americans Use Their Culture.* Chicago: University of Chicago Press.

Swinton, Katherine, and Carol Rogerson, eds. 1988. *Competing Constitutional Visions: The Meech Lake Accord.* Toronto: Carswell.

Tarrow, Sidney. 1992a. "Mentalities, Political Cultures, and Collective Action Frames: Constructing Meanings through Action." In *Frontiers in Social Movement Theory,* edited by A. Morris and C. Mueller. New Haven, Conn.: Yale University Press.

————. 1992b. "Costumes of Revolt: The Political Culture of Collective Action." Unpublished manuscript.

————. 1989a. *Struggle, Politics, and Reform: Collective Action, Social Movements, and Cycles of Protest.* Cornell Studies in International Affairs, Western Societies Papers, no.2.

————. 1989b. *Democracy and Disorder: Protest and Politics in Italy 1965-1975.* New York: Oxford.

————. 1988. "National Politics and Collective Action: Recent Theory and Research in Western Europe and the United States." *Annual Review of Sociology* 17:421-40.

Taylor, Verta. 1994. "Watching for Vibes: Bringing Emotions into the Study of Feminist Organizations." In *Feminist Organizations: Harvest of the New Women's Movement,* edited by Myra Marx Ferree and Patricia Yancey Martin. Philadelphia: Temple University Press.

————. 1989. "Social Movement Continuity: The Women's Movement in Abeyance." *American Sociological Review* 54:761-75.

————. Forthcoming. *Rock-a-Bye Baby: Feminism, Self-Help, and Postpartum Depression.*

Taylor, Verta, and Leila J. Rupp. 1993. "Women's Culture and Lesbian Feminist Activism: A Reconsideration of Cultural Feminism." *Signs* 19:32-61.

Taylor, Verta, and Nancy Whittier. 1993. "The New Feminist Movement." In *Feminist Frontiers III,* edited by Laurel Richardson and Verta Taylor. New York: McGraw-Hill.

————. 1992. "Collective Identity in Social Movement Communities: Lesbian Feminist Mobilization." In *Frontiers in Social Movement Theory,* edited by Aldon D. Morris and Carol McClurg Mueller. New Haven, Conn.: Yale University Press.

Thompson, E. P. 1966 [1963]. *The Making of the English Working Class.* New York: Vintage.

Thompson, John B. 1990. *Ideology and Modern Culture.* Oxford: Polity.

Thompson, W. I. 1967. *The Imagination of a Revolution: Dublin 1916.* Oxford: Oxford University Press

Thorndyke, P. W. 1977. "Cognitive Structures in Comprehension and Memory of Narrative Discourse." *Cognitive Psychology* 9.77-110.

Tillion, Germaine. 1966. *Le harem et les cousins.* Paris: Seuil.

Tilly, Charles. 1986. *The Contentious French.* Cambridge, Mass.: Harvard University Press.

————. 1978. *From Mobilization to Revolution.* Reading, Mass.: Addison-Wesley.

Touraine, Alain. 1985. "An Introduction to the Study of Social Movements." *Social Research* 52:749-87.

————. 1984. *Le retour de l'acteur.* Paris: Fayard.

————. 1978. *La voix et le regard.* Paris: Seuil.

————. 1974. *La production de la société.* Paris: Seuil.

Tronto, Joan C. 1987. "Beyond Gender Difference to a Theory of Care." *Signs* 12:644-63.

Turner, Jonathan. 1988. *A Theory of Social Interaction.* Stanford, Calif.: Stanford University Press.

Turner, Ralph H. 1983. "Figure and Ground in the Analysis of Social Movements." *Symbolic Interaction* 6, no.2: 175-81.

————. 1981. "Collective Behavior and Resource Mobilization as Approaches to Social

Movements." In *Research in Social Movements, Conflict and Change.* Vol. 4. Edited by Louis Kriesberg. Greenwich, Conn.: JAI Press.

———. 1969. "The Theme of Contemporary Social Movements." *British Journal of Sociology* 20:390-405.

Turner, Ralph H., and Louis M. Killian. 1987. *Collective Behavior.* 3d ed. Englewood Cliffs, N.J.: Prentice-Hall.

———. 1972. *Collective Behavior,* 2d ed. Englewood Cliffs, N.J.: Prentice-Hall.

Turner, Victor. 1969. *The Ritual Process.* Chicago: Aldine.

van Dijk, Teun A. 1992. "Discourse and the Denial of Racism." *Discourse and Society* 3:87-118.

———. 1987. *Communicating Racism: Ethnic Prejudice in Thought and Talk.* Newbury Park, Calif.: Sage.

———. 1979. "From Text Grammar to Interdisciplinary Discourse Studies." Paper for the La Jolla Conference of Cognitive Science, University of California, San Diego, La Jolla.

———. 1972. *Some Aspects of Text Grammars.* The Hague: Mouton.

van Schendel, Nicolas, 1994. "L'identité métisse ou l'histoire oubliée de la canadianité." In *La question identitaire au Canada francophone,* edited by Jocelyn Létourneau. Ste. Foy: Laval University Press.

Van Willigen, Marieke Minke. 1993. "Collective Identity and Activist Strategies in the Breast Cancer Movement." Unpublished master's thesis, Ohio State University.

Vickers, Jill. 1993. "The Canadian Women's Movement and a Changing Constitutional Order," *International Journal of Canadian Studies,* no.7-8 (Spring-Fall).

Viney, Linda L., and Lynne Bousfield. 1991. "Narrative Analysis: A Method of Psychosocial Research for AIDS-Affected People." *Social Science Medicine* 32:757-65.

Wachs, Eleanor. 1988. *Crime-Victim Stories.* Bloomington: Indiana University Press.

Weaver, Sally. 1981. *Making Canadian Indian Policy: The Hidden Agenda 1968-70.* Toronto: University of Toronto Press.

Weber, Max. 1968 [1920-22]. *Economy and Society: An Outline of Interpretive Sociology.* Berkeley: University of California Press.

———. 1958 [1904-5]. *The Protestant Ethic and the Spirit of Capitalism.* New York: Scribner's.

———. 1946a [1922-23]. "The Social Psychology of the World Religions." In *From Max Weber,* edited by H. H. Gerth and C. W. Mills. New York: Oxford University Press.

———. 1946b [1922-23]. "The Protestant Sects and the Spirit of Capitalism." In *From Max Weber,* edited by H. H. Gerth and C. W. Mills. New York: Oxford University Press.

Weed, Frank. 1990. "The Victim-Activist Role in the Anti-Drunk Driving Movement." *Sociological Quarterly* 31:459-73.

Weigert, Andrew J., J. Smith Teitge, and Dennis W. Teitge. 1986. *Society and Identity.* New York: Cambridge University Press.

Weller, J. M., and E. L. Quarantelli. 1974. "Neglected Characteristics of Collective Behavior." *American Journal of Sociology* 79:665-83.

Wertsch, James V. 1991. *Voices of the Mind.* Wheatsheaf: Sussex.

Wetherell, M., and J. Potter, 1992. *Mapping the Language of Racism.* Hemel Hempstead: Harvester/Wheatsheaf.

———. 1988. "Discourse Analysis and the Identification of Interpretative Repertoires." In *Analysing Everyday Explanation,* edited by C. Antaki. London: Sage.

Wexler, Richard. 1985. "Invasion of the Child Savers: No One Is Safe in the War against Abuse." *Progressive,* September, 19-22.

Wheaton Religious Gift and Church Supply. 1992. *Wholesale Catalog 1992-1993.* Wheaton, Ill.: Wheaton Religious Gift and Church Supply.

Whittier, Nancy. 1995. *Feminist Generations: The Persistence of the Radical Women's Movement.* Philadelphia: Temple University Press.

Williams, Raymond. 1977. *Marxism and Literature.* Oxford: Oxford University Press.
——. 1973. "Base and Superstructure in Marxist Cultural Theory." *New Left Review* 82 (November-December): 3-16.
Willis, Paul E. 1981. *Learning to Labor.* New York: Columbia University Press.
Wilson, John. 1990. *Politically Speaking: The Pragmatic Analysis of Political Language.* New York: Basil Blackwell.
Wolf, Eric R. 1969. *Peasant Wars of the 20th Century.* New York: Harper & Row.
Worsley, Peter. 1957. *The Trumpet Shall Sound: A Study of Cargo Cults in Melanesia.* London: MacGobbon and Kee.
Wuthnow, Robert. 1989. *Communities of Discourse: Ideology and Social Structure in the Reformation, the Enlightenment, and European Socialism.* Cambridge, Mass.: Harvard University Press.
——. 1987. *Meaning and Moral Order: Explanations in Cultural Analysis.* Berkeley: University of California Press.
Wuthnow, Robert, and Marsha Witten. 1988. "New Directions in the Study of Culture." *Annual Review of Sociology* 14:49-67.
Zajonc, Robert B. 1980. "Feeling and Thinking: Preferences Need No Inferences." *American Psychologist* 35 (February): 151-75.
Zald, Mayer N., and John D. McCarthy. 1987. *Social Movements in Organizational Society.* New Brunswick, N.J.: Transaction.
Zdravomyslova, Elena. 1992. The Role of Social Movements in the Creation of New Political Symbolism in Russia. Paper presented at the First European Conference on Social Movements, Berlin.
Zurcher, Louis, and David Snow. 1981. "Collective Behavior: Social Movements." In *Social Psychology: Sociological Perspectives*, edited by Ralph H. Turner and Morris Rosenberg. New York: Basic Books.

Contributors

Michael Billig is professor of social sciences at Loughborough University in Leicestershire. He is interested in rhetoric and political psychology. His books include *Arguing and Thinking* (1987), *Ideology and Opinions* (1991), and *Talking of the Royal Family* (1992).

Rick Fantasia is associate professor of sociology at Smith College in Northampton, Massachusetts. His book *Cultures of Solidarity: Consciousness, Action, and Contemporary American Workers* (1988) was co-winner of two American Sociological Association awards: the Sociology of Culture Section 1992 award for best book published within the past four years and the Collective Behavior and Social Movements Section 1990 award for books published in the two preceding years.

Gary Alan Fine is professor of sociology at the University of Georgia. He is author of *Rumor and Gossip: The Social Psychology of Hearsay* (with Ralph Rosnow) and *Manufacturing Tales: Sex and Money in Contemporary Legends*. He is currently completing a book on the structure and culture of the restaurant industry, and is beginning to write on persuasion and evidence in high school debate.

William A. Gamson is professor of sociology at Boston College and past president of the American Sociological Association. His most recent book, *Talking Politics* (1992), analyzes how working people think and talk about political issues and the ways in which they make use of media discourse and the larger political culture that it reflects. He co-directs the Media Research and Action Project at Boston College, a group focused on the media and public education strategies of social change organizations.

Eric L. Hirsch is associate professor of sociology at Providence College in Rhode Island. His publications include *Urban Revolt: Ethnic Politics in the Nineteenth Century Chicago Labor Movement* (1990), "Sacrifice for the Cause: Group Processes, Recruitment, and Commitment in a Student Social Movement" (1990), and "Protest Movements and Urban Theory" (1993). His research interests include the analysis of conflict processes in social movements, homelessness and poverty, and race and ethnic relations.

Jane Jenson is a research affiliate of the Center for European Studies at Harvard University and *professeure titulaire* in the Department of Political Science at the University of Montreal. For many years she was professor of political science at Carleton University in Ottawa. She is the coauthor of, among other works, *Mitterrand et les Françaises: Un rendez-vous manqué* (1994), *The Politics of Abortion* (1992), *Absent Mandate: The Politics of Electoral Change in Canada* (1990), and *The View from Inside: A French Communist Cell in Crisis* (1985), as well as coeditor of *The Feminization of the Labour Force* (1988) and author of numerous articles on politics and political economy in Canada and France.

Hank Johnston is a lecturer at San Diego State University, and in 1994 was a visiting professor at UCLA. The founding editor of *Mobilization: An International Journal,* he is the author of *Tales of Nationalism, Catalonia 1939-1979* (1991) and coeditor with Joseph Gusfield and Enrique Laraña of *New Social Movements: From Ideology to Identity* (1994). His book *Social Movement Theory* will appear in 1996. He has published numerous short works on social movements, resistance to state oppression, and nationalism, and in 1994 he received a National Endowment for the Humanities grant to study the role of art and literature in nationalist resistance in the former Soviet republics.

Bert Klandermans is professor of applied social psychology at Free University in Amsterdam. The emphasis in his work is on the social psychological consequences of social, economic, and political change. He has published extensively on the social psychological principles of participation in social movements and labor unions, and is one of the leading experts in the world in these areas. He has edited four volumes of *International Social Movement Research.* His *Social Psychological Principles of Movement Participation* will appear in 1995.

John Lofland is professor of sociology at the University of California, Davis. He is the author of, among other works, *Polite Protestors: The American Peace Movement of the 1980s* (1993) and coauthor, with Lyn H. Lofland, of *Analyzing Social Settings* (third edition, 1995).

Alberto Melucci is professor of cultural sociology and on the faculty of the postgraduate school of clinical psychology at the University of Milan. He has taught extensively in Europe and the United States and has contributed to many international journals. He is the author of more than ten books on social movements, cultural change, and personal and collective identity, including *Nomads of the Present* (1989), *Il gioco dell'io* (1991), and *Creatività* (1994).

Ann Swidler is associate professor of sociology at the University of California, Berkeley. Her works include *Organization without Authority* (1979) and, with R. N. Bellah, R. Madsen, W. M. Sullivan, and S. Tipton, *Habits of the Heart* (1985) and *The Good Society* (1991). She is currently completing *Talk of Love: How Americans Use Their Culture,* to be published by University of Chicago Press.

Verta Taylor is associate professor of sociology and a member of the graduate faculty of women's studies at Ohio State University. She is coauthor (with Leila J. Rupp) of *Survival in the Doldrums: The American Women's Rights Movements, 1945 to the 1960s* (1987), coeditor (with Laurel Richardson) of *Feminist Frontiers III* (third edition, 1989), and an associate editor of the University of Minnesota Press series Social Movements, Protest, and Contention and of the journal *Gender & Society*. Her research is on women's movements and gay and lesbian movements. She is currently writing a book on gender and the contradictions of women's self-help based on the postpartum depression movement.

Nancy Whittier is assistant professor of sociology at Smith College in Northampton, Massachusetts. She is the author of *Feminist Generations: The Persistence of the Radical Women's Movement* (1995).

Subject Index

Author Index